Indian Army Order of Battle

Richard A. Rinaldi and Ravi Rikhye

Orbat.com
for
Tiger Lily Books
A division of
General Data LLC

2011

The cover illustration is the formation badge of Army Headquarters.

The illustrations of Indian Army formation badges in this work are used with the kind permission of the Bharat Rakshak web site, who retain copyright on that material. The following individuals are credited for the particular badges:

Rupak Chattopadhyay: Western Command; some division badges
David Zothansanga: Southwestern and Training Commands; IX and XIV Corps; some division badges; all Area and Sub-Area badges
Amit Sharma: some division badges
Jagan Pillarisetti: all others

The map of India is from *The World Factbook* prepared by the CIA, at www.cia.gov/library/publications/the-world-factbook/geos/pk.html. US government publications are public domain documents.

Contents

Authors' Note

The Indian Army discloses little about its order of battle, strength, or composition. Its official website lists no formation below the command level, although it does refer to a few of the corps on command pages. Pages on the infantry regiments provide no information on their battalions, the Armoured Corps page has a single paragraph praising the "elan" and "operational success" of the Corps but no history or list of units, and pages on other arms and services are largely uninformative. While it does contain some information on peacekeeping and counterinsurgency, it notes that information on operations after 1948 is considered classified and the page on the history of wars and operations fought after 1948 lists a number of unofficial works, while noting that no official history of any of those wars or operations has been released.[1] Added to this penchant for secrecy is "[t]he tendency in India of poor recordkeeping and a general apathy to history…."[2]

The Bharat Rakshak web site on the Indian Army has the most order of battle information as well as information on operations and history. Unfortunately, the Armoured Corps and the infantry pages are little more than lists of regiments or battalions with virtually no information on raising or assignments, and essentially no information on units of field or air defence artillery, the engineers, or other arms and services. The other web site with extensive information on the Indian Army, that maintained by Global Security, clearly has taken much if not all of its order of battle information from Bharat Rakshak. However, it does have additional material on the Indian Army.

---

[1] Official histories have been written, and scans of those for the 1962, 1965 and 1971 wars are available and have been utilized for this work. Apparently these were leaked by *The Times of India*. We have not seen any leaked copies of the volume on Kargil 1999. The idea of forever secret official histories is especially alien to the American co-author, Rinaldi, who even as a high school student many years ago knew and appreciated the work of the US Army's Center of Military History. In addition to a vast amount of published material, they work with Army sc ools to ensure that "the study of history is a significant part of the training of officers and noncommissioned officers" and supports the use of history to foster unit pride and give soldiers an understanding of the Army's past (www.history.army.mil/html/about/overview.html).

[2] P. K. Gautam, *Composition and Regimental System of the Indian Army: Continuity and Change*, p 82. The author is a retired colonel, who suggests that even the poor primary sources that do exist may have been modified or edited "to suit current expedients" and points out that accurate studies of success and failure "are important for a military to adapt, improve and innovate" (p 83). Another retired officer commented on the problem of availability of information, stating war diaries "have hardly any useful information. Officers do not write diaries or notes. Regiments have hardly any." Lt Col (Retd) Gautam Sharma, *Indian Army (A Reference Manual)*, p x.

Another site with order of battle information is the Wikipedia article on the Indian Army. While it provides little beyond what could be found on the other two sites, it does seem to be more up to date on weapons and developments and its display of sources can be useful. Finally, there is the Indian Army portion of the Indian Military web site, which has corps and division identities and some summary information, but little beyond what can be found elsewhere..

Those four sites provided a starting point but were supplemented by a mass of other material. A major additional resource was the Orbat.com web site, created and run by Ravi Rikhye. As the site has grown and developed over the years, material on the Indian Army can be found in three different locations: History 1946-99, the TOE Library, and, most recently, the Center for Indian Military History. In addition, Mr. Rikhye has notes assembled over the years on a variety of historical material for the Indian Army, as well as prior published material on India and her Army. As noted earlier, scanned copies of the official histories of the 1962, 1965 and 1971 wars were available and utilized.

This work is based on open source, public domain information, which is incomplete and not always consistent. It represents the best effort by the authors to assemble and reconcile that information. Despite that, there remain some inconsistencies, especially in the orders of battle appendices. These simply cannot be reconciled from the available sources. In addition, given the nature of the sources, there may be some errors of fact. The authors are solely responsible for all opinions expressed in this work and for any errors of fact that it might contain.

As noted by the title, this book is an order of battle of the Indian Army: the units, organization and composition of that fighting force. It is not an administrative or operational history of the Indian Army, interesting as such a book can be,[3] and there is accordingly very limited discussion of operations.

---

[3] See, as a good example, Maj (Retd) K. C. Praval's *Indian Army After Independenc.* He was selected for this history by a Chief of the Army Staff and given at least some official support and access to official records. His book covers the period roughly through the mid 1980s.

Abbreviations

AA	Anti Aircraft
AD, ADA	Air Defence, Air Defence Artillery
AIFV	Armoured infantry fighting vehicle
AOR	Area of Responsibility
APC	Armoured personnel carrier
Armd	Armoured
ASC	Army Service Corps
ATGM	Anti-tank guided missile
Bde, bde	Brigade
Bn, bn	Battalion
BSF	Border Security Force: formed 1965 by federalizing state armed police battalions on border duty in the states bordering Pakistan; controlled by the Ministry of Home Affairs and has police powers as well as infantry weapons
CIH	Central India Horse
CO	Commanding Officer (sometimes shown as OC, or Officer Commanding)
COAS	Chief of the Army Staff; sometimes shown simply as Chief of Army Staff
COSC	Chiefs of Staff Committee (the three service heads)
Coy	Company
CI	counter insurgency
GOC	General Officer Commanding (used at division and corps level; at command level, the title is General Officer Commanding-in-Chief, or GOC-in-C)
gp	Group, generally in the sense of brigade group
GR	Gorkha Rifles
H and H	Home and Hearth: TA battalions intended for local defense
(I)	(Independent): part of a unit's designation
indep	independent
Inf	Infantry
IPKF	Indian Peace Keeping Force [in Sri Lanka]
ITF	Indian Territorial Force (pre-1939 Territorial Army)
J&K	Jammu and Kashmir
LOC	line of communications
MBT	Main battle tank
MG	Machine Gun
MLRS	Multiple Launch Rocket System
MMG	Medium Machine Gun
Mtn	Mountain

NEFA	North East Frontier Agency[4]
RAPID	Reorganized Plains Infantry Division
Regt, regt	Regiment
(Retd)	(Retired), used following the rank of a retired officer
RHQ	Regimental Headquarters
SAM	Surface to air missile
SATA	Surveillance and Target Acquisition
SF	Generally, State Forces: troops raised by the nominally sovereign princely states. All were disbanded are taken into the Army 1951-53. In the context of the Parachute Regiment, it means Special Forces.
SP	Self propelled
Sqn, sqn	Squadron
TA	Territorial Army
UAV	Unmanned aerial vehicle
u/c	under the control of
U/I	unidentified
wef	with effect from (e.g., date of assuming command)

[4] Became a Union Territory in 1972 as Arunachal Pradesh and a full State in 1987. Northeast India (or Northeast Region) as a term is more extensive than the old NEFA, comprising also the States of Assam, Meghalaya, Manipur, Mizoram, Nagaland, and Tripura. Sikkim was a protectorate from 1947 and a full State from 1975.

History

The current Indian Army came into existence 15 August 1947 on the partition of British India into the two new states of India and Pakistan. The Indian Army of the Raj was divided between the two, although the affected units were not necessarily located within the boundary of their new states when partition occurred.[5] The wartime army had been reduced to about 400,000 men, of which some 260,000 went to India. The rough division of strength and units was two-thirds to India and one-third to Pakistan. However, India did have an advantage in that most of the depots and virtually all of the military production facilities of the subcontinent fell within its borders.

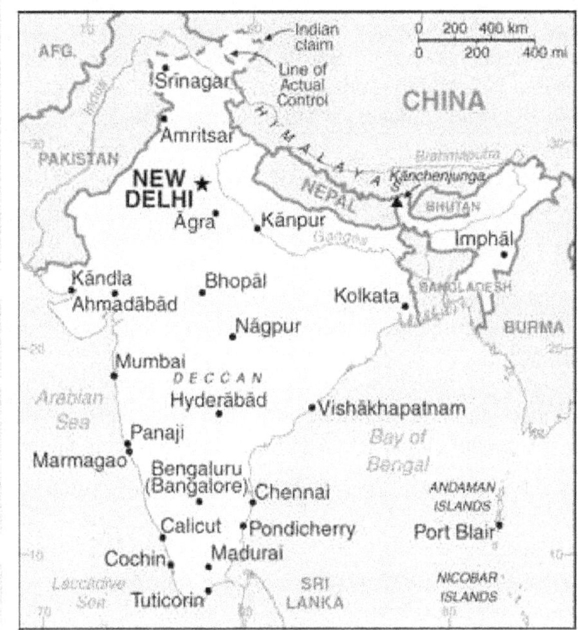

[5] The problems, chaos and violence attendant on dividing India and the Indian Army in August 1947 form the background to Jeffrey Archer's careful study, "The Punjab Boundary Force and the Problem of Order, August 1947," *Modern Asian Studies*, 8,4 (1974). One problem was that many regiments were of mixed communities, with each company or squadron a communal unit. Archer uses the 15th Punjab Regiment (which went to Pakistan) as an example: it was half Muslim, a quarter Hindu, and a quarter Sikh. Thus, half of its companies went to the Indian Army.

The new Army was created as its nation and Pakistan went to war over the state of Jammu and Kashmir,[6] surreptitiously beginning in October 1947 and officially from May 1948 when Pakistan committed regular military formations to combat. The two nations would go to war again in 1965, 1971 and 1999, the 1971 war resulting in East Pakistan becoming the independent nation of Bangladesh. India has also fought with China, contributed to peacekeeping operations, and battled local insurgencies.

India adopted a new constitution and declared itself a republic 26 January 1950; until then it was a Union within the British Commonwealth. For the Army this meant not only a new system of awards (see Appendix N) but the elimination of the word "Royal" and all other "non-Indian" associations in the names or titles of units.[7] The State Forces[8] had continued in existence after independence, in regional groupings under the Army's control. On 1 April 1951 those personnel and infantry units up to Indian Army standards were incorporated into existing regiments: e.g., 1st Patiala Infantry—which had served in Kashmir—became 15th Punjab (Patiala). State Force artillery was incorporated in 1948 and 1953 and engineers at various dates 1950-53.[9]

By 1953 the Indian Army had grown to a strength of 350,000 personnel. It had two corps headquarters, six divisions (one armoured and five infantry), and six independent brigades (one armoured, one parachute, and four infantry). On the eve of the 1962 war with India, the Army had grown to 550,000 personnel. It then had four corps headquarters—one raised that year, ten divisions (one armored and nine infantry), and nine independent brigades (one armoured, one parachute, and seven infantry).

While the Army grew in strength, modernization "was never taken seriously before 1962" and while the strength was sufficient, "it lacked the essential core

---

[6] While the name of the state is Jammu and Kashmir, it is often referred to by the shorter "J&K" or "JAK", or simply as Kashmir.

[7] While this is most evident in the titles of regiments or corps (e.g., the Royal Garhwal Rifles became the Garhwal Rifles and the Corps of Royal Indian Engineers became the Corps of Engineers), it also affected some infantry battalions. Until January 1950, 1st Sikh was officially 1st Bn (King George's Own)(Ferozepore Sikhs) of the regiment.

[8] The old India was divided between areas directly ruled by Britain and nominally independent princely states, some of which had modern military units that served alongside the old Indian Army in the world wars and the new Indian Army in Jammu and Kashmir and Hyderabad.

[9] The Jammu and Kashmir State Forces remained officially apart from the Indian Army until 1 January 1957.

in the way of equipment, training and general logistic support."[10] Following the disastrous war with China,[11] the Army was increased. The plan was to grow to a force of 10 mountain, 13 infantry, and two armoured divisions.[12] In the event, in 1971 India had 10 mountain, 14 infantry and one armoured divisions; the raising of the second armoured division was deferred for some ten years. Efforts were made to modernize equipment, leading to a standardized rifle, lighter and longer-range mortars, and a mountain gun for the artillery.[13]

Initial implementation of the 1962 plan called for a strength of 825,000 and four infantry divisions (36th, 39th, 54th and 57th) to be formed as cadres, to be expanded in case of emergency.[14] With the decision in 1966 that the cadre divisions had to be fully manned and organized, the manpower strength ceiling was increased to 950,000.

At the time of the 1965 war with Pakistan,[15] the Army had 745,500 personnel, five corps headquarters, ten infantry divisions, ten mountain divisions, an armoured division, three armoured brigades, and two parachute brigades. One consequence of the war was the US decision to stop supplying arms to India, leading to the importation of equipment from the USSR and other countries.

By 1971, on the eve of the next war with Pakistan, the Army totaled 833,800 personnel—still well below the 1966 plan.[16] There were six corps headquarters (one new), 14 infantry divisions, ten mountain divisions, one armoured

---

[10] S. N. Prasad (ed.), *History of Indo-Pak War, 1971*, p 269. As set out in greater detail in Praval, op. cit, Chapter Seven ("The Blunted Sword"), the government of Prime Minister Jawaharlal Nehru did not value the military and reduced the status of its personnel as well as restricting spending. Prasad also notes, however, that the Army Chiefs did not really stand up to the government and Ministry of Defence civilians in their treatment of the military.

[11] Orders of battle for this war are contained in Appendix G. One historian said that 1962 "saw the Indian Army at its nadir." Praval, op.cit., p 305.

[12] The Director of Military Operations at the time proposed an Army with two armoured, 12 mountain and 10 infantry divisions to face Pakistan and four divisions as Army HQ reserve. While officially disregarded by the new COAS, the adopted plan was not that different.

[13] Prasad, op. cit., pp 269-270 (on the equipment modernization).

[14] It appears that only the 57th was actually formed in cadre (in 1963); the 36th and 39th were raised in 1966 as standard infantry divisions, the 57th was brought to strength the same year as a mountain division, and the 54th was raised in 1967 as a standard infantry division.

[15] Orders of battle for this war are contained in Appendix H.

[16] The order of battle in December 1971 is contained in Appendix I.

division, four armoured brigades, two parachute brigades, and six infantry or mountain brigades.[17]

The Army continued to expand in the 1970s and 1980s. In 1986, General K Sundarji (COAS 1985-88) identified China, not Pakistan, as the future enemy. He proposed an expansion to four armoured, eight mechanised, seven RAPID, 19 mountain, and two air assault divisions. Although accepted by the government in principle, the expansion was never carried out because the Army was increasingly drawn into the Kashmir insurgency, which absorbed both its attention and its resources. In the early to mid 1990s India was hit by financial crises and resources were not available.[18]

General Sundarji also proposed a vast increase to the number of helicopters. He proposed giving IV and XXXIII Corps 200 helicopters each: 130 troop carrier for a one brigade lift, 40 gunships, and 30 light observation helicopters. In addition, 54th Infantry Division would get 500 helicopters to turn it into an air assault formation. These large numbers of helicopters (900 additional to the Army's existing ca.150) were completely out of the question resource wise. Even today the Army Aviation Corps has only around 200 helicopters. There are approved orders for 200 new light helicopters, but these appear intended to replace rather than augment the existing fleet.

Back in 1984, India launched Operation Meghdoot to seize control of the disputed Siachen glacier in Kashmir, gaining control of 900-1,000 square miles of territory. The final combat between the Indian and Pakistani Armies occurred in Kargil in 1999, when Pakistani paramilitary troops attempted to occupy territory on the Indian side of the Line of Control in Jammu and Kashmir.[19] There has been speculation that Pakistan hoped that this would result in an exchange of territory captured in Kargil for a withdrawal in the

---

[17] However, even in 1971 there were financial and other difficulties. In April 1971 the COAS told a Cabinet meeting that India's 1st (and only) Armoured Division had only 13 road-worthy Vijayanta tanks because the Finance Ministry would not released the funds to buy the necessary spare parts abroad. Needless to say the foreign exchange was quickly made available. Praval, op. cit., p 547.

[18] The one mechanized division formed was later converted to armoured; creation of the RAPIDs stopped after four infantry divisions converted; one division was designated air assault for a period but then reverted to infantry; two divisions were raised around 1985 and one formed in 2009. The Army stopped at 35 rather than General Sundarji's proposed 40, although c eation of two additional mountain divisions was recently approved and begun and another may form in 2011.

[19] The order of battle for this war is contained in Appendix K. In addition, the Army moved four brigades to Ladakh and one to Baramulah in Kashmir in case the war should spread.

Siachen; however, India's Operation Vijay regained control of at least 80% of the ground lost before hostilities ended.

Ironically, perhaps, the combat in Kashmir at the new Army's beginning was also its longest war, running just over 14 months. The disastrous 1962 war with China lasted 31 days. The second Kashmir war, in 1965, ran about two months, although there were some clashes outside that period. In the 1971 war, the fighting in the east and west were both over during the month of December. The final conflict, the 1999 Kargil War, had around three months of active fighting (May-July), although the infiltration from Pakistan began that February and there was some skirmishing prior to May.

These relatively brief periods of conventional state versus state war do not constitute the Indian Army's only combat experience. The new nation and its Army have been actively involved in peacekeeping operations from the end of the Korean War in 1953 through to the present. Those under UN auspices did not always result in fighting, but some of them (Congo twice and Somalia) certainly did. Finally, there was the more than two-year experience of the Indian Peace Keeping Force (IPKF) in Sri Lanka, which became more of a counterinsurgency (CI) operation than a peacekeeping effort.[20]

India is a very large nation, with a diverse population and varied geography, much of it difficult jungle or mountain. As a result, the nation has faced a number of insurgencies, some of them widespread and long lasting.[21] This has led to varying levels of Army involvement in CI operations. In a few cases, new divisions were formed for CI purposes. As one author noted, "As against the intermittent commitment in conventional wars, the Indian Army has been fighting insurgency almost continuously since independence....Counter-insurgency operations have provided the staple operational fare for the Indian Army...."[22]

An insurgency in the state of Punjab began in the late 1970s, the result of socioeconomic changes growing out of agricultural changes—including both prosperity for some and dispossession from the land by others, concern by some Sikhs of being absorbed into the Hindu fold, and political moves by the

---

[20] Peacekeeping operations are reviewed in Appendix O.

[21] A 2001 post in a Strategy Page forum (www.strategypage.com/militaryforums/72-90.aspx) lists an almost unbelievable number of militant, foreign, separatist or terrorist groups in the following states in India: Assam, Jammu and Kashmir, Manipur, Meghalaya, Nagaland, and Tripura.

[22] Brig SP Sinha, "CI Operations in the Northeast," *Indian Defence Review*, Vol 21.2 (Jan 2007). A summary of these operations, through the mid 1980s, can be found in Praval, op.cit., pp 517ff.

Congress Party to deal with a regional party in Punjab. Ultimately, a Sikh preacher and his followers became disruptive in the province and, in June 1984, took over Sikhism's holiest shrine, the Golden Temple complex in Amritsar. After negotiations failed, the Army was ordered to storm the complex , requiring a 24-hour firefight—with tanks and artillery—to clear it.[23] Concurrent with and following the fighting at the Golden Temple, many divisions were deployed in the Punjab and other areas to keep the peace.[24] Results of this action (Operation Blue Star) included a mutiny by some elements of the Sikh Regiment and—that September—the assassination of Prime Minister Indira Gandhi by her Sikh bodyguards.

In 1988, Kashmiri Muslims launched an armed struggle, including bombings, kidnappings, and attacks on Hindu civilians. The Army was sent into the area in December 1989 and the struggle gradually escalated. The by now secessionists received aid and safe haven from Pakistan, and the two counties exchanged gunfire at times in 1990 and 1991. By the spring of 1999 there were 95 battalions from the Indian Army, 36 battalions of the Rashtriya Rifles—created specifically for CI operations in Jammu and Kashmir—and around 110 battalions from the Border Security Force and Central Reserve Police Force.[25] Of course, some of those troops would be stationed there in any case for protecting the border. In fact, as one of our authors noted elsewhere, "[t]he Indian Army, without any equivocation, believes its mission is defense against external aggression and not in internal security....[and therefore] from the start the Indian Army has been against any involvement in the Kashmir CI."[26] The Rashtriya Rifles, ordered increased after the 1999 Kargil War, were an effort to

---

[23] The most complete account, with information on the Army units involved, is Operation Blue Star, 05 June 1984, by Bharat Rakshak (www.bharat-rakshak.com/LAND-FORCES/History/1972-99/283-Operation-Blue Star.html). The 9th and 15th Infantry Divisions provided troops: 16th Cavalry, 1st Para-Commando, 10th Guards, 8th Mechanised Infantry, 26th Madras, 10th Dogra, 9th Garhwal Rifles, 9th and 15th Kumaon, and 12th Bihar.

[24] 1st Armoured and 4th, 7th, 9th, 14th, 15th, 16th, 18th, 23rd, 29th, 36th, 39th and 54th Infantry Divisions. According to Rikhye, this larger deployment is the proper Operation Blue Star and the storming of the Temple was Operation Metal. However, as with the Bharat Rakshak article, Blue Star has become associated solely with the fighting at the Golden Temple.

[25] An example of a CI operation in this area was Sarp Vinish, one of the biggest single CI operations in the Indian Army's history. Launched in May 2003 in the CI sector covered by Romeo Force in West Kashmir (Kaka Hills area, Surankote, which lies in the Pir Panjal Range between Srinager and Jammu regions). Romeo Force had 9th Parachute (Special Forces) under direct command, along with the 163rd Infantry Brigade (4th and 15th Garhwal Rifles, 2/4 Gorkha Rifles, and an unidentified infantry battalion), and the 12th Sector Rashtriya Rifles (16th and 20th Rashtriya Rifles).

[26] Ravi Rikhye, Indian Forces in the Kashmir Insurgency: A Note (2003).

free regular infantry battalions from CI duty by creating a force specifically organized for that role, albeit staffed by Regular personnel on two-three year tours. In recent years there was enough perceived stability to allow the withdrawal of two Army divisions.

However, the longest and most intractable were the insurgencies in Assam and the Northeast. Insurgency in Nagaland began in the 1950s and was largely quelled by the 1980s, although violence returned beginning in 1993.[27] Mizoram saw conflict from the 1960s through the early 1980s.[28] An insurgency in neighboring Manipur was largely suppressed by the 1990s. Tripura has seen terrorist activities. Army divisions were involved in CI activities in these areas on a regular basis. For example, the 23rd Infantry Division was raised in 1960 and given responsibility for Nagaland. When it shifted elsewhere in 1962, the 8th Mountain Division was raised to replace it for CI duties in Nagaland.

One long-lasting insurgency that the Army has apparently largely been kept out of is the Maoist Naxalite insurgency. Beginning in 1967 in West Bengal, this movement spread across rural areas of eastern and central India. In 2007, Prime Minister Manmohan Singh said that the Maoists posed the most serious threat to national security in India.[29] While it appears that only police and paramilitary forces were employed against the Naxalites, a June 2010 *Times of India* article suggested that Army HQ was drawing up a plan to keep around five divisions in readiness for anti-Naxal operations if necessary. Central Command would be responsible for training and re-orienting the selected troops.[30] Unofficially, in

---

[27] The first Army commitment was an infantry brigade in April 1956, and it was soon apparent that much larger forces would be needed. A state of Nagaland came into effect in 1963 and the Army formed the Naga Regiment in 1970.

[28] This conflict led to the 1968 raising of a few "30-series" battalions organized as light infantry especially for CI operations. All were converted to standard battalions by about 1972.

[29] "Senior Maoist 'arrested' in India." BBC News, 19 December 2007, news.bbc.co.uk/2/hi/south_asia/7151552.stm. By 2010, the insurgency affedted about 200 of India's 588 districts. "A bumpier but freer road", 397 *The Economist* 8702 (October 2nd-8th 2010), p 77.

[30] *The Times of India*, 17 June 2010, timesofindia.indiatimes.com/india/Army-training-50000-men-to-tackle-Naxals/articleshow/6056573.cms. The Naxalist insurgency was the subject of several articles in the *USI Journal*, the most recent (and interesting) by Maj Gen (Retd) Y K Gera, "Naxalism: A Threat to India's Security." *USI Journal*, Jul - Sep 2009,Vol CXXXIX, No.577. General Gera makes clear his preference for the Army being involved only in an advisory capacity, and noted an increase of 10,000 in the Central Reserve Police Force (CRPF) to form Combat Resolute Action Battalions (COBRA) to improve security. He also notes that the "Army is being closely associated with planning of operations, to be able to intervene, if the situation so demands." The 2010 *Times of India* article may reflect that "just in case" planning.

July 2010 the 6th Mountain, 23rd Infantry, 27th Mountain and 54th Infantry Divisions were identified as those selected to begin pre-deployment training for operations against the Maoist rebels.

In noted contrast to the other descendent of the pre-1947 Army, the Pakistani, the Indian Army has never questioned the supremacy of the civilian government over the military nor has it intervened in politics.[31]

---

[31] It is not quite true to say that the Indian is the "only apolitical army" in Asia or Africa (Lt Gen S. K. Sinha, in the Foreward to Praval, op.cit., p xi); Praval himself noted more accurately that "[i]t is a matter of pride for the Indian Army that it has kept out of politics while in post other developing countries of Asia and Africa, the armed forces have not only dabbled in politics but have also seized power in many of them." (pp 564-565).

Class and Demographics

India has a large population, estimated at more than 1.1 billion in July 2010, and one that is extremely diverse as well.[32] The 2001 census showed the following religious breakdown: Hindu 80.5%, Muslim 13.4%, Christian 2.3%, Sikh 1.9%, and other or unspecified 1.9%. There are six different languages spoken by at least 5% of the population, and four more by 3% to 4.5%. (The largest group, at 41%, are Hindi speakers.) De facto, English "is the most important language for national, political, and commercial communication...." There are 15 official languages not including English, which is a subsidiary official language.

"Class", as applied to the Indian Army,

> means a type of Indian recognized as distinct from others by the Army authorities for purposes of recruitment and organization. The basis of the distinction may be difference of race, language, religion, caste, domicile or any two or more of these.[33]

While India is officially a secular state, and discrimination based on class is forbidden by the constitution, the effects of religion, caste, and other factors still affect the society and thus its armed forces as well. Regional languages also affect an individual's identity, e.g., as a Gujarati or a Marathi. In fact, the very names of certain infantry regiments reflect their origins, composition or primary recruiting areas: e.g., the Sikh Regiment, the Rajputana Rifles, the Maratha Light Infantry, the Garhwal Rifles. The goal may be units that are "All India All Classes"—certainly the most efficient in the use of manpower—but most regiments of infantry and many of the Armoured Corps still have distinct ethnic or other identity, with no mixing below battalion/regiment or company/squadron level.[34]

---

[32] Statistical data in this section is from the CIA World Factbook section on India, www.cia.gov/library/publications/the-world-factbook/geos/in.html.

[33] Report of the 1945 Willcox Committee (set up to examine the reorganization of the Indian Army and Air Force), quoted in P. K. Gautam, op. cit., p 6.

[34] These are discussed in the sections on each infantry regiment, and in Appendix E for armoured regiments. There have been some who argued that these unmixed units improve recruiting in their home areas as well as increased regimental esprit-de-corps, a conclusion that Gautam comes to in his study (see, e.g., p viii and pp 83-84).

The National Emblem

The National Emblem of India figures prominently in Army heraldry, particularly in rank insignia and regimental badges. Officially the National Emblem is known as the Ashok Chakra, and is described as follows:[35]

> State emblem is an adaptation from the Sarnath Lion Capital of Ashoka. In the original, there are four lions, standing back to back, mounted on an abacus with a frieze carrying sculptures in high relief of an elephant, a galloping horse, a bull and a lion separated by intervening wheels over a bell-shaped lotus. Carved out of a single block of polished sandstone, the capital is crowned by the Wheel of the Law (Dharma Chakra).
>
> In the state emblem adopted by the Government of lndia on 26 January 1950, only three lions are visible, the fourth being hidden from view The wheel appears in relief in the centre of the abacus with a bull on right and a horse on left and the outlines of other wheels on extreme right and left. The bell-shaped lotus has been omitted. The words 'Satyameva Jayate' from Mundaka Upanishad’, meaning 'Truth Alone Triumphs', are inscribed below the abacus in the Devanagari script.

Unofficially, this emblem is commonly called the Ashoka Lions, less often the Sarnath Lions, and Ashoka Lions is generally used in this work. When used in badges or other insignia, the words below the abacus (Satyameva Jayate) are almost always omitted.

---

[35] Offiical page at ari.nic.in/National Emblem details.htm.

Indian Army Outline Orbat

- *6th Mtn Div (Bareilly) [Army HQ reserve]
- Northern Command (Udhampur, Jammu and Kashmir)
  - 39th Mtn Div (Palampur) [Command reserve]
  - XIV Corps (Leh, Ladakh)
    - 3rd Inf Div (Leh), 8th Mtn Div (Dras)
  - XV Corps (Srinagar, Jammu and Kashmir)
    - 19th Inf Div (Baramulla), 28th Inf Div (Gurez)
  - XVI Corps (Nagrota, Jammu and Kashmir)
    - 10th Inf Div (Akhnoor), 25th Inf Div (Rajauri)
- Western Command (Chandigarh, Punjab)
  - II Corps (Ambala, Haryana)
    - 1st Armd Div (Ambala), 14th RAPID (Derhradun), 22nd Inf Div (Meerut)
  - IX Corps (Yol, Himachal Pradesh)
    - 26th Inf Div (Jammu), 29th Inf Div (Pathankot)
    - 2nd, 3rd and 16th Ind Armd Bdes
  - XI Corps (Jalandhar, Punjab)
    - 7th Inf Div (Firozpur), 9th Inf Div (Meerut), 15th Inf Div (Amritsar)
    - 23rd Ind Armd Bde, 55th Ind Mech Bde
- South Western Command
  - I Corps (Mathura, Uttar Pradesh)
    - 4th Inf Div (Allahabad), 33rd Armd Div (Hisar), 36th RAPID (Sagar)
  - X Corps (Batinda, Punjab)
    - 16th Inf Div (Sri Ganganagar), 18th RAPID (Kota), 24th RAPID (Bikaner)
    - 6th Ind Armd Bde
- Southern Command (Pune, Maharashtra)
  - XII Corps (Jodhpur, Rajasthan)
    - 11th Inf Div (Ahmedabad), 12th Inf Div (Jodhpur)
  - XXI Corps (Bhopal, Madhya Pradesh)
    - *23rd Inf Div (Ranchi), 31st Armd Div (Jhansi), *54th Inf Div (Secunderabad)
    - 91st Inf Bde [Amphib]
- Central Command (Lucknow, Uttar Pradesh)
- Eastern Command (Kolkata, West Bengal)
  - III Corps (Rangapahar [Dimapur], Nagaland)
    - 56th Mtn Div (Zakhama), 57th Mtn Div (Leimakhong)
  - IV Corps (Tezpur, Assam)
    - 2nd Mtn Div (Dibrugarh), 5th Mtn Div (Bomdila), 21st Mtn Div (Rangia)
  - XXXIII Corps (Siliguri, West Bengal)
    - 17th Mtn Div (Gangtok), 20th Mtn Div (Binnaguri), *27th Mtn Div (Kalimpong)

* Unofficially identified in 2010 to begin pre-deployment training for operations against the Maoist rebels in eastern and central India.

The Indian Army Today

Army Headquarters is at New Delhi and the senior officer is the Chief of the Army Staff (COAS).[36] The heads of the six operational commands and of the Training Command have equal status with the Vice-Chief of the Army Staff (VCAOS). There are now two Deputy COAS positions: Planning and Systems, and Information System and Training. Some of the other senior staff positions reflect the British origins of the Indian Army: Adjutant General, Quartermaster General, and Master General of the Ordnance, along with the Engineer-in-Chief and Military Secretary.[37]

The COAS is a member of the Chiefs of Staff Committee (COSC), which has its own Chairman. There are some other integrated defence staffs positions and organizations, e.g., Strategic Nuclear Command, Integrated Service Command. The Ministry of Defence provides overall direction and policy to the Armed Forces, with a Defence Planning Staff Directorate which provides the COSC with an overall view of the situation (including finances) facing the Armed Forces.

India has the largest all-volunteer Army in the world. Its strength in 2002 was given as 980,000. There were 300,000 first line reservists (those within five years of regular service) and 500,000 second line reservists (those out more than five years but under 50). The Territorial Army had 40,000 first line troops (generally in organized units) and 160,000 second line.[38] A more recent estimate is 1,414,000 personnel on active duty and about 1,800,000 reservists of all types.[39]

The main operational headquarters are the six commands, which control all of the corps (13),[40] divisions (35), and brigades of the Army. There is also a Training Command.

The Army has 35 divisions: three armoured divisions,[41] four RAPID [Reorganised Army Plains Infantry Division],[42] 11 mountain[43] and 17 infantry

---

[36] Appendix A provides a list of all Chiefs of the Army Staff.
[37] The Military Secretary maintains all officer personnel records and handles postings, transfers, retirements, etc. Thus, these matters are not handled by the Additional Director General of Personnel Services in the Adjutant General's Branch.
[38] Figures from Bharat Rakshak and repeated in the Global Security section on India.
[39] Wikipedia.
[40] I, II, III, IV, IX, X, XI, XII, XIV, XV, XVI, XXI, and XXXIII.
[41] 1st, 31st and 33rd.
[42] 14th, 18th, 24th and 36th.

divisions.[44] (Two additional mountain divisions were authorized and have begun formation in 2010 with a target standup date of 2012, and another may begin formation in 2011.) There are also two artillery divisions,[45] with one more recently authorised. In addition to the divisions, there are eight independent armoured brigades[46] and seven independent infantry brigades,[47] as well as a parachute brigade.[48] There are 15 independent artillery[49] and four engineer brigades as well.[50]

Air defence has two SAM groups and 13 air defence brigades.[51] Each of the three strike corps is to have an air defence brigade (sometimes called a group) of three regiments: one SA-6, one SA-8b, and one ZSU-23-4 Shilka or Tunguska-M1.

A retired officer characterized India's post-1971 strategic doctrine as "one of deterrence based on counter offensive capability" later modified to include—in the face of proxy wars by Pakistan—" a greater offensive bias in its military doctrine" including the proactive doctrine of "Cold Start."[52] He noted that the eighties saw a shift from the defensive posture of the 1970s to an offensive posture, including a more aggressive mode of offensive operations.[53]

As with other armies, India conducts various large-scale exercises. Operation Brasstacks, beginning November 1986, was intended to simulate full-scare war on the western border, involving 16 divisions. After the 13 December 2001 attack on the Indian Parliament, Operation Parakram saw tens of thousands of troops massed along the border with Pakistan: some 500,000 by January

---

43 2nd, 5th, 6th, 8th, 17th 20th, 21st, 27th, 39th, 56th and 57th.
44 3rd 4th, 7th, 9th, 10th, 11th, 12th, 15th, 16th, 19th, 22nd, 23rd, 25th, 26th, 28th, 29th and 54th.
45 40th and 41st.
46 2nd, 3rd, 4th, 6th, 14th, 16th, 23rd and 140th.
47 These include 55th and 340th Mechanised and 91st Infantry (with amphibious training).
48 The 50th.
49 Four are known: 97th, 261st, 401st (Independent) and 374th Composite.
50 Three are known: 471st, 474th and 475th.
51 A few brigade designations are known: 611th Independent, 612th Mechanised, 615th, 616th and 617th Independent. The 312th and 342nd Independent were in the eastern sector and the 322nd and 332nd were in the western sector during the 1971 war and some or all may still be active.
52 Col (Retd) Ali Ahmed, "India's Strategic and Military Doctrines: A Post 1971 Snapshot." *USI Journal*, Oct - Dec 2009,Vol CXXXIX, No.578
53 Ibid. This is one basis for the move to greater mechanisation and air mobility discussed earlier. As noted there and below, and by Col Ahmed in his article, financial problems held up both mechanisation and modernisation in general.

2002.[54] Pakistan likewise deployed troops to the border. Tensions escalated in May following attacks on the dependents of Indian military personnel, and there were some clashes between the two armies. However, the situation began to deescalate in June, and demobilization along the border started October 2002. In addition to its use as a security response, the operation also tested Indian Army warfighting doctrine (e.g., going from a "cold start" to massive offensive operations into Pakistan).[55]

An early 2004 article noted the problem of aging and obsolescent equipment, especially artillery and air defence weapons, and many of those old systems are still part of the inventory six years later. Other shortages or problems included various types of radars, 155mm ammunition, unmanned aerial vehicles (UAVs), and secure short range radio sets. The Indian Army, according to the author, "has acquired the reputation of being a first rate army equipped with mostly second rate equipment. It seriously lacks a potent firepower punch, especially in the mountain sector, and the reconnaissance, surveillance and target acquisition (RSTA) assets necessary for the optimum exploitation of even the existing firepower assets."[56]

A more recent article did not find the situation much better. "Almost everything that a soldier needs, from the clothes and boots to the weapon he carries, is at present well below par." The author found fault with the small arms available, the lack of artillery modernization, surveillance and target acquisition capability, air defence missiles, and communications equipment. The only arm where "upgradation and modernization has by and large been on track" was Armour, thanks to introduction of the T-90. In addition to equipment problems, he also noted the "the serious shortage of junior officers."[57]

Another journal article felt that "the Indian military machine is falling apart due to acute shortages, …." This author also referred to the outdated artillery and air defence weapons and radars as well as the shortage of officers—"army

---

[54] India blamed Pakistan-based groups for the attack; that country suggested that India staged the attack to smear the groups, who were part of the struggle in Kashmir.

[55] For two views of Operation Parakram, see Sunil Sainis, "Thoughts on Operation Parakrama," www.bharat-rakshak.com/LAND-FORCES/History/Millenium/321-Op-Parakram.htm, and Y. I. Patel, "Dig Vijay to Divya Astra: a Paradigm Shift in the Indian Army's Doctrine," www.bharat-rakshak.com/LAND-FORCES/History/Millenium/324-A-Paradigm-Shift.html.

[56] Brig Gurmeet Kanwal, "Equipment Acquisition Imperatives of the Indian Army," *Indian Defence Review*, Vol 18(4) (Oct-Dec 2003). Appendix L discusses Indian Army equipment.

[57] Lt Gen Vinay Shankar, "Army's Capability Accretion," *Indian Defence Review*, Vol 25.1 (Jan-Mar 2010). It appears that the general is retired.

alone needs twelve thousand lieutenants, captains and majors"—and the loss of status resulting from pay reductions.[58] These concerns were echoed in 2007 by a retired lieutenant general: "While military experts have been pre-occupied with the deficiency in manpower, particularly the officer cadre in the Armed Forces, it is the poor state of military hardware that should cause greater concern."[59]

In summary, then, the Indian Army is large and well-disciplined, clearly subordinate to the civil government, with one actively hostile country to its west and one of concern to the north, facing ongoing insurgencies (some sponsored and supported from outside the country), with problems of equipment modernization and the recruitment and retention of junior officers. The Army, like the rest of the Armed Forces, thought one officer, may also be facing loss of a positive image among the general public.[60]

---

[58] Bharat Verma, "Declining Military Prowess," *Indian Defence Review*, Vol 25.2 (Apr-Jun 2010). Mr Verma is the *Review*'s editor.

[59] Lt Gen (Retd) S P M Tripathi, "The Truth about Military Hardware in our Armed Forces." *USI Journal*, October-December 2007,Vol CXXXVII, No.570. General Tripathi expressed concern not only about the lack of modern equipment but the undesirability of dependence on foreign governments for equipment, which is both expensive and time-consuming (especially when setting up production facilities in India) and felt that "[n]ot only should we aim to equip our Armed Forces with modern equipment, made in India, but we should also aim to enhance exports of our military hardware and earn valuable foreign exchange." Some of the equipment problems are discussed in Appendix Q.

[60] See Lt Cdr Yogesh B Athawale, "Image of the Armed Forces – Arresting Negative Trends." *USI Journal*, April-June 2006, Vol CXXXVI, No 564. He discusses a number of reasons for this erosion as well as methods for addressing them. He ends: "[i]nternal reforms, mutually beneficial partnerships with external agencies and unflinching support from the Government are the basic pre-requisites for preserving the venerated image of the Armed Forces, which thrives on the essentials of public confidence and adherence to the values of democracy." *The Times of India* seems to be replete with articles about the arrests of officers (including generals) on one charge or another and allegations of corruption in procurement. Such articles cannot help the Army's general image.

Formation Badges

The Indian Army has a comprehensive system of formation badges, from Army HQ down to areas and sub-areas. All of them are based on shields, and are standardized depending on type of formation. In some cases, the current design harks back to the Second World War badge of the same-numbered formation.

Army HQ, New Delhi, has a shield divided red over black with a gold (or saphron yellow) Chakra in the center. This is the cover illustration.

Commands all wear a shield divided red-black-red with the central black bar somewhat narrower than the red above and below. Their details are given below with the entry on each command.

Corps badges are shields similarly divided, red-white-red. (Some appear to have a very narrow black border to the central white bars.) They are also detailed in the entry on each corps.

Armoured divisions (and independent armoured brigades) all have a yellow shield with a thin red edging. Infantry and mountain divisions all use black shields, as do separate infantry brigades. Artillery divisions use dark blue shields, but there are no confirmed pictures of their formation badges. Those badges known are detailed in the entry for the division.

50th Parachute Brigade has a maroon shield. Prior to 1952 it had a light blue Belleraphon astride Pegasus, the formation badge used by all British airborne formations and (with the word "India") by wartime Indian formations. Its current badge is the winged Shatrujeet [sometimes Shatrujit] (a mythical king with a winged steed) in silver metal pinned onto the maroon shield.

Areas and sub-areas all use a red shield. The few areas and sub-areas known are listed under their respective commands but their badges are not described.

Known formation badges down to division level are illustrated in the entry for each formation.[61] Those for areas and sub-areas are grouped on a page following the section for divisions.

---

[61] These illustrations come from the Bharat Rakshak web site (www.bharat-rakshak.com/LAND-FORCES/) and are used in this work by their kind permission.

Commands

The pre-1947 Army had three regional commands (Northern, Eastern and Southern) and an independent district (Western) with the status of a command. Each of the commands had several district (renamed 1947 as area) headquarters below them. The Southern and Eastern Commands were retained in the new Indian Army, although not necessarily with the original boundaries. A new Western Command was created shortly after independence, with additional commands formed in later years. The General Officer Commanding-in-Chief of a command is a lieutenant general.[62]

Commands have a territorial and administrative role, with areas and sub-areas to carry out these responsibilities.[63] Information on these is incomplete but given where known. In wartime, commands have an operational responsibility, serving effectively as an army headquarters. Formations such as divisions and independent brigades are normally under the command of a corps, but some have been earmarked from time to time as Army or command reserves.

Southern Command

With its headquarters at Poona (now Pune), Maharashtra, this was the largest of the pre-war commands. However, given its distance from the wartime front in Burma and northeastern India—or the often unstable northwestern frontier with Afghanistan—it largely had a training and support role. It was only with the creation of Pakistan that the command abutted an international boundary. Even then, its first operational role came in September 1948 when it commanded the entry of troops into Hyderabad,[64] and its next came only in 1961 with the seizure of Goa from the Portuguese (removing the last European-occupied part of India); it first participated in combat with an external foe during the 1965 war.

---

[62] Which means the command GOC-in-C and a corps GOC are the same rank. Apparently only the COAS is a full general.

[63] Area commanders are major generals, and sub areas and independent sub areas are commanded by brigadiers.

[64] Like the ruler of Jammu and Kashmir, the Nizam of Hyderabad attempted to become an independent state. State forces and irregulars opposed the Indian Army, but the fighting was over in 100 hours.

In August 1947, Southern Command had the Deccan, Madras and Bombay Areas (with HQs at Kamptee, Madras and Bombay). By the 1990s the command had two area HQs: one at Mumbai (formerly Bombay), the Maharashta Goa and Gujarat Area (MG&G Area), responsible for those states; and one at Chennai, the Andhra, Tamil Nadu, Karnataka and Kerala Area (ATNK&K Area) responsible for Andhra Pradesh, Tamil Nadu, Karnataka and Kerala. There were some changes to the command's boundaries in April 2005 when a new South Western Command was established.

In October 1962, Southern Command had two infantry brigades, one of which was considered Army HQ Reserve.

During the 1965 war, the Command had the 11th Infantry Division.

In December 1971 the Command had the 11th and 12th Infantry Divisions. It was only in 1987 that a corps HQ (XII) was established for these two divisions.

Operational units within Southern Command now come under the XII Corps (Jodhpur) and XXI Corps (Bhopal).

The Command's formation sign is a shield, divided vertically red-black-red, with the Southern Cross: four yellow stars.[65]

Eastern Command

Another of the existing commands, with headquarters at Ranchi from 1942. From April 1942 to October 1943, the command was designated as Eastern Army and responsible for operations against the Japanese. (In October 1943, HQ Fourteenth Army was formed for combat operations and Eastern Command was reestablished, at Tollygunge, Calcutta.) Headquarters returned to Ranchi in March 1947. On independence, Eastern Command had the United Provinces, Bighar and Orissa, Bengal and Assam, and Delhi and East Punjab areas (with their HQs at Lucknow, Dinapore, Calcutta and Delhi). When the Punjab Frontier Force disbanded 15 September 1947, the Delhi and East Punjab area was separated as a new command.

---

[65] The pre-independence Southern Command had essentially the same formation sign, except that it was a rectangle rather than a shield.

Command HQ moved to Lucknow in February 1955 and to Fort William, Calcutta (now Kolkata), West Bengal, in May 1963, when the new Central Command was established at Lucknow. The command has had involvement in combating various insurgencies and border skirmishes with China.

In October 1962, the Command had HQ XXXIII Corps, responsible for CI in Nagaland and the border with East Pakistan, and HQ IV Corps (raised that month), which would be responsible for the North East Frontier Area. There were three infantry divisions (4th, 20th and 23rd) and an independent infantry brigade. There was a plan to raise a HQ Fourteenth Army following the 1962 war, but it was cancelled and the two corps remained under Eastern Command.

Eastern Command was not involved in the 1965 war. At the time, it had IV Corps (2nd, 5th and 23rd Mountain Divisions), XXXIII Corps (7th and 15th Inantry and 4th Mountain Divisions), 8th Mountain Division (considered a command reserve but mainly involved in CI operations), and the 9th Infantry Division.

In December 1971, Eastern Command was responsible for the invasion of East Pakistan. It had II Corps (4th Mountain and 9th Infantry Divisions), IV Corps (8th, 23rd and 57th Mountain Divisions), and XXXIII Corps (6th and 20th Mountain Divisions) along with the 50th Parachute Brigade. In addition, two full mountain divisions (17th and 27th) and some additional units were left along the border with China under the rear HQs of IV and XXXIII Corps.

Operational units are now under III Corps (Dimapur), IV Corps (Tezpur) and XXXIII Corps (Siliguri). The former 101 Communications Zone is now 101 Area (North East). There is also Bengal Area. There is no information on other area HQs within the Command.

The Command's formation sign is a shield, divided vertically red-black-red, with a gold or yellow rising sun, base on the bottom of the black bar and five rays going to the side and top edges of the shield.

Western Command

When the Punjab Frontier Force was disbanded 15 September 1947, the Delhi and East Punjab Area of Eastern Command was separated and elevated as the Delhi and East Punjab Command (popularly, the DEP Command). While responsible for part of the border with Pakistan, the first responsibility was dealing with the ongoing violence in the Punjab and then the accession of Jammu and Kashmir to India and the war there. On 18 January 1948 it was redesignated as Western Command. In June 1972, the northern portion of the command went to the new Northern Command. Command HQ is at Chandimandir (now Chandigarh), Punjab.

In October 1962 the Command had XV Corps (19th, 25th and 26th Infantry Divisions and two infantry brigades) and XI Corps (5th, 17th and 27th Infantry Divisions and two infantry brigades). It had some other infantry brigades, mainly in Uttar Pradesh, which later went to the new Central Command.

During the 1965 war, the Command had the I, XI and XV Corps, with 1st Armoured Division in Command Reserve and a few separate brigades. In May 1965, I Corps had only 14th Infantry Division; XI Corps had 4th Mountain and 7th and 15th Infantry Divisions; and XV Corps had 3rd, 19th, 25th and 26th Infantry Divisions. I Corps was reorganized in September with the 1st Armoured, 6th Mountain, and 14th and 26th Infantry Divisions.

In December 1971, Western Command had XV Corps (3rd, 10th, 19th, 25th and 26th Infantry Divisions); I Corps (36th, 39th and 54th Infantry Divisions); and XI Corps (1st Armoured and 7th, 14th and 15th Infantry Divisions) as well as a few independent brigades.

Operational units are currently under the II Corps (Ambala), IX Corps (Yol), and XI Corps (Jalandhar).

The Command's formation sign is a shield, divided vertically red-black-red, with a gold Ashoka Chakra in the center.

Central Command

Central Command was established at Lucknow, Uttar Pradesh, on 1 May 1963, taking over part of the territory of Eastern Command.

I Corps HQ and 36th Infantry Division were located within the Command in 1971, but both went to Western Command upon mobilization for the war that December.

The command has I Corps (Mathura) located within its area. However, that corps was transferred to the new South Western Command sometime before early 2007. There is an Uttar Pradesh Area. There is no information on other areas.

The Command's formation sign is a shield, divided vertically red-black-red, with a gold stylized noonday sun in the center.

Northern Command

This command was established June 1972 with headquarters at Udhampur, Jammu and Kashmir. Its principal responsibility has been defence and counterinsurgency in Jammu and Kashmir.

The XIV Corps (Leh), XV Corps (Srinagar) and XVI Corps (Nagrota) control the operational units in Northern Command. 71 Independent Sub Area is part of the Command. III Corps and its 57th Mountain Division were shifted into the command as a reserve for Operation Parakram 2001-2002.

The Command's formation sign is a shield, divided vertically red-black-red, with a yellow symbolic compass North Point as used in cartography.[66]

South Western Command

Newest of the territorial commands, raised 15 April 2005 and fully operational 15 August 2005, with headquarters at Jaipur, Rajasthan.

Operational units are under the control of I Corps (Mathura), formerly under Central Command,[67] and X Corps (Batinda), formerly under Western Command.

The Command's formation sign is a shield, divided vertically red-black-red, with a silver streak going from upper right to lower left, behind a golden-yellow seven-pointed star. The silver streak symbolizes "offensive strike action, communication and Information Warfar" while the star heralds "the Seventh Command and with it, assured decisive victory."[68]

---

[66] The pre-independence Northern Command used the identical formation sign, except that the North Point was in white.

[67] I Corps remains located within Central Command, but was transferred to South Western Command sometime prior to Exercise Ashwamedh in Rajasthan (24 April-4 May 2007), its first exercise after the transfer.

[68] From the Command's page on the official Indian Army web site.

Indian Army Training Command

The Indian Army Training Command, or ARTRAC, was established at Mhow, Madhya Pradesh, on 1 October 1991, "with the requisite infrastructure and resources to meet all aspects of concepts and doctrine development, training policies and institutional training."[69] In essence, it formulates doctrine and is responsible for institutional training in the Army. Headquarters moved to Shimla, Himachal Pradesh, on 31 March 1993.

The Command's formation sign is a shield, divided vertically red-black-red, with two crossed golden swords in front of the torch of learning (yellow flames and white base).

[69] Indian Army web site, ARTRAC.

Corps Headquarters

No corps headquarters survived the demobilization following World War II. The XV, XXI, XXXIII and XXXIV Indian Corps were formed during the war, and three of the numbers would later be used by the new Army. In addition, the British IV Corps served in India and Burma and was sometimes (but inaccurately) referred to as IV Indian Corps.

The first corps HQ of the Indian Army was the V (later XV) raised in 1948, followed by the XI in 1950. The first corps in the east, XXXIII, was raised in 1959, joined by IV in 1962 just ahead of the war with China. Another corps (I) was raised just ahead of the 1965 war and another (II) just before the 1971 war. A seventh (XVI) was formed just after the war, in 1972. X Corps was raised in 1976 and two more during the 1980s (III and XII). The former HQ IPKF became the XXI Corps in 1990; the XIV Corps was formed in 1999 following the Kargill War, and the last corps (IX) was raised only in 2005.

I Corps

I Corps, at Mathura, Uttar Pradesh, is a strike corps under South Western Command.[70] It has three divisions: 4th Infantry, 33rd Armoured and 36th RAPID. It also has the 23rd Artillery Brigade and an unidentified air defence brigade.

Corps HQ was raised mid May 1965 and moved to Kalachack under Western Command by 4 September 1965, just ahead of active operations in the Sialkot sector. (In May it was in command of the still forming 14th Infantry Division.) 26th Infantry Division from XV Corps came under command 4 September; and the Corps added 1st Armoured Division and 6th Mountain Division (shifted from the Himalayan border with only two of its brigades) to the 14th Infantry Division.

Following hostilities, the corps HQ was established within Central Command. I Corps served under Western Command in December 1971. It had the 36th, 39th and 54th Infantry Divisions.

The formation sign is a shield, vertically divided red-white-red, with a black numeral "I" inside a thin black outlined circle in the center.

---

[70] The corps remains within the territory of Central Command, to which it belonged until the transfer to South Western Command.

II Corps

II Corps, also known as the Kharga Corps, at Ambala, Haryana, is a strike corps under Western Command. It has three divisions (1st Armoured, 14th RAPID and 22nd Infantry) and an independent armored brigade (14th). The corps also has artillery, air defence(612th Mechanised), and engineer (474th) brigades.

The corps was raised 7 October 1971 at Krishna Nagar in West Bengal (Eastern Command) specifically to control formations attacking western East Pakistan.. In December 1971 it had 4th Mountain and 9th Infantry Divisions. After the fall of Jessore HQ II Corps shifted to Bhatinda in the Punjab; 9th Infantry Division started shifting on December 16. II Corps took over Fazila-Ganganager; the arrival of 9th Infantry Division would have allowed 14th Infantry Division to reconcentrate its brigades which had been dribbled ad hoc to reinforce other formations. Then 1st Armoured and 14th Infantry Divisions under HQ II Corps would have attacked after the Pakistan II Corps offensive was launched.[71] The early ceasefire ended these plans. The corps remained in the west following the war.

The formation sign is a shield, vertically divided red-white-red, with a kharga in white with black outline and details and a black hilt in the center of the shield.[72]

III Corps

III Corps, at Rangapahar (Dimapur), Nagaland, is under Eastern Command. It has two divisions: 56th and 57th Mountain. The corps also has an artillery brigade.

The corps was raised in 1986, taking over 8th and 57th Mountain Divisions for CI; 23rd Mountain Division also became involved in CI under the corps, although it was also tasked for the border with Burma. (57th Mountain Division sent to Sri Lanka with the IPKF, probably in 1988; the IPKF withdrew late 1989-March 1990 and the division

---

[71] 1st Armoured and 14th Infantry Divisions were intended to be paired as a strike corps for offensive operations. XI Corps, to which they had been assigned, was overextended and lacked the command and control to plan a successful attack as well as perform its other responsibilities.

[72] The kharga, a sickle or sythe with a sharp edge and is associated with the Goddess Kali.

returned to III Corps.) While oriented to CI operations, the III would serve as an additional corps with Eastern Command in the event of a war with China. It was in Jammu and Kashmir for a period around 1990. 8th Mountain Division went with it to Jammu and Kashmir in 1990 and never returned. The corps HQ and 57th Mountain Division shifted to the west as a reserve for Northern Command during Operation Parakram 2001-2002. The corps had only a single division after 1990 until 56th Mountain Division was raised in 2009.

The formation sign is a shield, vertically divided red-white-red, with an upright bayonet (white blade, black hilt) in front of crossed Naga spears (black with a red covering where they cross).

IV Corps

IV Corps, at Tezpur, Assam, is under Eastern Command. It has three divisions: 2nd, 5th and 21st Mountain. The corps also has an artillery brigade.

IV Corps was raised 4 October 1962 at Tezpur and given responsibility for the Northeast Frontier Agency (NEFA), taking over 4th Infantry Division from XXXIII Corps. That division was destroyed in the 1962 war with China and withdrawn the next year. 5th Infantry Division was brought in to take over its sector. 2nd Infantry Division was raised in October 1962 as part of the corps. 23rd Infantry Division at Rangia was added in 1963. All three were converted to mountain divisions in 1963.

In December 1971 it was part of the force assembled by Eastern Command for the invasion of East Pakistan. IV Corps had the 8th, 23rd and 57th Mountain Divisions. It left a Rear HQ to control forces remaining on the Chinese border.

At some point after 1972 (1978?) 23rd Mountain Division left Bhutan to become Eastern Command reserve. 21st Mountain Division was raised 1978 and placed under IV Corps, to replace 23rd Mountain Division.

The formation sign is a shield, vertically divided red-white-red, with a black elephant in the center.[73] The corps nickname is Gajraj (King Elephant).

---

[73] The British IV Corps, which served in eastern India and Burma during the Second World War, had the identical black elephant on a red rectangle as its formation sign.

IX Corps

IX Corps, also known as the Rising Star Corps, is at Yol, Himachal Pradesh, under Western Command. It has three divisions (26th and 29th Infantry and 39th Mountain) and three independent armored brigades (2nd, 3rd and 16th).

The corps was formed 1 September 2005, taking over two divisions (26th and 29th Infantry) formerly under XVI Corps.

The formation sign is a shield, vertically divided red-white-red, with a nine-pointed star (green with gold edging) containing an open gold circle in the center.[74]

X Corps

X Corps, at Bhatinda, Punjab, is under South Western Command. It has three divisions (16th Infantry and 18th and 24th RAPID) and the 6th Independent Armored Brigade. The corps also has artillery, air defence (615th) and engineer (471st) brigades.

The corps was raised at Bhatinda ca. 1976. It took over the 16th Infantry Division as well as the new 18th Infantry Division, which was also raised in 1976. When the 24th Infantry Division was raised in 1978, it was added to X Corps.

The formation sign is a shield, vertically divided red-white-red, with a black rearing horse with the torso of a man launching a spear in the center.

XI Corps

XI Corps, at Jalandhar, Punjab, is under Western Command. It has three divisions (7th, 9th and 15th Infantry) and two independent brigades (23rd Armoured and 55th Mechanised). The corps also has an artillery brigade.
This corps was raised in 1950 in Punjab as a strike formation for operations against Pakistan. Upon

[74] This has also been shown as a black star with a gold outline circle in the center.

formation it took command of 4th Infantry Division (Ambala) and 5th Infantry Division (Ranchi and then Ferozepur). 27th Infantry Division, raised 1953 in West Bengal, was shifted to Jullunder by 1960 and came under XI Corps. 17th Infantry Division was rasied 1961 at Jullunder, replacing the 4th which was moved to the NEFA.

All three of its divisions were shifted to the northeast, the 5th in 1962 and the 17th and 27th in 1963. Two new divisions were raised in 1964: 7th Infantry Division at Ferozepur and 15th Infantry Division at Dehradun.

The corps, under Western Command, had an active role in the 1965 war.[75] In May it had the 15th Infantry Division (HQ Amritsar), 4th Mountain Division (HQ Fazilka), 7th Infantry Division (HQ Bhikiwind), and 2nd (Independent) Armoured Brigade. By August it had added 29th and 57th Infantry Brigades; 50th (Independent) Parachute Brigade joined 10 September 1965 and was placed under 15th Infantry Division. 41st Mountain Brigade was under command 12-19 September when it then went to 4th Mountain Division. (However, that division's 7th Mountain Brigade then came under direct Corps control 19 September.) 67th Independent Infantry Brigade Group was assigned 5 September to cover the Fazilka sector, joined later by 105th Independent Infantry Brigade.

The corps served under Western Command in December 1971. It had the 7th, 14th and 15th Infantry Divisions, 1st Armoured Division, 51st (Independent) Parachute Brigade, 14th (Independent) Armoured Brigade, and two additional infantry brigades (67th and 163rd). 1st Armoured and 14th Infantry Divisions were transferred to II Corps, which came west after initial operations in East Pakistan.[76]

Following the war, the corps reverted to control of 7th and 15th Infantry Divisions. However, 9th Infantry Division moved into the corps area (Meerut) in 1972. It is usually shown as being part of XI Corps, but there is at least some question about that.

The formation sign is a shield, vertically divided red-white-red, with a black stylized Triphul (trident) inside a thick black outlined circle in the center.

---

[75] In XI Corps in 1965, two division commanders, three brigade commanders, and a dozen battalion commander were relieved of their commands during operations for insufficient aggressiveness.

[76] 1st Armoured and 14th Infantry Divisions were intended to operate as a pair in a strike corps; XI Corps had inadequate command and control to plan the offensive and perform its other responsibilities, and had in fact broken up the 14th to meet changing tactical requirements.

XII Corps

XII Corps, also known as the Desert Corps, is at Jodhpur, Rajasthan, under Southern Command. It has two divisions (11th and 12th Infantry) and two brigades (4th Armored and 340th Mechanized). The corps also has an artillery brigade.

The corps was raised in February 1987 at Jodhpur, taking over the existing 11th and 12th Infantry Divisions in Southern Command. Prior to that, they had come directing under Command HQ.

The formation sign is a shield, vertically divided red-white-red, with an eight-pointed star, white with black details, in the center.

XIV Corps

XIV Corps, at Leh, Ladakh, is under Northern Command. It has two divisions: 3rd Infantry and 8th Mountain. The corps also has an artillery brigade. The speculative designation for this corps before it was actually raised was XVII.

The corps was raised in 1999 after the Kargil War revealed that the XV Corps was too extended. 3rd Infantry Division had been part of XV Corps, while 8th Mountain Division of III Corps was in the area on extended temporary duty for CI operations. These were the two divisions used in the Kargil War. Two new independent infantry brigades are due to be raised, one for the northwest Nepal border and one for Ladakh, probably to shorten 3rd Infantry Division's AOR.

The formation sign is a shield, vertically divided red-white-red, with a design in the center. Tridents are associated with Ladakh (see 3rd Infantry Division) but we are unsure of the meaning of crossed flaming tridents, and are also unsure of the exact meaning of the central device.

XV Corps

XV Corps, also known as the Chinar Corps, is at Srinagar, Jammu and Kashmir, under Northern Command. It has two divisions: 19th and 28th Infantry. The corps nickname derives from its formation sign, which features a Chinar leaf with a battle axe on it.

XV Corps was raised in October 1948 at Srinagar as V Corps, from HQ Jammu and Kashmir Force, which had been established in late 1947 to control operations in that state. (Two divisions had been established there May 1948: Sri [later 19th] and JA [later 26th], both of which remained under command.) It was later (1955 perhaps, definitely before 1962) renumbered as XV Corps, and may have been located for a time at Udhampur. HQ moved to Badami Bagh, Cantt Srinagar in 1972 when Northern Command was established.

The corps, under Western Command, had an active role in the 1965 war. 3rd Infantry Division, under command, appears to have played no real part in operations. Other formations assigned were the 19th, 25th and 26th Infantry Divisions and the 163rd Infantry Brigade, 41st Mountain Brigade, and the 121st and 191st Infantry Brigade Groups. 28th Infantry Brigade was later shifted to the corps from Command Reserve. 52nd Mountain Brigade came under command 11 September. HQ 10th Infantry Division came into the corps just after the outbreak of war, taking over several brigades.

XV Corps served under Western Command in December 1971. It had five infantry divisions under command: 3rd, 10th, 19th, 25th and 26th. Following the war, in June 1972, the 10th and 26th Infantry Divisions passed to the new XVI Corps.

XV Corps was responsible for Indian forces involved in the 1999 Kargil War (3rd Infantry and 8th Mountain Divisions, both reinforced).[77] This war indicated that the corps was responsible for too long a front. Following the war, part of the corps sector (3rd Infantry and 8th Mountain Divisions) went to the new XIV Corps at Leh, Ladakh. In mid 2005, 25th Infantry Division went to XVI Corps.

---

[77] 8th Mountain Division, of III Corps, was on extended CI duty and placed under XV Corps for the Kargil War in place of the missing 28th Mountain Division.

The formation sign is a shield, vertically divided red-white-red, with a gray-green Chinar leaf containing a gold battle axe in the center.[78]

XVI Corps

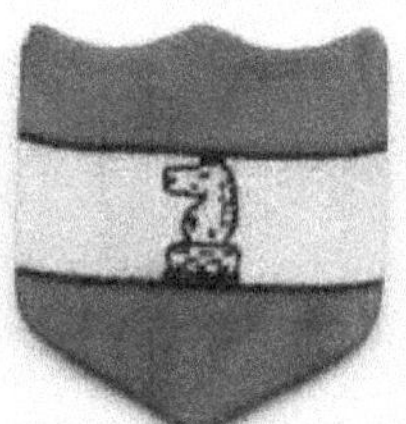

XVI Corps, also known as the Nagrota Corps or the White Knight Corps, is at Nagrota, Jammu & Kashmir, under Northern Command. It has two divisions (10th and 25th Infantry) and may have an armored brigade.[79] The corps also has an artillery brigade. The corps nicknames derive from its HQ city and the white knight Chess piece on its formation sign.

The corps was raised 1 June 1972, taking over 10th and 26th Infantry Divisions from XV Corps. 29th Infantry Division was assigned in 1984 when it was raised. During times of crisis, 39th Mountain Division (normally serving as a Command reserve) came under XVI Corps to cover the long gap between its 10th and XV Corps' 25th Infantry Divisions, making it effectively the largest formation in the Indian Army. Two divisions (26th and 29th Infantry) and part of the corps area of responsibility went to the new IX Corps in mid 2005. The corps then took over 25th Infantry Division from XV Corps.

The formation sign is a shield, vertically divided red-white-red, with a white Chess knight (black outline and details). General JFR Jacobs, the first commander, chose the design. He was an avid Chess player and said he liked the idea of a knight because it jumped over the enemy.

XXI Corps

XXI Corps, also known as the Sudarshan Chakra Corps, at Bhopal, Madhya Pradesh, is a strike corps under Southern Command. It has three divisions: 23rd Infantry, 31st Armoured and 54th Infantry. (36th RAPID, often shown under this corps, is currently with the I Corps.) The corps also has artillery, air defence and engineer (475th) brigades. In 2009 the 91st Infantry Brigade, intended for amphibious operations, was formed and assigned.

---

[78] There was a XV Indian Corps in the Second World War. Its formation badge was a geometric design of three Vs (Roman numeral for 5) in black or white on a red rectangle or red circle.

[79] If so, this might be the 140th (I) Armoured Brigade, which has been referred to as the first formation to receive the Arjun MBT but is otherwise unknown.

This corps was initially established as the Indian Peace Keeping Force (IPKF) which deployed to Sri Lanka following a peace pact in July 1987. However, it became involved in the renewed fighting, until leaving in March 1990. In April 1990 the HQ was redesignated XXI Corps and it was established at Bhopal in July 1990.

The formation sign is a shield, vertically divided red-white-red, with a Black Chakra in the center.

XXXIII Corps,

XXXIII Corps, at Siliguri, West Bengal, is under Eastern Command. It has three divisions: 17th, 20th and 27th Mountain. The corps also has an artillery brigade.

The corps is responsible for the Indo-Tibetan border, moving to its current location when raised in 1959, taking over the 4th Infantry Division, which was shifted from Ambala. In 1962, just before the war with China, part of its front and 4th Infantry Division were given to the new IV Corps when GOC XXXIII Corps resisted the government's forward policy along the border. 20th Infantry Division, at Ranchi, was placed under command in October 1962. 17th Infantry Division (Ambala, XI Corps) arrived during the 1962 war and 27th Infantry Division (also ex XI Corps) in 1963, as did 20th Infantry Division from Ranchi. All three then converted as mountain divisions, remaining with the Corps to the present day.

In December 1971 it was part of the force assembled by Eastern Command for the invasion of East Pakistan. XXXIII Corps had the 6th and 20th Mountain Divisions, a brigade from 8th Mountain Division, and the 50th (Independent) Parachute Brigade—which later shifted to the west. It left a Rear HQ to control forces remaining on the Chinese border.

The formation sign is a shield, vertically divided red-white-red, with a crossed black spear and trident in the center with black wings to either side.[80]

---

[80] The Second World War XXXIII Indian Corps had a device with a crossed sword and trident (although reversed from the trident and spear of the current design) and wings, all in white on a black rectangle. This was actually the second badge used by the wartime corps, and adopted when its intended role changed to that of an amphibious expeditionary corps: the trident represented the Royal Navy, the sword the Army, and the wings the Royal Air Force. Despite the intent, it actually served in ground combat in eastern India and Burma.

Phantom Corps Headquarters

VI Corps: This was a planned 1981 raising to take over the 11th and 12th Infantry Divisions in Southern Command. However, due to the CI in the Northeast, priority was given to raising HQ III Corps there. When a new corps HQ for Southern Command did raise, it was numbered as XII Corps.

VIII Corps: HQ VIII Corps was reported as raising at Mathura in 1967 but the corps was never actually formed.

XVII Corps: The speculative designation for what was raised at Leh as XIV Corps.

XIX Corps

A deception HQ raised for Operation Parakram[81] and located at Kathua in the Jammu-Pathankot corridor.

LX Corps: In 1972 there were reports that HQ LX Corps had been raised in 1971. This does not appear to have been a deception measure and is probably a mistaken report as nothing more was ever heard about such a corps.

Corps Artillery

While artillery brigades are shown for a few of the corps, each corps contains GHQ artillery regiments. Artillery in a plains corps is usually four regiments, including a rocket regiment. A mountain corps usually has one-two medium regiments and two 105mm howitzer regiments.

---

[81] The mobilization and movement of troops to the border with Pakistan following the December 2001 attack on the Indian Parliament. It continued through October 2002.

Divisions

Most divisions of the Indian Army were demobilized following the Second World War. By independence in August 1947, only five were still in existence. (One division headquarters went to Pakistan.) The 2nd Airborne Division was disbanded 14/15 August 1947, with one parachute brigade and some divisional units going to Pakistan and the other two brigades and remaining units to India. The 4th Infantry Division had been transformed into the Punjab Boundary Force (PBF) in July 1947, serving to help with the division of that province between the two new states and tring to deal with the widespread violence there. The Punjab Boundary Force was disbanded 1/2 September 1947.

Thus, only the 1st Armoured Division HQ (at Secunderabad, with its armoured brigade under command and the lorried infantry brigade with the PBF) and the 5th Infantry Division HQ (at Ranchi, with two infantry brigades under command) went to the new Indian Army in August; 4th Indian Division resumed its former identity after the PBF disbanded the beginning of the next month. For the most part, then, the new army had no tactical headquarters above brigade level. However, it may have formed another one that year, and did raise three more in 1948.[82] Only two divisions were formed in the 1950s, but the next decade saw a full dozen divisions raised. More were formed in the 1970s and later, ultimately bringing the total to the current 35 divisions.[83]

While only the three divisions still active in 1947 have a clear lineal claim to the old Indian Army, a number of divisions have adopted variants on the formation signs of the same-numbered division of the Second World War, often

---

[82] Two were provisional divisions formed in Jammu and Kashmir May 1948 for the final months of the war, later regularized as the 19th and 26th. If the 20th was not raised until 1948, as seems most likely, then four divisions were formed.

[83] In early 2008, according to *The Times of India*, the Army began preparations to raise two more mountain divisions. They would be in place "only by the middle of the next decade." The article was dated 7 February 2008. See timesofindia.indiatimes.com/ Two_mountain_units_to_counter_Pak_China/articleshow/2762650.cms. A 2009 article indicated that one of the new mountain divisions would be headquartered in central Nagaland or Assam. While there are CI operations in the area, "sources say the division could also have the task of keeping an eye on the Chinese border in neighbouring Arunachal Pradesh…." *The Times of India*, 11 September 2009, timesofindia.indiatimes.com/india/New-N-E-division-with-eye-on-China/ articleshow/4995973.cms. Apparently, the Army began to post officers to the new divisions by March 2010, and the plan was to have both fully operational by 2012. *The Times of India*, 31 March 2010, timesofindia.indiatimes.com/india/Future-war-on-two-and-a-half-fronts/articleshow/5744073.cms.

taking the same nickname as well when it was derived from the formation sign. Some appear to make an explicit claim to be a new raising of the wartime division, although it is unclear if there is an official policy on this. At least in the early years, new divisions were given the numbers of divisions with distinguished World War II service records.

The bulk of Indian divisions were infantry. After the 1962 war, some infantry divisions were converted to mountain divisions, and over time additional divisions were raised as mountain. Some divisions have converted from mountain back to infantry, and some infantry divisions later converted to mountain. There was only a single armoured division until 1972 when the second formed, and a mechanised division later became the third. A 1985 plan had called for wholesale mechanisation of most plains divisions. The original concept was tested in a 1986-87 exercise, and four divisions converted to Reorganized Plains Infantry Divisions (RAPIDs). With attention drawn to the Kashmir insurgency in the 1990s, no more RAPID divisions were created, nor was there any further effort to increase the mechanisation of the remaining infantry divisions.

1st Armoured Division

The division is at Ambala, Haryana, under the command of II Corps, Western Command. It is known as the Airawat (Black Elephant) Division. The formation sign is a yellow shield with a thin red edging and a black elephant (white details) centered.[84] (The GOC is referred to as the Ankush – the instrument used by the Mahout to guide the elephant.) The division is composed of the 1st, 43rd and 98th Armoured Brigades. The first two brigades have been with the division continuously since 1947, although the 43rd was formerly a lorried infantry brigade.

One of two divisions that went to the new Indian Army in August 1947, headquarters and the assigned 1st Armoured Brigade were at Secunderabad. The other assigned brigade—43rd Lorried Infantry Brigade—had been sent to the Punjab Boundary Force in July 1947 and returned later. The division relocated ca 1948 to Jullunder (Jalandhar).[85] In September 1948 the division and some

[84] The World War II 1st (later 31st, later 1st again) Armoured Division wore a plain black elephant on a green rectangle.

[85] 1st Armoured Division Engineers were sent to Jammu and Kashmir in early 1947 and served as JAK Division Engineers in 1948, returning in 1949.

attached infantry entered Hyderabad for a 100-hour war when that state attempted to maintain independence outside of India. (The division had 1st Armoured and 7th and 9th Infantry Brigades under command for this operation.) The division was based at Secunderabad 1948-50, moving back to Jullunder 1950, then going to Jhansi in 1954, with the armoured brigade at Babina.

In October 1962, the division was in Army HQ Reserve. It controlled the 1st Armoured and 43rd Lorried Infantry Brigades. At some point the division moved to Meerut.

In the 1965 war the division, then at Patiala, was initially part of Western Command Reserve. It shifted to I Corps at the beginning of September. The division still comprised the 1st Armoured and 43rd Lorried Infantry Brigades. It relocated to Jhansi in 1970.

In December 1971 the division was under XI Corps, Western Command; still with 1st Armoured and 43rd Lorried Infantry Brigades. It was soon transferred to II Corps for offensive operations but the cease fire came before the operation could be planned and implemented. Following the war, the division was reorganized with the 1st and 43rd Armoured Brigades and relocated (1972) to Ambala. In 1984, it was reorganized with the 1st, 43rd and 98th Armoured Brigades.

2nd Mountain Division

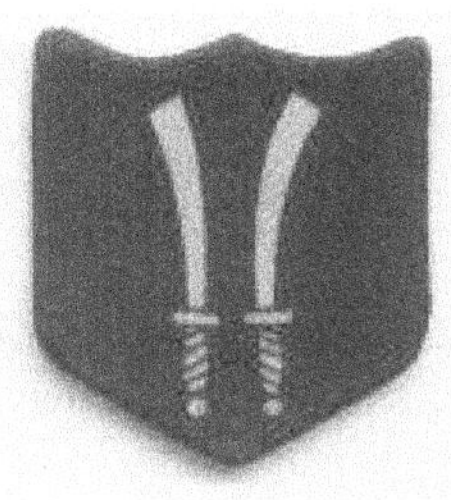

This division is at Dibrugarh, Assam, as part of IV Corps, Eastern Command. The formation sign is a black shield with two tulwars (curved swords dating back to medieval India).[86]

This division was raised ca. October 1962 (HQ at Teju) during the war with China as 2nd Infantry Division under IV Corps, and located in the extreme northeast of Arunachal Pradesh.[87] It took over 11th Infantry Brigade, formerly with 4th Infantry Division, which was on the front, and the 5th and 181st Infantry Brigades, which played no role in the fighting. It

86 There was a 2nd Indian Infantry Division in the Second World War, but it was deception formation created from lines of communication troops in Iraq. The number was next used in 1945 when 44th Indian Airborne Division was renumbered as the 2nd. That division was disbanded on partition.

87 23rd Division Engineers, in Nagaland, were redesignated 2nd Division Engineers and transferred.

was responsible for East NEFA. It was redesignated 1963 as 2nd Mountain Division.

In 1965 2nd Mountain Division was at Tezu under IV Corps.

In December 1971, 5th Mountain Brigade was under 101 Communications Zone. The remainder of the division remained on the China border under Rear HQ IV Corps.

The division was involved in CI operations in Assam 2002-2003. It currently includes the 181st Mountain Brigade.

3rd Infantry Division

This division is at Leh, Ladakh, under XIV Corps, Northern Command. It is nicknamed the Trishul (Trident) Division. The formation sign is a black shield with outlines of three snow-capped mountains in row, along with a trishula (traditional Indian trident) in the center.[88] The 3rd has always been an infantry division because the Ladakh plateau permits use of vehicles, so there was never a need to make this into a mountain division configuration.[89]

This division was raised 26 October 1962 in Ladakh (HQ Leh) following the start of the war with China, coming under XV Corps. It took over 114th Infantry Brigade (Chushul), along with 70th Infantry Brigade (Demchok) and 163rd Infantry Brigade (in reserve at Leh). The 114th Infantry Brigade was destroyed in the initial Chinese attacks.

By early 1965 3rd Infantry Division may have had control of five infantry brigades, including 68th Infantry and 121st (I) Infantry Brigades; however, two brigades were withdrawn for the Pakistan front. In the 1965 war it was under XV Corps, Western Command, but apparently not involved in fighting. At that time it controlled 70th, 114th and 163rd Infantry Brigades.

---

[88] In the Second World War, 3rd Indian Infantry Division was simply a cover designation for Special Force (The Chindits).

[89] However, some sources have shown it as 3rd Mountain Division at various times. It may have been unofficially called 3rd Himalayan Division in its early years; see, e.g., Praval, op. cit., who refers to the raising of "3 Himalayan Division" at p 292.

In December 1971 the 3rd was still under XV Corps, Western Command; it controlled 70th and 114th Infantry Brigades and 121st (I) Infantry Brigade. Its 163rd Infantry Brigade was detached and did not return.

The division participated in the 1999 Kargil War, controlling the 70th and 102nd Infantry Brigades.[90] The next year, the division transferred to the new XIV Corps. It is currently the only division with two rather than three brigades.

4th Infantry Division

The 4th has been both an infantry and a mountain division during its existence. It is currently at Allahabad, Uttar Pradesh, under I Corps, South Western Command. It is nicknamed the Red Eagle Division. The formation sign is a black shield with a red eagle in full flight.[91]

4th Infantry Division was used to form Punjab Boundary Force 17 July 1947 with HQ at Lahore. It controlled its own 5th and 11th Infantry Brigades, 14th Parachute Brigade (which would go to Pakistan), 43rd Lorried Infantry Brigade, and 114th Infantry Brigade. The PBF disbanded 1 September 1947 and the division HQ moved to Jullundur. The division moved 1948 to Ambala as reserve for Western Command. When XI Corps was formed in 1950, 4th Infantry Division was assigned to it. In 1958 the division was given the task of building residential accommodations for itself at Ambala, completing some 1,400 houses by early 1959.[92]

The division moved to NEFA and the Chinese border area 1959, with 5th, 7th and 11th Infantry Brigades, coming under XXXIII Corps. Transferred to the new IV Corps October 1962; division HQ was at Tezpur; 11th Infantry Brigade was in Nagaland on CI duties. (11th Infantry Brigade went to new 2nd Infantry

---

[90] Despite being part of the division, the 102nd was officially 102nd (Independent) Infantry Brigade.

[91] This is similar to the formation sign of the Second World War 4th Indian Infantry Division, which was a red eagle in flight on a dark blue rectangle. The division was formed September 1939 from HQ Deccan District and known as HQ Force K4 until numbered as a division 5 October 1939. It served in North Africa, Eritrea, Italy and Greece, returning to India January-February 1946.

[92] Praval, op. cit., p 199. One might wonder about the effect on training and morale to use a combat division as labourers and then, a few months later, move them out of their new and partially self-constructed cantonment to an area requiring construction of yet another cantonment. (Engineers and civilian workers were also involved in the project.)

Division November 1962 during war with China.) 7th Infantry Brigade was destroyed in the 1962 war, during which the division was given control of 48th Infantry Brigade (ex 17th Division), 62nd Infantry Brigade (ex 20th Division), 65th Infantry Brigade (ex Southern Command), 67th Infantry Brigade, and 82nd Infantry Brigade (ex Southern Command). It became responsible for West NEFA, with new 2nd Inantry Division taking over East NEFA.

Following the 1962 disaster it was withdrawn and rebuilt in 1963 at Ambala as 4th Mountain Division. (5th and 11th Infantry Brigades remained in NEFA and went to other formations.) The division was reorganized with 7th Mountain Brigade, 33rd Mountain Brigade (newly raised), and 62nd Mountain Brigade (ex 20th Infantry Division). It moved back to the Northeast and was oriented to what became the State of Himachal Pradesh: its 33rd Brigade was in Sugar Sector facing Tibet; 61st Brigade was at Solan-Dagshai, and 7th Brigade was in Ambala as the division reserve.

In the 1965 war, 33rd Mountain Brigade was left behind in its old Sugar sector (later going to 39th Division); the division gained 41st (I) Mountain Brigade (ex XV Corps reserve) but then its own 7th Mountain Brigade went into XV Corps reserve.

In 1970-71 the division shifted to the East partly to assist in anti-Naxalite operations in West Bengal, and partly because India assessed that Sugar sector would remain a low risk sector. It was placed under I Corps 1970, by which time it had moved to Central Command. In December 1971 it was under II Corps for the invasion of East Pakistan and controlled the 7th, 41st and 62nd Mountain Brigades. The division returned to I Corps afterwards. The 4th converted 1972 back to an infantry division.

The division, with two of its brigades, went to Sri Lanka in 1988 as part of the IPKF. The IPKF withdrew late 1989-March 1990.

5th Mountain Division

5th Mountain Division, at Bomdila, Arunachal Pradesh, under the command of IV Corps, Eastern Command, was initially an infantry division. Its nickname is the Ball of Fire Division. The formation sign is a black shield with a red circle or ball of fire (chakra, or ball of fire, is a divine weapon in Hindu mythology).[93]

---

[93] The World War II 5th Indian Infantry Division wore a red circle on a black square., referring to it as a ball of fire. The division HQ was formed June 1940 from HQ Deccan District. The division served Eritrea, Iraq and Cyprus (garrison duties), and North Africa. It returned to India May-June 1942, serving later against the Japanese in

5th Infantry Division was one of the two infantry divisions of the new Indian Army in August 1947. Headquarters was at Ranchi, along with the assigned 161st Infantry Brigade, while the 123rd Infantry Brigade was at Ramgarh. The division HQ later shifted to Ferozepur. When XI Corps was formed in 1950, 5th Infantry Division was assigned to it.

In October 1962 the division was still under XI Corps in Western Command. HQ was still at Ferozepur. In late November 1962, in response to Chinese aggression, 5th Infantry Division moved to the foothills in Arunachal Pradesh province, remaining in that area since then. It was converted to a mountain division in 1963. In 1965 it was at Bomdila under IV Corps.

In December 1971 the 5th remained on the border with China under Rear HQ IV Corps, except for its 167th Mountain Brigade which was detached.

It has been involved in CI operations as well as its border defence mission.

6th Mountain Division

This division is at Bareilly, Uttar Pradesh, and functions as an Army HQ reserve. It has been shown as under I Corps, South Western Command.[94] Its formation sign is a black shield with mountains represented by white lines and a gold Himalayan eagle.[95]

Raised 26 March 1963 with the 9th, 69th and 99th Mountain Brigades and sent to the Himalayan border (HQ at Naini Tal). (The 99th had served in the Congo 1961-63.) The new division was oriented toward the western Uttar Pradesh sector, between Himachal Pradesh and the west Nepal border; the region is now a separate State called Uttarakhand. Soon the Army decided this secondary sector represented no real threat and 6th Division, while remaining at its previous cantonments,

---

the Arakan, eastern India, and Burma. It went to Singapore in September 1945, and then Java, returning to India April-May 1946.

[94] I Corps is located within the territory of Central Command but is no longer assigned to it. 6th Mountain Division is located within the same area.

[95] A 6th Indian Infantry Division existed during the Second World War, serving on garrison duties in Iraq.

became an Army HQ reserve. At that point 9th Mountain Brigade was made independent and left to cover the border segment.

The division shifted to I Corps, Western Command, in early September 1965 with its two brigades: (69th and 99th Mountain); 35th Infantry Brigade from 14th Infantry Division came under command after arrival.

In December 1971 the 6th was under XXXIII Corps, although initially tasked as the Army HQ Reserve for Bhutan and it remained in that area with its 9th and 99th Mountain Brigades; 71st Mountain Brigade from 8th Mountain Division was placed under its command two days after the war began.

The division shifted to Leh 1986-87 and then relocated to Bareilly. It was unofficially identified in July 2010 as one of four divisions to begin pre-deployment training for operations against the Maoist rebels in eastern India.

7th Infantry Division

This division is at Ferozepur (Firozpur), Punjab, under XI Corps, Western Command. It is nicknamed the Golden Arrow Division. Its formation sign is a black shield with a golden arrow, point upwards and to the left.[96]

The division was raised in 1964 at Ferozepur and placed under XI Corps, Western Command.

In the 1965 war, it served under XI Corps, and initially had the 48th, 65th and 67th Infantry Brigades, and (by September) the 48th and 65th plus the 29th, which was detached to a sector north of 15th Infantry Division. (The 67th was detached to the Fazilka sector as an independent brigade.)

December 1971, under XI Corps, Western Command, the 7th controlled its own 29th, 48th and 65th Infantry Brigades and 35th Infantry Brigade from 14th Infantry Division.

[96] Essentially the same as the Second World War 7th Indian Infantry Division, which had a gold or yellow arrow on a black rectangle. It was likewise known as the Golden Arrow Division. Ironically, 7th Infantry Division was the only division HQ to go to Pakistan in 1947.

8th Mountain Division

This division is currently at Dras, Jammu and Kashmir, under XIV Corps, Northern Command. Its AOR is from Matayan to west of the Siachin. The formation sign is a black shield with overlapping gold circles (representing the number "8") and a red bayonet, point upwards through the intersection of the circles.[97]

Raised 1962 to replace 23rd Infantry Division for CI duty in Nagaland and to act as NEFA reserve; its HQ was formerly HQ GOC Nagaland. (The HQ was located at Kohima until 1990.) At one point late in the 1960s it had some 30 battalions under command, including the paramilitary Assam Rifles and police units. In 1965 it was considered a reserve for Eastern Command in addition to CI duties.

In the 1971 war the 8th was under IV Corps for the East Pakistan campaign., with the 59th and 81st Mountain Brigades, 1st East Bengal Brigade, and five BSF battalions. Its 71st Mountain Brigade was initially under XXXIII Corps and then placed under 6th Mountain Division; its 95th and 167th Mountain Brigades were under 101 Communications Zone; its 303rd Mountain Brigade was left along the border with China under Rear HQ XXXIII Corps. Finally, its 56th Brigade was on CI duties in Nagaland and Manipur.[98]

The division served on CI duties 1972-1990 and was placed under III Corps when it was formed in 1986. (That year it had 56th, 59th and 81st Mountain Brigades; 56th had six battalions.) Moved 1991 to Kashmir for CI duties, with HQ at Sharifabad, and responsible for the Punch, Rajouri, and Mendhar districts. Officially it was on temporary duty but it never returned to III Corps.

The 8th was shifted 1 June 1999 to XV Corps for the Kargil conflict, taking over vacant positions formerly held by 28th Mountain Division. It controlled the 50th (I) Parachute Brigade; its own 56th, 79th and 192nd Mountain Brigades; and 121st (I) Infantry Brigade. At one point the division exceeded 30,000 personnel and had 30 infantry battalions. The shift to Kashmir became permanent after 1999, with the division placed under the new XIV Corps.

---

[97] There was a Second World War 8th Indian Infantry Division, which served in Italy after garrison duties in the Middle East; it was disbanded in 1946.

[98] Per John H. Gill, *An Atlas of the 1971 India-Pakistan War*, which contains the most detailed order of battle for December 1971. However, it is hard to imagine one division with seven assigned brigades.

9th Infantry Division

This division is at Meerut, Uttar Pradesh, under XI Corps, Western Command. It is nicknamed the Pine Division. Its formation sign is a black shield with a grey pine tree.[99]

The division was raised in 1963 at Ranchi.

In December 1971 it was under II Corps for the invasion of East Pakistan, commanding the 32nd, 42nd and 350th Infantry Brigades.

In 1976 the division moved to Meerut. It is usually shown as being under XI Corps from that date, although there has been some question about the assignment. 9th Infantry Division provided some of the troops for Operation Bluestar June 1984.

10th Infantry Division

The 10th is at Akhnoor, Jammu and Kashmir, under XVI Corps, Northern Command. It is nicknamed the Dah Division. (Dah is Sanskrit for torment, grieve or burn.) The formation sign is a black shield. Originally it had two crossed sabers (gold hilts and silver blades) but now has two crossed tulwars in silver.[100]

Raised in 1965 at Belguam, Karnataka. The division was still in the process of formation when its HQ was shifted to Akhnoor and XV Corps late August, taking over the 191st (I) Infantry Brigade Group and the 80th Infantry Brigade from 25th Infantry Division. (The HQ was at about 30% of establishment and transferred without any divisional troops.) It then added 41st (I) Mountain Brigade from XV Corps reserve, 28th Infantry Brigade (which had replaced the 41st in corps reserve, but then went to the 10th), and finally the 52nd Mountain Brigade. The division thus ended up with 15 battalions for its defence of Akhnur against Pakistani attack.

---

[99] The Second World War 9th Indian Infantry Division was one of two lost at Singapore in 1942.

[100] The World War II 10th Indian Infantry Division served in the Middle East and Italy and was disbanded January 1947. It used diagonal bands of red and blue on a black square.

In December 1971 the 10th was under XV Corps, Western Command, controlling the 28th, 52nd, 68th and 191st Infantry Brigades, along with 3rd (I) Armoured Brigade. In June 1972 it transferred to the new XVI Corps.

11th Infantry Division

This division is at Ahmedabad, Gujarat, under XII Corps, Southern Command. Its nickname is the Golden Katar Division. The formation sign is a black shield with a gold Katar (Rajput dagger).[101] Currently includes 31st Armoured Brigade.

The division was raised in 1965. It was in the Rajashtan sector September 1965, which transferred from Western to Southern Command that month. Its 30th Infantry Brigade was involved in operations. HQ 85th Infantry Brigade arrived mid September 1965 and took over two battalions from the 30th.

It was under Southern Command in December 1971, with the 31st, 85th and 330th Infantry Brigades.

The division was placed under XII Corps when it was raised in February 1987.

12th Infantry Division

This division is at Jodhpur, Rajasthan, as part of XII Corps, Southern Command. It is nicknamed the Battle Axe Division. Its formation sign, accordingly, is a black shield with a gold battle axe.[102]

The division was formed 3 November 1966 from forces in the Barmer sector of the border with Pakistan.

In December 1971 the 12th was under Southern Command, with the 30th, 45th and 322nd Infantry Brigades. The division was assigned to attack Rahim Yar Khan and cut the north-south highway (Karachi to Rawalpindi) and rail line. The division's offensive was thrown off by a hurried attack by a Pakistan brigade. The GOC of the division refused to advance after that, despite the COAS's best efforts. The GOC Southern

---

[101] The 11th Indian Infantry Division of World War II was lost at Singapore in 1942.
[102] 12th Indian Infantry Division was used as a deceptive designation in Persia during the Second World War, similar to the 2nd.

Command also refused to get the division moving. Sam Manekshaw, the COAS, could not remove the commanders because he himself had initiated the policy of not changing commanders during war time.

The division was placed under XII Corps when it was raised in February 1987.

14th Infantry Division [RAPID]

Formerly a standard infantry division, the 14th is at Dehradun, Uttarakhand, under II Corps, Western Command. It is nicknamed the Golden Key Division. The formation sign is a black shield with a golden key.[103] The division contains the 58th Armoured Brigade (Roorkee) and the 35th and 116th Infantry Brigades (Dehradun). It is considered an "offensive" RAPID.

14th Infantry Division was raised in 1964. It was still in the process of raising when assigned to I Corps around May 1965. It had the 35th and 58th Infantry Brigades, with the 116th Infantry Brigade joining in August 1965. (However, 35th Infantry Brigade was sent to 6th Mountain Division early September and 58th Infantry Brigade sent to Pathankot.)

In December 1971 the division was under XI Corps, Western Command, with the 116th Infantry Brigade. Its 35th Infantry Brigade was detached to 7th Infantry Division and its 58th Infantry Brigade was detached to 15th Infantry Division. The division was soon transferred to II Corps for offensive operations (and recombined) but the cease fire came before the operation could be planned and implemented.

15th Infantry Division

Stationed at Amritsar, Punjab, under XI Corps, Western Command. It is nicknamed the Panther Division. The formation sign is a black shield with a gold panther's head, details in black, with white teeth and a red tongue.

The division was raised 1 October 1964 at Clement Town, Dehradun and placed under XI Corps. In the

[103] There was a 14th Indian Infantry Division in the Second World War. It fought in the Arakan 1942-43 and then served as a training formation until disbanded in 1946.

1965 war it was under XI Corps, Western Command, with the 38th and 54th Infantry Brigades. 96th Infantry Brigade was detached as part of the corps reserve, but returned later. 50th (I) Parachute Brigade came under command during September.

In December 1971 the 15th was under XI Corps, Western Command; it controlled its own 38th, 54th, 86th and 96th Infantry Brigades along with 58th Infantry Brigade from 14th Infantry Division. It provided some of the troops for Operation Bluestar June 1984.

16th Infantry Division

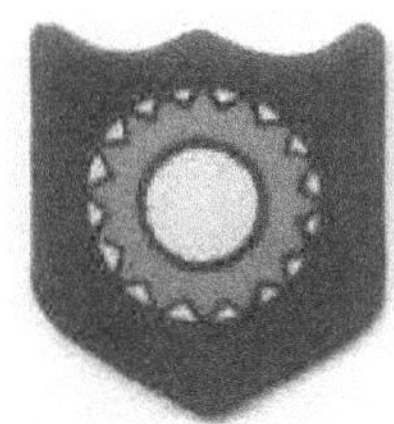

This division is at Sri Ganganagar, Rajasthan, under X Corps, South Western Command. It is nicknamed the Sudarshan Chakra Division. The formation sign is a black shield with the Sudarshan Chakra (with 16 points) in red on a white circle.

Foxtrot Sector, raised ad hoc in 1971 at Fazilka, South Punjab, became 16th Infantry Division in 1972. In 1976 it was placed under the newly-raised X Corps.

17th Mountain Division

Formerly an infantry division, 17th Mountain is at Gangtok, Sikkim, under XXXIII Corps, Eastern Command. It is nicknamed the Black Cat Division. The formation sign is a black shield with a black cat outlined in gold.[104]

17th Infantry Division was raised 15 November 1960 at Ambala to replace 4th Infantry Division as a reserve in Punjab, coming under XI Corps. (It was raised with the 48th, 63rd and 99th Infantry Brigades; the 99th was detached in 1961 and sent to the Congo.[105]) In 1961 it was used to seize Goa from the Portuguese, eliminating the last European-occupied territory in India. It commanded its own 48th and 63rd Infantry Brigades and 50th (I) Parachute Brigade for that operation.

---

[104] The World War II 17th Indian Infantry Division wore a black cat on a khaki square. Raised in June 1941, it had extensive experience in Burma and eastern India against the Japanese; it was disbanded January 1947 in Burma. The British Army also used this number, having a 17th Gurkha Infantry Division in Malaya 1952-1971.

[105] These were the same numbers as the brigades with the division at the end of the Second World War.

In October 1962 the division was XI Corps in Western Command. HQ was at Ambala and it included the 48th, 63rd and 164th Infantry Brigades. The division moved to Sikkim in November 1962 and came under XXXIII Corps. It converted the next year to a mountain division. It was still under XXXIII Corps in 1965.

In December 1971 the 17th remained along border with China under Rear HQ XXXIII Corps.

There was some talk of India providing a division for service in Iraq during the insurgency following the 2003 US invasion. 17th Mountain Division may have been alerted for use in Iraq, although any such plans ultimately fell through and it is unclear how serious the possibility was.

18th Infantry Division [RAPID]

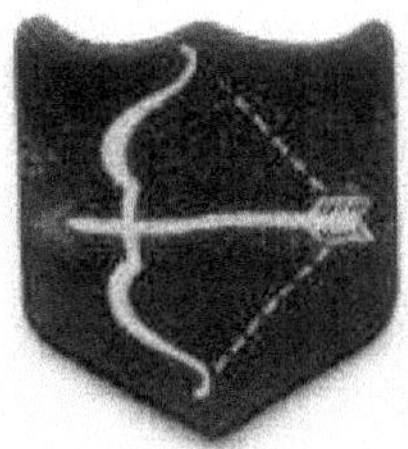

This division is at Kota, Rajasthan, under X Corps, South Western Command. The formation sign is a black shield with a gold fully-drawn bow and arrow (red arrowhead). The division includes 27th Armoured Brigade and 44th Mountain Brigade. It is considered a "defensive" RAPID.

The division was raised in 1976 and placed under the newly-raised X Corps.

19th Infantry Division

This division is at Baramulla, Jammu and Kashmir, as part of XV Corps, Northern Command. The formation sign is a black shield with a golden hand and forearm thrusting a dagger downwards.[106]

19th Infantry Division was raised May 1948 at Srinagar, and initially designated the Sri Division.[107] It began with control of 161st and 163rd (ex "Z") Infantry Brigades and

---

[106] 19th Indian Infantry Division in the Second World War wore a yellow dagger in a clenched hand on a red rectangle. It served in Assam and Burma, and was disbanded there in 1946.

[107] 2nd Airborne Division Engineers assigned as Sri Division Engineers 21 May 1948. They later shifted to 26th Infantry Division.

77th Parachute Brigade. In October 1962 the division was under XV Corps in Western Command. HQ was at Baramula, and its brigades were 104th Infantry (Tithwal), 161st Infantry (Uri), and 268th Infantry (Baramula)
In the 1965 war, the 19th was under XV Corps, Western Command; it commanded the 104th, 161st and 268th Infantry Brigades and the normally independent 68th Infantry Brigade was also under command.

In December 1971 the division was still under XV Corps, Western Command, with the 104th, 161st and 268th Infantry Brigades along with three sector commands.

20th Mountain Division

Formerly an infantry division, the 20th is at Binnaguri, West Bengal, under XXXIII Corps, Eastern Command. It is nicknamed the Kirpan Division. A kirpan is a Sikh religious article resembling a sword. The formation sign is a black shield with a white kirpan.[108]

20th Infantry Division has been reported as being at Ranchi as early as 1947, although this is disputed, and 1948 is more likely.[109]

In October 1962 the division came under XXXIII Corps in Eastern Command. HQ was at Ranchi, moving 16 November 1962 to Gangtok. The division had 66th and 165th Infantry Brigades. It converted 1963 to a mountain division. In 1965 the 20th was at Binaguir under XXXIII Corps.

In December 1971 it remained under XXXIII Corps for East Pakistan operations, with the 66th, 165th and 202nd Mountain Brigades and 340th Mountain Brigade Group. The last-named later moved to Kutch.

---

[108] The Second World War 20th Indian Division had a very similar design in appearance, although it was a silver clenched hand holding a tulwar on a black circle. That division served in Assam and Burma, going to Indochina following the war. it returned to India in early 1946 and was disbanded.

[109] In September 1956, 632 Corps Troops Engineers moved to Kohima and were redesignated as 20th Division Engineers. In September 1959, 20th Division Engineers were transferred to the new 23rd Infantry Division and redesignated accordingly.

21st Mountain Division

This division is stationed at Rangia, Assam, under IV Corps, Eastern Command. It is nicknamed the Red Horns Division. The formation sign is a black shield with a small white buffalo head with long red horns.[110]

The division was raised in 1978 to replace 23rd Mountain Division.

22nd Infantry Division

This division is at Meerut, Uttar Pradesh, under II Corps, Western Command. It is nicknamed the Ram Division. The formation sign is a black shield with a golden ram's head (details in purple).

The division was raised in 1978. It was originally named X Division to confuse Pakistani intelligence.

23rd Infantry Division

This division is at Ranchi, Jharkhand, under XXI Corps, Southern Command. It is nicknamed the Seval Division. (Seval is the red rooster heralding the dawn by calling for the sun to rise.) The formation sign is a black shield with a red fighting cock within a narrow red circle outline.[111]

The division was raised 1 September 1959 for the Nagaland insurgency when GOC Assam was redesignated as GOC 23rd Infantry Division.[112] In October 1962 it was moved to Rangia and placed under XXXIII Corps in Eastern Command.[113] It included the 73rd and 301st Infantry

---

[110] A 21st Indian Infantry Division existed as an ad hoc formation during 1944. It had the white buffalo head and red horns on a blue square.

[111] The Second World War 23rd Indian Infantry Division had a red fighting cock on a light yellow circle. It fought in northeast India and Burma, going to the Dutch East Indies following the war. The division later moved to Malaya late 1946 and was disbanded early the next year.

[112] Divisional engineers were formed by transfer and redesignation of 20th Infantry Division Engineers.

[113] 23rd Division Engineers were redesignated 2nd Division Engineers November 1962 and transferred.

Brigade and possibly the 192nd Infantry Brigade. Converted as a mountain division 1963 and placed under IV Corps. (It was also tasked as Eastern Command Reserve.) In 1965 it was still under IV Corps. 23rd Mountain Division was shifted from Assam to Western Command toward the end of the 1965 war but arrived too late to be of use.

In December 1971 it was under IV Corps for East Pakistan campaign; controlled 83rd, 181st and 301st Mountain Brigades along with 61st Mountain Brigade from 57th Mountain Division.

In 1976 the division left Bhutan for Ranchi to again serve as Eastern Command reserve and was reorganized in 1983 as 23rd Infantry Division. (It was often shown as being under III Corps.) Unofficially identified in July 2010 as one of four divisions to begin pre-deployment training for operations against the Maoist rebels in eastern India.

24th Infantry Division [RAPID]

This division is at Bikaner, Rajasthan, under X Corps, South Western Command. The details of the formation sign are unknown. The division includes the 180th Armoured Brigade (Bikaner) and 25th Infantry Brigade (Bhatinda), with another infantry brigade at Lalgarh Jattan. It is considered a "defensive" RAPID.

This division was raised in 1978 and placed under the newly-raised X Corps..

25th Infantry Division

This division is at Rajauri, Jammu and Kashmir, under XVI Corps, Northern Command. It is nicknamed the Ace of Spades Division. The formation sign is a black shield with a red outline of an ace of spades.[114]

The division was raised in 1948.

In October 1962 the division was under XV Corps in Western Command. HQ was at Poonch, and its brigades were 80th, 93rd and 120th Infantry.

[114] The 25th Indian Infantry Division in World War II wore a black ace of spades on a green square. It served in the Arakan and Burma. It moved into Malaya following the war and was disbanded there in early 1946.

In the 1965war , under XV Corps, Western Command, 25th Infantry Division contained the 62nd Mountain Brigade and the 80th,93rd and 120th Infantry Brigades. In September, 80th Infantry Brigade was placed under 10th Infantry Division, shortening the division's front.

In December 1971 the 25th was still under XV Corps, Western Command; it controlled the 80th, 93rd and 120th Infantry Brigades and 33rd Infantry Brigade from 39th Infantry Division.

The division transferred mid 2005 to XVI Corps.

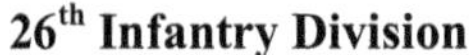

26th Infantry Division

Stationed at Jammu [City], Jammu and Kashmir, as part of IX Corps, Western Command. It is nicknamed the Tiger Division. The formation sign is a black shield with a yellow Royal Bengal tiger (mouth in red and other details in black) stepping through a blue triangle.[115]

The division was raised May 1948 in Jammu, and known initially as the JA Division.[116]

In October 1962 the division was under XV Corps in Western Command. HQ was at Jammu, and its brigades were 19th, 36th and 168th Infantry.

In the 1965 war, the 26th was still under XV Corps, Western Command, with the 19th, 162nd and 168th Infantry Brigades. It shifted to I Corps the beginning of September 1965, with the 162nd and 168th Infantry Brigades and was joined after operations started by 52nd Mountain Brigade.

In December 1971 it was still under XV Corps, Western Command, with the 19th, 36th and 162nd Infantry Brigades; its 168th Infantry Brigade was under X Sector (later 39th Infantry Division) in I Corps, Western Command.

---

[115] The Second World War 26th Indian Division also had a yellow Royal Bengal tiger (details in black), stepping out of a narrow blue triangle, but set on a black triangle. It served in the Arakan and Burma. It went to Sumatra following the war, leaving October-November 1946 and was disbanded January 1947 in India.

[116] 1st Armoured Division Engineers served as JA Division Engineers from early November 1947, returning to their parent formation in 1949. 2nd Airborne Division Engineers (from Sri—later 19th—Division) formed the basis for 26th Infantry Division Engineers.

In June 1972 the division transferred to the new XVI Corps. In mid 2005 it was transferred to the new IX Corps.

27th Mountain Division

Another former infantry division, the 27th is at Kalimpong, West Bengal, under XXXIII Corps, Eastern Command. It is nicknamed the Striking Lion Division. The formation sign is a black shield with a golden lion (details in black). It includes 123rd Mountain Brigade. At some point after 1988 the division was tasked for commitment against Pakistan in case of war.

The division was based in Kalimpong, West Bengal, when raised in 1953 and later (by 1960) moved to Jullundar. While often shown under XI Corps, it was actually an Army HQ reserve formation.

In October 1962 the division was with XI Corps in Western Command. HQ was still at Jullundur; it included the 64th and 123rd Infantry Brigades; the third brigade designation is unknown. It converted to a mountain division in 1963 and moved to Sikkim, coming under XXXIII Corps. In 1965 it was still in Sikkim under XXXIII Corps.

In December 1971 the 27th remained along border with China under Rear HQ XXXIII Corps. The division moved to Jammu from XXXIII Corps for Operation Parakram in 2001-2002. It was split up to reinforce other formations, but the main body was at Sundarbani (XVI Corps).

27th Mountain Division was moved to Kashmir during the 1999 Kargil War. It was relocated back to its original area of responsibility in Kalimpong in 2008 as part an Army initiative to withdraw two divisions from Kashmir.[117] The 27th was unofficially identified in July 2010 as one of four divisions to begin pre-deployment training for operations against the Maoist rebels in eastern India.

28th Infantry Division

This division is at Gurez, Jammu and Kashmir, under XV Corps, Northern Command. The design of the formation sign is unknown. The division includes 53rd Mountain Brigade.

---

[117] *Times of India*, 19 December 2009, timesofindia.indiatimes.com/iplarticleshow/5353950.cms.

The division was raised as 28th Mountain Division in 1984 for the Kargill sector. When the insurgency in Kashmir heated up in the 1990s, it was sent to Kupwara (NW of Srinager) to reduce 19th Infantry Division's AOR. Thus, the division was missing during the 1999 Kargil War, although one of its brigades was shifted to Ladakh in case the war expanded. Following the war the division was permanently assigned to XV Corps, and later redesignated 28th Infantry Division.

29th Infantry Division

This division is at Pathankot, Punjab, under IX Corps, Western Command. It is nicknamed the Silver Mace Division. The formation sign is a black shield with a silver gada (mace) with details in red.

The division was raised in 1984 and placed under XVI Cops. In mid 2005 it transferred to the new IX Corps.

31st Armoured Division

This division is at Jhansi, Uttar Pradesh, under XXI Corps, Southern Command. It is nicknamed the White Tiger Division. The formation sign is a yellow shield with a thin red border containing a charging white tiger (details in black). It contains the 34th, 94th and 224th Armoured Brigades.

The division was raised in 1972 at Jhansi with the new pattern of two armoured brigades.[118] It changed in 1984 to three armoured brigades. The formerly independent 2nd Armoured Brigade was assigned in 1972, remaining until replaced in 1992 by 224th Armoured Brigade.[119]

---

[118] The 1st Armoured Division had been numbered as the 31st from October 1941 to October 1945, making “31” a logical numerical designation for an armoured division.

[119] The 2nd had been in existence as an independent armoured brigade from the first day of the new Indian Army, and there was lobbying against its inclusion in the new armoured division early on. Finally, HQ 224th (I) Armoured Brigade was traded with it, restoring the 2nd to its former independent status.

33rd Armoured Division

This division is at Hisar, Punjab, under I Corps, South Western Command. It is nicknamed the Dot Division. The formation sign is a yellow shield with a thin red border with a red dot within four black lines, representing a tank caught within a gun sight. It contains the 39th, 57th and 88th Armoured Brigades.

The division was originally formed as a mechanized division (four tank regiments and six mechanized infantry battalions) at Hisar, possibly in 1978. Following the decision to create RAPIDs in 1986-87, the 33rd was converted as an armoured division. There has been some commentary to the effect that the Army was never quite sure what role a mechanised division was intended to play and, ultimately, that another armoured division (with the reverse mix of tank and infantry units) made more sense.

36th Infantry Division [RAPID]

This division is at Sagar, Madhya Pradesh, as part of I Corps, South Western Command. The formation sign is a golden falcon.[120] The division includes the 18th Armoured Brigade (Gwalior) and 72nd and 115th Infantry Brigades (Gwalior and Dhana, respectively).

Originally intended for raising as a cadre division, it was raised in 1966 at Sagar as a standard division. The division, like I Corps HQ, was within the bounaries of Central Command.

In December 1971 the division was under I Corps, Western Command; it controlled the 18th and 115th Infantry Brigades; its 72nd Infantry Brigade was under 39th Infantry Division, also in I Corps. That division's 87th Infantry Brigade was later transferred to the 36th.

The 36th was the second division sent to Sri Lanka as part of the IPKF, probably landing in 1987. It controlled the 41st, 72nd and 115th Infantry Brigades. The IPKF withdrew late 1989-March 1990.

---

[120] A 36th Indian Infantry Division was formed in 1942, but it had a large British Army element and was redesignated in 1944 as the [British] 36th Infantry Division.

39th Mountain Division

This division is at Palampur, Himachal Pradesh, serving as a reserve for Northern Command. It is nicknamed the Talwar Division. The formation sign is a black shield with a silver clenched fist hold a talwar (heavy Indian sword).[121]

The division was one of four planned to be raised as a cadre. However, it was raised at standard strength (without an armoured regiment) 1966 at Jhansi as 39th Infantry Division, to serve as XV Corps reserve. It moved to Yol, Himachal Pradesh in 1969.

In December 1971 it was under I Corps, Western Command; it had the 87th Infantry Brigade along with 72nd Infantry Brigade from 36th Infantry Division and 2nd (I) Armoured Brigade. Its 33rd Infantry Brigade was with 25th Infantry Division, XV Corps, Western Command and its 323rd Infantry Brigade was under X Sector, I Corps. The 87th Infantry Brigade was later shifted to 36th Infantry Division. The 39th later took over X Sector, regaining its 323rd Infantry Brigade and also gaining control over 168th Infantry Brigade of 26th Infantry Division.

The division was converted ca. 1995 to mountain. It was moved into the Kashmir Valley to strengthen the CI effort in the 1990s. (Its base was shifted to Palmpur in 2005 when the new IX Corps took over its space at Yol.) In 2009 it returned to its base in Palampur.[122]

40th Artillery Division

Stationed at Ambala under Western Command. It is sometimes shown as being with I Corps. The formation sign is on a dark blue shield but the design is not known. Raising date and other details are unknown.

---

[121] The World War II 39th Indian Light Division had a white tulwar held in a clenched brown fist, all on a dark green circle. It began life as the 1st Burma Division, being renumbered in 1942 and serving as a training division from 1943 until disbanded in 1946.

[122] *Times of India*, 19 December 2009, timesofindia.indiatimes.com/iplarticleshow/5353950.cms.

41st Artillery Division

Raised in April 2002 for Southern Command and located at Pune. The formation sign is on a dark blue shield but the design is no known. Raising date and other details are unknown.

54th Infantry Division

This division is at Sikandrabad (Secunderabad), Uttar Pradesh, under XXI Corps, Southern Command. It is nicknamed the Bison Division. The formation sign is a black shield a white bison head (details in black, ears in red and nose in blue). It has trained for amphibious tasks.

The division was raised in 1967 at Secunderabad. While planned as one of the cadre divisions, it was raised at full strength.

In December 1971 the division was under I Corps, Western Command; it controlled its own 47th, 74th and 91st Infantry Brigades along with 16th (I) Armoured Brigade.

Conversion of the 54th to an airmobile division, as 54th Air Assault Division, was approved in 1985.[123] Elements of the division participated in Exercise Brass Tacks in 1986-87. However, given the lack of helicopter assets "the division's 'air assault' designation meant in reality only that it was adept at quickly loading and unloading from transport aircraft."[124]

While in its nominal air assault role, the division was the first to be sent to Sri Lanka as part of IPKF, landing in August 1987. It controlled the 47th, 76th and 91st Infantry Brigades. The IPKF withdrew late 1989-March 1990. Following the withdrawal, the 54th was redesignated as an infantry division. It has been unofficially identified in July 2010 as one of four divisions to begin pre-deployment training for operations against the Maoist rebels in eastern India.

---

[123] 47th Infantry Brigade received some light airmobile training in January 1987 during Operation Trident, flying from Hyderabad to Delhi.

[124] Ken Conboy, *Elite Forces of India and Pakistan*, p 15. Gen Sundarji, then COAS, envisaged two air assault divisions and a massive increase in the Army Air Corps, but financial and operational considerations prevented this. It has been reported that Gen Sundarji did not ask the US Military Attache for the war establishment of an air assault division until after he announced the conversion of 54th to air assault.

56th Mountain Division

This division was raised in 2009, with its HQ at Zakhama, Nagaland, under III Corps, Eastern Command. The formation sign is unknown.

57th Mountain Division

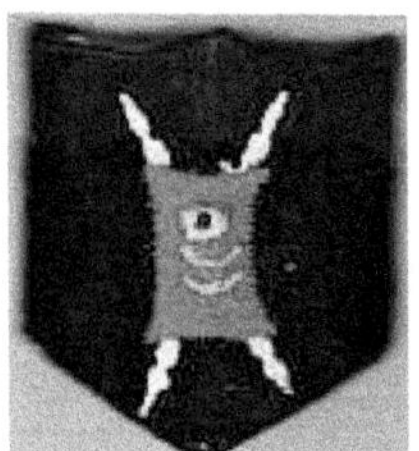

This division is at Leimakhong, Manipur, under III Corps, Eastern Command. It is nicknamed the Red Shield Division. The formation sign is a black shield in front of two Naga spears.

The division was raised at Mizoram in 1963 as 57th Infantry Division. Initially formed as a cadre division, it was raised to standard strength 1966 as 57th Mountain Division and took over 61st Infantry Brigade. It was intended to serve as a command reserve and was in Nagaland.

In December 1971 the division was under IV Corps for East Pakistan operations; it had the 73rd and 311th Mountain Brigades, with its 61st Mountain Brigade under 23rd Mountain Division in the same corps.

The 57th served in Punjab on CI duties 1986-87 in a roving role being deployed near Tarn Taran, later Mahajan and then Phalodi. The division was placed under III Corps when it was formed in 1986. Trained in jungle warfare, the division was sent to Sri Lanka, probably in 1988, as part of the IPKF. The IPKF withdrew late 1989-March 1990. The division then returned to III Corps, and went with it to Jammu and Kashmir for Operation Parakram 2001-2002. The corps and division later returned to the Northeast.

New Divisions

In addition to the 56th Mountain Division, another division was supposed to be raised in Eastern Command in 2009. However, that was postponed and is expected to start raising in 2011.

Apart from this, in early 2008 the Army began preparations to raise two more mountain divisions in Northern Command. Originally, they would be in place "only by the middle of the next decade".[125] However, the Army began to post

---

[125] *The Times of Indai* in an article was dated 7 February 2008. See timesofindia.indiatimes.com/Two_mountain_units_to_counter_Pak_China/articleshow/2762650.cms. A 2009 article indicated that one of the new mountain divisions would

officers to the new divisions by March 2010, and the plan was to have both fully operational by 2012.[126]

The Army proposed raising a third artillery division, in Eastern Command. When formed, it is to have two brigades of 155mm howitzers and one of multiple-launch rocket systems.[127] There are no details of when the division will be raised or become operational; the number "42" would be a logical but unconfirmed designation for it.

---

be headquartered in central Nagaland or Assam. While there are CI operations in the area, "sources say the division could also have the task of keeping an eye on the Chinese border in neighbouring Arunachal Pradesh…." *The Times of India*, 11 September 2009, timesofindia.indiatimes.com/india/New-N-E-division-with-eye-on-China/articleshow/4995973.cms.

[126] *The Times of India*, 31 March 2010, timesofindia.indiatimes.com/india/Future-war-on-two-and-a-half-fronts/articleshow/5744073.cms.

[127] *The Times of India*, 2 July 2009, timesofindia.indiatimes.com/Eye-on-China-more-muscle-for-East/articleshow/4725693.cms.

Areas and Sub-Areas

This section shows the formation badges for the known areas and sub-areas.

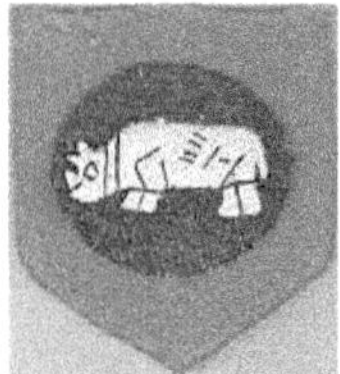

101 Area (North East)

Andhra Tamil Nadu Karnataka & Kerala Area (ATNK&K Area)

Andhra Sub-Area

Bengal Area

Delhi and Rajasthan Area

Madhya Pradesh and Bihar Area

Maharashtra Goa & Gujarat Area (MG & G Area)

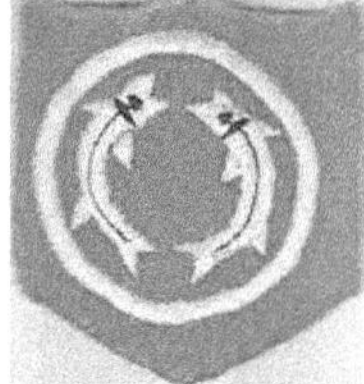

Uttar Pradesh Area

71 Independent Sub-Area (Northern Command)

Punjab Haryana & Himachal Pradesh Independent Sub-Area

Armoured Corps

The new Indian Army inherited 12 armoured regiments from the old one.[128] Ten regiments were equipped with tanks: six Sherman, three Stuart, and one Churchill.[129]

1st Horse (Skinner's Horse)
2nd Lancers (Gardner's Horse)
3rd Cavalry[130]
4th Hodson's Horse
7th Light Cavalry
8th Light Cavalry
9th Deccan Horse
14th Scinde Horse
16th Light Cavalry
17th Poona Horse
18th Cavalry
21st Central India Horse

There was also a ceremonial unit, the Governor General's Bodyguard, officially the Viceroy's Bodyguard but still called by its old name. When India became a republic in January 1950 this was redesignated as the **President's Bodyguard**. It is a mounted (horsed) unit, with a strength of 180; other ranks are equal parts Sikhs, Jats and Rajputs while officers are recruited on an all India basis. It has BTR-60 APCs in addition to its horses, and some personnel are parachute trained.[131]

---

[128] Royal titles from the Raj period have been omitted as they were dropped in 1950 when India officially became a Republic. Thus the first two units had been Skinner's Horse (1st Duke of York's Own) and 2nd Royal Lancers (Gardner's Horse). The 1922 reorganization merged 39 cavalry regiments into 21, of which three then became training units. The former 5th, 6th, 10th, 11th, 13th and 19th regiments went to Pakistan. The former 12th, 15th and 20th regiments (the training units) had been disbanded in 1941. See Appendix D for details on the lineage and titles of the original cavalry regiments of the new Indian Army.

[129] The US M4 Sherman was the main Allied medium tank of the Second World War; the M3 Stuart was a light tank limited to recce tasks in Europe by 1944; the Churchill was a British infantry tank, slow and heavily armoured and intended to assist infantry.

[130] This regiment had been lost at Singapore in 1942 and reformed April 1946 as the reconnaissance regiment for the 2nd Airborne Division.

[131] The unit's web page is at presidentofindia.nic.in/presidentsbodyguards.html. Detachments have served in the 1965 war, with the IPKF in Sri Lanka, Siachen, and with the UN in Somalia Sierra Leone and Angola.

The first post-war armoured regiment was not raised until 1956 when the 20th Lancerr reformed, followed by two more regiments the next year. However, from 1965 to 1989 the number of armored regiments increased from 15 to 55, and the total is now 63. New regiments were designated as cavalry until 1966 when the designation armoured regiment replaced cavalry.[132]

61st Cavalry, raised in 1953 at Jaipur from State Force units, is a horsed cavalry regiment. Initially intended as a mounted recce unit for the desert ion wartime, it was reorganized in 1975 as a purely ceremonial unit.

The Armoured Corps has employed a wide variety of tanks over the years. After the 1965 war, when the US ended arms shipments, it began switching to tanks and other equipment from the USSR. British- and Soviet-designed tanks have been produced locally under license. The first locally designed and developed tank, the Arjun Mk 1 began to enter service in 2009 after years of trials, development and other problems.

Year	Regiments	Equipment[133]
1947	12	3 Stuart, 6 Sherman, 1 Churchill,[134] 2 armoured car
1957	16	3 Stuart, 7 Sherman, 4 Centurion, 1 unknown
1965	17	7 Sherman, 4 Centurion, 2 AMX-13, 1 T-54/55, 2 PT-76
1971	26	4 Centurion, 12 T-54/55, 2 PT-76, 6 Vijayanta, 2 unknown
1976	32	4 Centurion, 13 T-54/55, 2 PT-76, 12 Vijayanta, 1 unknown
1979	37	1 Centurion, 16 T-54/55, 1 PT-76, 16 Vijayanta, 3 unknown
1982	45	16 T-54/55, 1 PT-76, 16 Vijayanta, 6 T-72, 4 unknown
1994	57	12 T-55, 14 Vijayanta, 27 T-72, 4 unknown
2009	63	10 T-55, 35 T-72M1, 11 Vijayanta, 5 T-90S, 1 Arjum Mk 1 (undergoing trials), 1 unknown

The Armoured Corps Centre and School was formed on 23 August 1948 at Ahmadnagar from various training establishments created by the old Indian Army. It is second only to the Artillery Centre in size and its commandant is a lieutenant general. There is the Basic Training Centre, the Driving and

132 The exception was the 45th Cavalry, which was allowed to claim a link to the wartime unit of the same designation. The 1956 regiment used the 20th Lancers designation of a disbanded unit. As with Pakitan, the Indian Army filled in missing numbers between 1 and 21 with new units.

133 This table represents a best effort to reconcile inconsistent data from several sources with the established raising dates of regiments.

134 Later changed to Shermans.

Maintenance Regiment (training vehicle drivers), the Armament and Electronics Regiment (trains gunners and communication personnel), the Automotive Regiment (the Driver Maintenance Group to 1991; technical training for AFV drivers and upgrade courses for other personnel), and the School of Technical Training, which took over the advanced training wings from other regiments. The Centre also has the School of Armoured Warfare, which trains students from all arms and services in command from troop to battalion level. There is also an Armoured Corps Depot, performing a variety of administrative tasks for the Indian Armoured Corps.

The current armoured regiments of the Indian Army are contained in the list below. Each regiment has its own badge, the old regiments generally using a variant of the pre-1947 badge with crowns or other non-Indian elements removed.[135] Most regiments include crossed lances as part of their badges, although some have stylized tanks or other designs.[136]

1st Horse — Aug 1947: Dera Ismail Khan [Churchills, in place of Stuarts]. [Switched back to Stuarts for 1948 operations in Kashmir, and Hyderabad (1st Armd Bde), then reverted to Churchills.] Shermans 1957-1965, followed by T-54 1965 and T-55 later.] Sep 1965: with 15th Inf Div. Dec 1971: 2nd Armd Bde [T-55]. [T-72 from 1979.]
Motto: Himmat-e-mardan, madad-e-khuda (Bravery of man is by the grace of God)
Honours:[137] Harar Kalan, Punjab 1971.

2nd Lancers — Aug 1947: in Malaya [Shermans]. 1965: u/c 1st Armd Div for operations (had been with 26th Inf Div) [Shermans]. Dec 1971: 1st Armd Bde [Vijayanata]. [T-72 by late 1990s.]
Honours: Punjab 1965.

---

135 However, 1st Horse did retain the White Rose [of York] at the intersection of the crossed lances, a reference to their prior designation which included "Duke of York's Own."

136 Photographs of many of the badges can be found at empiretocommonwealth.webs.com/armyreg04.htm.

137 In all lists of honours, specific battle honours are given first, followed by the relevant theatre honour. Only the former are emblazoned on regimental colours.

3rd Cavalry	Aug 1947: Rawalpindi. 1948: 1st Armd Bde, Hyderabad [Shermans]. 1965: 2nd (I) Armd Bde [Centurions]. Dec 1971: 3rd Inf Div [Centurions]. *Motto*: Kirti aur vivek *Honours*: Asal Uttar, Punjab 1965; Shehjra, Punjab 1971.
4th Horse	Aug 1947: (Ahmednagar) 2nd Armd Bde. 1965: 1st Armd Bde [Centurions]. Dec 1971: 16th Armd Bde [Centurion]. *Motto*: Tayar bar tayar *Honours*: Butur Dograndi, Phillora, Punjab 1965; Basantar River, Punjab 1971.
5th Armoured	Raised 1 Dec 1983 at Jodhpur, later moved to Patiala. [Vijayanta tanks late 1990s. First regiment to get T-90 MBT.]
6th Armoured	Raised Feb 1984. [Vijayanta tanks late 1990s.]
7th Lt Cavalry	Aug 1947: in Japan [Stuarts/armd cars]. Served in Kashmir [Stuarts/armd cars] 1947-48. Oct 1962: B Sqn [Stuarts] with 4th Inf Div in Ladakh. Sep 1965: 2nd (I)Armd Bde [PT-76]. Redesignated 7th **Cavalry** after 1965. Dec 1971: 2nd Armd Bde [T-55]. [Later T-72] *Honours*: Srinagar, Naushera, Jhangar, Zoji La, Jammu & Kashmir 1947-48; Punjab 1965; Mian Bazaaar, East Pakistan 1971; Punjab 1971.
8th Lt Cavalry	Aug 1947: Calcutta area. Sep 1965: 2nd (I)Armd Bde [AMX-13]. Redesignated **8th Cavalry** after 1965. Dec 1971: 3rd Armd Bde but with 26th Inf Div [Vijayanta]. *Honours*: Punjab 1965.
9th [Deccan] Horse	Aug 1947: (Secunderabad) 1st Armd Bde [Shermans]. 1965: 2nd (I) Armd Bde, then 4th Inf Div [Sherman IV/V]. Dec 1971:10th Inf Div [T-54]. [T-72 by late 1990s.] *Motto*: Sanghe Shakti *Honours*: Asal Uttar, Punjab 1965.
10th Armoured	Raised Apr 1984. [Vijayanta tanks late 1990s.]
11th Armoured	Raised May 1984. [Vijayanta tanks late 1990s.] *Motto*: Jeet hi jeet
12th Armoured	Raised 1 Oct 1984. [Vijayanta tanks late 1990s.] *Motto*: Shauryamev Jeevanam (Life only with valour)

13th Armoured	Raised Sep 1984. [Vijayanta tanks late 1990s.]
14th [Scinde] Horse	Aug 1947: 2nd Armd Bde (Ahmednagar). Sep 1965: with 15th Inf Div [Sherman V]. Dec 1971: 2nd Armd Bde [T-55].]. [T-72 by late 1990s.] *Motto*: Man dies but the regiment lives *Honours*: Dograi; Punjab 1965; Malakpur, Punjab 1971.
15th Armoured	Raised Mar 1985. [Vijayanta tanks late 1990s.]
16th Lt Cavalry	Aug 1947: (Ahmednagar) 2nd Armd Bde. 1965: 1st Armd Bde [Centurions]. Redesignated **16th Cavalry** after 1965. Dec 1971: 16th Armd Bde [Centurion]. Participated in Operation Blue Star Jun 1984. *Honours*: Punjab 1965.
17th Horse	Aug 1947: (Risalpur?) 3rd Armd Bde.[138] 1948: 1st Armd Bde, Hyderabad [Shermans] 1965: 1st Armd Bde [Centurions]. Dec 1971: 16th Armd Bde [Centurion]. [T-72 by late 1990s.] PVC: two[139] *Motto*: Ranvir jai sada *Honours*: Phillora, Buttur Dograndi; Punjab 1965; Basantar River, Punjab 1971.
18th Cavalry	Aug 1947: (Risalpur?) 3rd Armd Bde.[140] 1965: 26th Inf Div [Sherman V]. Dec 1971: 14th Armd Bde [T-54]; sqns with 67th Inf Bde, 51st Para Bde, Juliet Sector. [T-54 replaced by T-72 in 1983.] *Motto*: Sahas aur samman *Honours*: Jammu & Kashmir 1965; Tilakpur-Muhadipur, Punjab 1965; Punjab 1971.
19th Armoured	Raised Mar 1985. [Vijayanta tanks late 1990s.]

---

[138] This brigade HQ went to Pakistan on independence.

[139] Param Vir Chakra, India's highest gallantry award. Lt Col Ardeshir Burzorji Tarapore (15 Oct 1965) (P [posthumous]); 2/Lt Arun Khetarpal (16 Dec 1971) (P). These are the only two PVCs earned by members of the Armoured Corps.

[140] This brigade HQ went to Pakistan on independence.

20th Lancers	Raised 1956 [Churchill].[141] 1962: part of B Sqn [AMX-13] to 114th Inf Bde Ladakh.[142] Sep 1965: XV Corps [AMX-13]. Dec 1971: 12th Inf Div [AMX-13]. *Honours*: Jammu & Kashmir 1965.
[21st] Central India Horse	Aug 1947: Ahmednagar [2nd Armd Bde?]. Served in Kashmir 1948 [Stuarts]. 1965: [Shermans]; with 7th Inf Div?. Dec 1971: 3rd Armd Bde but with 26th Inf Div [T-55]. [T-72 by late 1990s.] *Motto*: Fortune Favours the Brave *Honours*: Rajaori; Jammu & Kashmir 1947-48; Burki, Punjab 1965.
41st Armoured	Raised 1 Jul 1980 at Ahmednagar. [T-72 tanks late 1990s.]
42nd Armoured	Raised Jan 1981. [T-55 tanks late 1990s.]
43rd Armoured	Raised Feb 1981. [Vijayanta tanks late 1990s.]
44th Armoured	Raised Dec 1981.
45th Cavalry	Raised 16 May 1965.[143] Served as an armoured delivery regiment in 1965 war. Dec 1971: 3rd (I) Armd Bde but detached to 9th Inf Div [PT-76], A Sqn to 4th Mtn Div. [Later T-55 tanks] *Motto*: Veer Bhogya Vasundhara *Honours*: Darsana, East Pakistan 1971
46th Armoured	Raised Jul 1982. [Vijayanta tanks late 1990s.]
47th Armoured	Raised Nov 1982. [T-72 tanks late 1990s.]
48th Armoured	Raised Dec 1982. [T-55 tanks late 1990s.]
49th Armoured	Raised Oct 1983. [Vijayanta tanks late 1990s.]

---

[141] Considered as re-raising of 20th Lancers, a training regiment disbanded in 1941.
[142] Two troops, later increased to a full squadron known as the Himalayan Detachment, which remained until 1966.
[143] Considered as a re-raising of 45th Cavalry, which was active 1941-46 and then disbanded.

50th Armoured	Raised May 1989. [T-72 tanks late 1990s.] *Motto*: Digvijay (Victory in all directions)
51st Armoured	Raised Jul 1989. [T-72 tanks late 1990s.] Motto: Har maidan fateh
52nd Armoured	Raised May 1994. [T-72 tanks late 1990s.]
53rd Armoured	Raised 2002.
54th Armoured	Raised after 2002.
55th Armoured	Raised after 2002.
56th Armoured	Raised after 2002.
57th Armoured	Raised after 2002.
58th Armoured	Raised after 2002.
59th Armoured	Raised after 2002.
61st Cavalry	Raised 1 Oct 1953 at Gwalior from State Forces as a horsed regiment.[144] 1965: 57th Inf Bde. One sqn at Delhi from 1970, later disbanded. A purely ceremonial unit after 1975.[145] *Motto*: Ashwa Shakti Yashobal
62nd Cavalry	Raised 31 Mar 1957 at Ambala Cantonment [Shermans].[146] 1965: 26th Inf Div but u/c 1st Armd Div [Shermans]. Dec 1971: 14th Armd Bde [T-55] but with Mike Force, I Corps. [T-72 tanks late 1990s.] *Motto*: Dhaiya evam shaurya (Fortitude and valour)

---

144 The source units were the Gwalior Lancers, Jodhpur/Kachhawa Horse, Mysore Lancers, Saurashtra Cavalry Sqn, and B Sqn, 2nd Patiala Lancers—the only State Force cavalry to survive 1951. It was designated New Horsed Cavalry Regiment (perhaps the worst title ever given to a regiment) until January 1954.

145 Famed for its polo playing members, the regiment has a page on the IndiaPolo.com web site: www.indiapolo.com/Polopedia/Genesis/Indian_Army/61st_Cavalry/61st_cavalry.html.

146 The regiment has also been shown as raised in 1956 and equipped with Churchill tanks at first.

63rd Cavalry	Raised 1957 [Stuarts]. 1961-62: provided indep armoured car sqn with 99th Inf Bde Congo. Sep 1965: Eastern Cmd [PT-76]. Dec 1971: 3rd (I) Armd Bde but under XXXIII Corps [T-55], B Sqn 9th Inf Div. *Motto*: Prakram hi dharma hai *Honours*: Bogra, East Pakistan 1971.
64th Cavalry	Raised 31 Mar 1966 with volunteers from other regiments [Shermans]. Dec 1971: 14th Armd Bde [T-54]. [T-72 tanks late 1990s.] *Motto*: Veerta hi maan (Ever by courage and honour)
65th Armoured	Raised Sep 1966.[147] Dec 1971: 1st Armd Bde [Vijayanata]. Served with IPKF in Sri Lanka. [T-72 tanks late 1990s.]
66th Armoured	Raised 1966 [Vijayanta]. Dec 1971: [Vijayanta]. [T-72 tanks late 1990s.] *Honours*: Punjab 1971.
67th Armoured	Raised Sep 1967. Dec 1971: 1st Armd Bde [Vijayanata]. [Later T-72]
68th Armoured	Raised 14 Mar 1968 [Vijayanata]. Dec 1971: 1st Armd Bde [Vijayanata]. [T-72 tanks late 1990s.] *Motto*: Vijay aur samman (Victory and honour)
69th Armoured	Raised 1 Oct 1968 [PT-76]. Dec 1971: 3rd (I) Armd Bde but under XXXIII Corps [PT-76]. [T-72 tanks late 1990s.] Honours: Bogra, East Pakistan 1971.
70th Armoured	Raised Jan 1968 [SS-11 ATGM regt]. Dec 1971: 14th Armd Bde [SS-11] but with Foxtrot Sector. Converted as normal armd regt 1975 [T-55]. *Motto*: Sattar Number Karke Rahenge
71st Armoured	Raised Jan 1971. Dec 1971: 14th Armd Bde but with 86th Inf Bde/15th Inf Div [T-55]. [Still T-55 late 1990s.] *Motto*: Shatrunash

[147] Raised initially as 65th Cavalry and then became first unit designated as an armoured regiment.

72nd Armoured	Raised Jul 1971. Dec 1971: 3rd Armd Bde [T-55]. [Still T-55 late 1990s.] *Motto*: Vivek, veerta, vijay *Honours*: Chamb, Jammu & Kashmir 1971.
73rd Armoured	Raised 3 Dec 1971 [T-55]. [Still T-55 late 1990s.] *Motto*: Purity, Determination and Valour
74th Armoured	Raised Jun 1972 [T-55]. [Still T-55 late 1990s.]
75th Armoured	Raised 12 Mar 1972 [T-55].[148] [Still T-55 late 1990s.] May be firt regiment to receive Arjun MBT and an element of 140th (I) Armd Bde.[149] *Honours*: Sindh 1971 (earned by component squadrons)
76th Armoured	Raised Mar 1985. [Vijayanta tanks late 1990s.]
81st Armoured	Raised Oct 1973. [T-72 tanks late 1990s.]
82nd Armoured	Raised Oct 1975. [T-72 tanks late 1990s.]
83rd Armoured	Raised Jan 1976. [T-55 tanks late 1990s.]
84th Armoured	Raised Jul 1976. [T-72 tanks late 1990s.] *Motto*: Aham ver yuddh sthale
85th Armoured	Raised Oct 1976. [T-72 tanks late 1990s.] *Motto*: Sarvasva Vijay
86th Armoured	Raised 1 Mar (or Jan?) 1977. [T-55 tanks late 1990s.]
87th Armoured	Raised Jul 1979. [T-72 tanks late 1990s.] *Motto*: Nishchay ay kar apni jeet karon
88th Armoured	Raised Feb 1980. [T-72 tanks late 1990s.]
89th Armoured	Raised Feb 1980. [Vijayanta tanks late 1990s.]

---

[148] Raised by consolidation of 3rd, 4th and 5th (I) Armoured Squadrons at Gadra Road in Pakistan, the only regiment raised outside India.

[149] According to a discussion thread in a Bharat Rakshak forum on armoured vehicles; forums.bharat-rakshak.com/viewtopic.php?f=3&t=5530&start=120.

90th Armoured Raised Jul 1979.[150] [T-72 tanks late 1990s.]

Independent squadrons have existed from time to time, and there were ten in 1971. The 1st to 6th were designated as independent armoured squadrons and the 90th to 93rd as independent reconnaissance squadrons. The 3rd, 4th and 5th were consolidated in March 1972 to form 75th Armoured Regiment; the 90th to 92nd were consolidated in July 1979 to form the 90th Armoured Regiment. The others were presumably disbanded by that date.

	Affiliation	Assignment	Equipment
1st	7th Cavalry	IV Corps	PT-76
2nd	21st Cavalry	16th (I) Armd Bde[151]	AMX-13
3rd	1st Horse	Southern Cmd	T-55
4th	9th Horse	Southern Cmd	upgunned Sherman
5th	63rd Cavalry	IV Corps	PT-76
6th		Southern Cmd	T-55
....			
90th	17th Horse	16th (I) Armd Bde	AMX-13
91st	14th Horse	2nd (I) Armd Bde	AMX-13
92nd	18th Cavalry	14th (I) Armd Bde	PT-76
93rd		1st Armd Div	AMX-13

There have been ad hoc squadrons from time to time, such as one raised for service in the Congo during the early 1960s.

---

[150] Formed from three existing independent reconnaissance squadrons, from the 17th Horse, 18th Cavalry and 65th Armored Regiments [numbered as 90th-92nd]..

[151] Possibly assigned in lieu of 92nd Recce Squadron, which was detached to 163rd Infantry Brigade, Foxtrot Sector.

Selected Armoured Regiment Badges

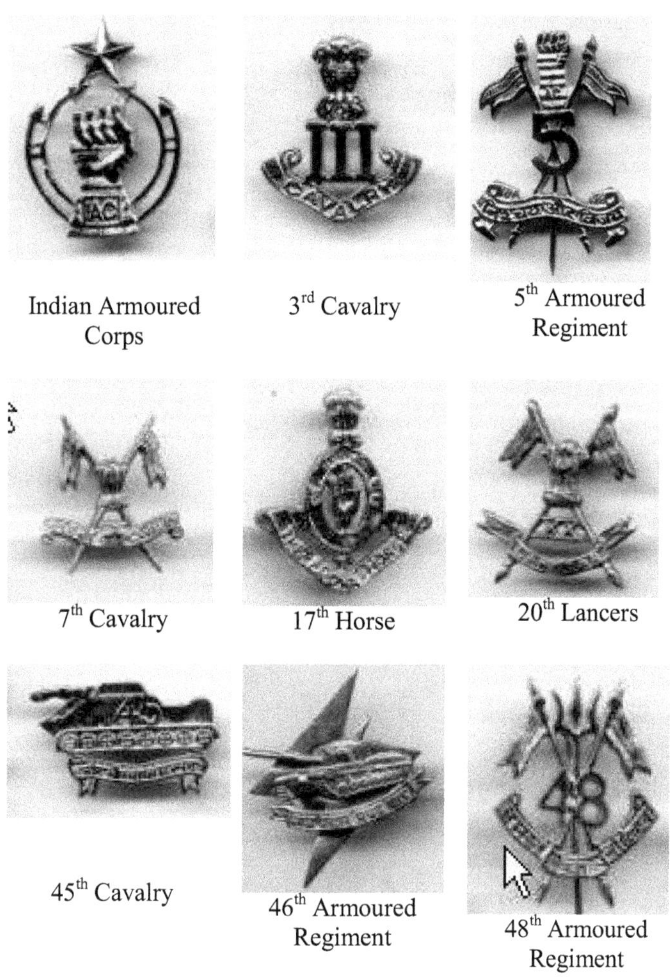

Indian Armoured Corps

3rd Cavalry

5th Armoured Regiment

7th Cavalry

17th Horse

20th Lancers

45th Cavalry

46th Armoured Regiment

48th Armoured Regiment

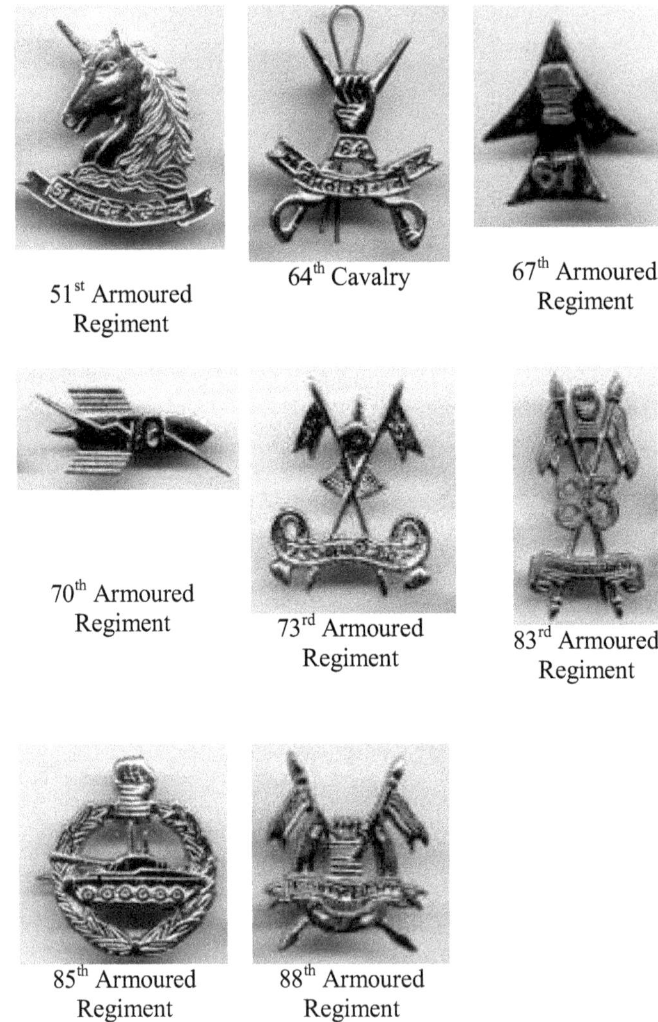

51st Armoured Regiment

64th Cavalry

67th Armoured Regiment

70th Armoured Regiment

73rd Armoured Regiment

83rd Armoured Regiment

85th Armoured Regiment

88th Armoured Regiment

All of the regimental badges appearing in this book are from the private collection of Jagan Pillarisetti, and generously made available by him.

Infantry

The regular regiments of the old Indian Army were numbered from 1st to 19th, although all but the Punjab regiments—most of which went to Pakistan—eliminated the numerical designations in October 1945 following the war.[152] The following regiments (with their old numbers in brackets and any royal titles ignored) were transferred to the new Indian Army:

2nd Punjab Regiment
[3rd] Madras Regiment
[4th] Grenadiers
[5th] Maratha Light Infantry
[6th] Rajputana Rifles
[7th] Rajput Regiment
[9th] Jat Regiment
[11th] Sikh Regiment
[17th] Dogra Regiment
[18th] Garhwal Rifles
[19th] Kumaon Regiment[153]

In addition, a few regiments formed during the Second World War were retained on the establishment and went to the new Indian Army:

The Sikh Light Infantry
The Assam Regiment
The Bihar Regiment
The Mahar Machine Gun Regiment

Finally, the old Army had ten regiments of Gurkhas. Four of these (2nd, 6th, 7th and 10th) went to the British Army,[154] while the following—restyled as Gorkha—went to the Indian Army following a November 1947 treaty:

1st Gorkha Rifles (The Malaun Regiment)

---

[152] The 1922 reorganization created 19 new multi-battalion infantry regiments from the more than 100 mainly single-battalion regiments then in existence. The intent was for each regiment to have a training battalion, designated as the 10th. These did not survive as actual units following the Second World War and some regiments have chosen not to re-use the number..

[153] Renamed from 19th Hyderabad Regiment following the war.

[154] As will be seen in the regimental sections, not all of the personnel in the four regiments chose to go to the British Army, and a few of their battalions transferred almost intact to regiments staying in India.

3rd Gorkha Rifles
4th Gorkha Rifles
5th Gorkha Rifles (Frontier Force)
8th Gorkha Rifles
9th Gorkha Rifles

Some units from the former princely states became battalions of one or another of these regiments in 1951. Only the Jammu and Kashmir Infantry were taken into the Army as a distinct regiment, in 1957.

Additional regiments were formed after 1947. The 11th Gorkha Rifles were newly raised January 1948. In August 1949, the Brigade of The Guards was formed taking over the four most senior battalions in the Army. It was given precedence as the senior infantry regiment. A distinct Parachute Regiment was created in 1952, ranking after the Guards. The Jammu and Kashmir Infantry (later Rifles) were nominally apart from the Indian Army until 1957. The Naga Regiment was formed in 1970. In 1976, militia units in Kashmir were regularized as the Jammu and Kashmir Light Infantry. In April 1979, the 14 existing mechanised (APC-mounted) infantry battalions were used to form a new regiment, The Mechanised Infantry. It was given precedence after the Parachute Regiment, making it third overall among the infantry.

The Naga Regiment notwithstanding, the government and Army have resisted calls for new provincial-named or class-based regiments. Those calls began shortly after independence and have continued to the present.[155] Thus, the Infantry largely reflects the inheritance from the pre-independence Army, with the Brigade of The Guards created as a deliberately "All India" regiment and the Parachute and Mechanised Infantry Regiments the outcome of their distinct roles.

Brigade of The Guards

Although ranked as the senior infantry regiment, this all-class mixed regiment was raised in August 1949, taking over the four most senior battalions (2nd Punjab, 1st Grenadiers, 1st Rajputana Rifles and 1st Rajput) as its initial battalions.[156] The new regiment was the creation of the first Indian Chief of the

---

[155] See Gautam, op. cit., pp 57-58.

[156] These battalions may include their former titles as a parenthetical, e.g., 4th Guards (1st Rajput). Mechanised Guards battalions may now have "(Mechanised)" appended at the end of their designation.

Army Staff, General (later Field Marshal) K.M. Cariappa.[157] At the time, infantry regiments were class-based as a regiment, or recruited various classes but segregated by company. The Brigade of The Guards was to recruit from all classes, and its units were mixed down to the section (platoon) level.[158] The regiment has the privilege of choosing its own officers.

As it expanded some battalions were formed as anti-tank guided missile units, and from 1986 it gradually began to convert others to mechanised (APC-mounted); all but four were so converted by March 1999, and the remainder may have been by now. The four ATGM battalions were later converted to the recce and support role, with ATGM platoons assigned to infantry battalions.

1st Bn (2nd Punjab)	Raised Aug 1949 (ex 2nd Punjab). Sep 1965: 121st Inf Bde [but also shown with 163rd Inf Bde]. Dec 1971: 66th Mtn Bde.
2nd Bn (1st Grenadiers)	Raised Aug 1949 (ex 1st Grenadiers). Dec 1971: 268th Inf Bde.
3rd Bn (1st Rajputana Rifles)	Raised Aug 1949 (ex 1st Rajputana Rifles). Sep 1965: 30th Inf Bde [but also shown with 48th Inf Bde]. Dec 1971: 35th Inf Bde.
4th Bn (1st Rajput)	Raised Aug 1949 (ex 1st Rajput). Dec 1971: 311th Mtn Bde.
5th Bn	Oct 1962: 48th Inf Bde (Ambala); sent to NEFA to oppose Chinese invasion. 1965: 48th Inf Bde. Dec 1971: 41st Mtn Bde. Tour of duty in Siachen 1986.
6th Bn	Sep 1965: 268th Inf Bde [but also shown with 163rd Inf Bde]. Dec 1971: 66th Mtn Bde.
7th Bn	Dec 1971: 121st Inf Bde. Tour of duty in Siachen mid 1989.
8th Bn	Dec 1971: 202nd Mtn Bde. Tour of duty in Siachen mid 1989.
9th Bn	Dec 1971: 59th Mtn Bde.
10th Bn	Dec 1971: 115th Inf Bde. Participated in Operation Blue Star Jun 1984.
11th Bn	Dec 1971: 19th Inf Bde.
12th Bn[159]	Dec 1971: Western Cmd [SS-11].

---

[157] As a young officer in 1932, Field Marshal Cariappa spent time attached to 2nd Bn Coldstream Guards, a source of his inspiration of the new regiment. The other was his desire for a regiment completely devoid of regional or class ties.

[158] This has changed somewhat over the years. Gautam, op.cit., in the entry for this regiment in Table 5.4 (p 47) indicates that two battalions are composed of hill tribes (possibly the 13th and 14th) and one is composed of South India Communities. Sharma, (op. cit., p 87) notes the two battalions of hill tribes and indicates that some battalions are restricted to zones (northern, western, central, southern, etc.) while two battalions take all classes from Bihar, UP, MP and Orissa.

[159] First ATGM battalion, initially equipped with ENTAC and later with Milan.

13th Bn	Converted from 31st Bn. Dec 1971: 95th Mtn Bde. Served with IPKF in Sri Lanka.
14th Bn	Converted from 32n Bn. Dec 1971: 73rd Mtn Bde.
15th Bn[160]	{recce and support}
16th Bn	Served with IPKF in Sri Lanka. Served in Angola (UNAVEM III) 1995-97.
17th Bn[161]	Detachments [ATGW] with 8th Mtn Div 1999 Kargill War. {recce and support}
18th Bn	
19th Bn[162]	Detachments [ATGW] with 3rd Inf Div and detachment [ATGW] with 8th Mtn Div 1999 Kargill War. {recce and support}
31st Bn	Raised under modified establishment for counter-insurgency operations in the Northeast. *Reorganized as 13th Bn*
32nd Bn	Raised under modified establishment for counter-insurgency operations in the Northeast.. *Reorganized as 14th Bn*

Two TA battalions are associated with the Brigade of the Guards: 117th Infantry Bn (TA) at Tiruchi and 125th Infantry Bn (TA) at Secunderabad.

Regimental Centre: Began as an affiliate (wing) of the Rajputana Rifles Regimental Centre; separated and established 1956 at Kota, Rajasthan; moved 1976 to Kamptee, near Nagpur in Maharashtra.

Regimental Insignia: Garuda (a mythological eagle mount of the Hindu god Vishnu) in standing position above a scroll reading "BRIGADE OF THE GUARDS".

Motto: Pahla Hmesha Pahla (First Always First; also translated as Ahead Always Ahead)

PVC: one[163]

Honours:[164] Naushera (2nd Punjab [1], 1st Rajput [4]), Gurais (1st Grenadiers [2]), Jammu and Kashmir 1947-48 (2nd Punjab [1], 1st Grenadiers [2], 1st Rajput

---

160 Raised as an ATGM battalion, with Milan.

161 Raised as an ATGM battalion, with Milan.

162 Raised as an ATGM battalion, with Milan.

163 Lance Naik Albert Ekka, 14th Bn (3 Dec 1971)(P).

164 As with the Armoured Corps, specific battle honours are shown first, followed by the applicable theatre honours. The parentheses indicate the specific battalion(s) which earned the honours shown. The four original battalions brought all of their battle and theatre honours (including pre-1947) with them.

[4]); Burki (5), Punjab 1965 (5); Gadra Road (3), Rajasthan 1965 (3); Hilli (8), Sylhett (9), Ganga Sagar (14), Akhaura (4), East Pakistan 1971 (4, 5, 8, 9, 14); Shingo River Valley (7), Jammu and Kashmir 1971 (7, 11, 12).

The Mechanised Infantry

This regiment was raised 1 April 1979, taking over the 14 battalions from existing regiments that had been mounted in APCs. Until battalions from the Brigade of Guards were converted, it was the only unit with mechanised infantry. Despite being the youngest regiment in terms of formation, it was given precedence as third, behind the Guards and the Parachute Regiment.

After the regiment's formation, the 14 original battalions were gradually changed from one class to all India mixed, and all new battalions were raised as all India. However, in 2001 a decision was made to convert the first 14 back to their original class composition, thus aligning them with their former regiments.[165] As with the Guards, redesignated battalions were allowed to retain their former title as a parenthetical; they are not shown in the first column of the table since they appear with the 1 April 1979 raising date.

1st Bn	Raised 1 Apr 1979 (ex 1st Madras).
2nd Bn	Raised 1 Apr 1979 (ex 1st Jat).
3rd Bn	Raised 1 Apr 1979 (ex 1/8 Gorkha Rifles). Served with IPKF in Sri Lanka.
4th Bn	Raised 1 Apr 1979 (ex 1st Sikh).
5th Bn	Raised 1 Apr 1979 (ex 14th Kumaon).
6th Bn	Raised 1 Apr 1979 (ex 1st Garhwal Rifles). Served with IPKF in Sri Lanka.
7th Bn	Raised 1 Apr 1979 (ex 1st Dogra).
8th Bn	Raised 1 Apr 1979 (ex 7th Punjab). Participated in Operation Blue Star Jun 1984.
9th Bn	Raised 1 Apr 1979 (ex 7th Grenadiers).
10th Bn	Raised 1 Apr 1979 (ex 20th Maratha LI).
11th Bn	Raised 1 Apr 1979 (ex 18th Rajputana Rifles).
12th Bn	Raised 1 Apr 1979 (ex 16th Mahar).
13th Bn	Raised 1 Apr 1979 (ex 18th Rajput). Served with IPKF in Sri Lanka.
14th Bn	Raised 1 Apr 1979 (ex 16th J&K Rifles).
15th Bn	Served with IPKF in Sri Lanka.
16th Bn	Served with IPKF in Sri Lanka.
17th Bn	{recon & support}

[165] Gautam, op.cit., regimental entry in Table 5.4 (p 47) and pp 66-67.

18th Bn	
19th Bn	{recon & support} Served with IPKF in Sri Lanka.
20th Bn	
21st Bn	One coy served in Angola (UNAVEM III) 1995-97.
22nd Bn	
23rd Bn	{recon & support}
24th Bn	Raised 1993 (ex 20th Rajput).
25th Bn	{recon & support}

Regimental Centre: Ahmednagar, Maharashtra. When battalions of the Brigade of The Guards began to mechanise, that aspect of their training was handled at this centre. It also conducts all-arms technical training for Army personnel.

Regimental Insignia: A rifle bayonet point upwards mounted on a BMP-1, with a scroll below reading "MECH INF REGT".

Motto: Veerta aur vishwas (Valour and Faith)

Honours: the regiment itself has not earned any battle or theatre honours. However, the 14 original battalions brought with them all of their honours, which have thus been inherited by the regiment. [The earning battalion numbers are those of the new regiment. It appears that the former regiments did not lose any battle or theatre honours even where the transferring battalion was the sole earner of those honours.] Srinagar (4), Tithwal (1, 4), Jammu and Kashmir 1947-48 (1, 4, 6); Chushul (3), Ladakh 1962 (3); Kalidhar (1), Jammu and Kashmir 1965 (1, 5); Asal Uttar (7, 11), Dograi (8), Punjab 1965 (1, 7, 8, 11); Gadra Road (6), Rajasthan 1965 (6); Akhaura (13), East Pakistan 1971 (8, 10, 13); Basantar River (11), Punjab 1971 (7, 11).

The Punjab Regiment

Formed as 2nd Punjab Regiment from 67th Punjabis [1st Bn], 69th Punjabis [2nd Bn], 72nd Punjabis [3rd Bn], 74th Punjabis [4th Bn], 87th Punjabis [5th Bn], and 2nd Bn/67th Punjabis [10th Bn]. (The 4th Bn was disbanded in 1939. The 5th Bn was lost at Singapore in 1942 and not reformed.) Known wartime units included the 6th, 7th, 8th, 25th, 26th and 27th Bns. 2nd Punjab Regiment retained the numerical designation until 1947 (the 1st and other numbered Punjab Regiments went to Pakistan), then becoming The Punjab Regiment. In 1946, the 1st Bn was converted to the parachute role, later becoming a battalion of the new Parachute Regiment.

The regiment recruits Sikhs and Dogras from the Punjab.[166]

In 1951, the regiment added four former State Forces battalions (Jind Infantry, Nabha Akal Infantry, and the 1st and 2nd Patiala Infantry)—all former princely states in the Punjab—as its 13th to 16th Battalions.

1st (Para) Bn	Aug 1947: 77th Para Bde (Multan). Served in Kashmir 1947-48 (161st Inf, 50th Para, 19th Inf Bdes). *Transferred Apr 1952 as 1st Para.*
2nd Bn	Aug 1947: Lahore. Served in Kashmir 1948 (50th Para Bde). *Transferred Aug 1949 as 1st Guards.*
3rd Bn	Aug 1947: Ranchi. Sep 1948: 9th Inf Bde. Served a tour with UN force in Gaza. Dec 1971: 81st Mtn Bde. Served with IPKF in Sri Lanka. 1999: 121st Inf Bde Kargil War.
6th Bn	
7th Bn	Aug 1947: Jubbulpore. Sep 1965: 96th Inf Bde. Dec 1971: 32nd Inf Bde [mech: SKOTs]. *Transferred Apr 1979 as 8th Mech Inf.*
9th Bn	Raised ca 1947.[167] Sep 1948: Hyderabad operation. 1962: 7th Inf Bde. Sep 1965: 191st Inf Bde.
10th Bn	
11th Bn	
12th Bn	
13th Bn (Jind)	Raised 1 Apr 1951 (ex Jind Inf). Sep 1965: 54th Inf Bde. Dec 1971: 35th Inf Bde. Served in 1999 Kargil War.
14th Bn (Nabha Akal)	Raised 1 Apr 1951 (ex Nabha Akal Inf).[168] Sep 1965: 67th (I) Inf Bde. Dec 1971: 42nd Inf Bde. Served in Angola (UNAVEM III) 1995-97.
15th Bn (Patiala)[169]	[1st Patiala Inf served in Kashmir 1947-48 with 268th Inf, 80th Inf, 50th Para and 77th Para Bdes.] Raised 1 Apr 1951 (ex 1st Patiala Inf). Dec 1971: 29th Inf Bde but under 35th Inf Bde. Served on CI duties in J&K 1992-95.
16th Bn (Patiala)	Raised 1 Apr 1951 (ex 2nd Patiala Inf). Sep 1965: 65th Inf Bde.
17th Bn	Sep 1965: 121st Inf Bde [also shown with70th Inf Bde].
18th Bn	Dec 1971: 121st (I) Inf Bde.

---

[166] Information on recruitment classes for the Infantry are from Gautam, op. cit., Table 5.4 (pp 47-50). This has been supplemented in some cases by information in the regimental entries in Sharma, op. cit.

[167] To absorb additional Sikhs and Dogras rendered surplus by Punjab regiments that went to Pakistan.

[168] The battalion continued its prior State Force composition as 75% Sikh and 25% Dogra.

[169] The battalion continued its prior State Force composition as an all Sikh unit.

19th Bn[170]	Aug and Sep 1965: 68th Inf Bde. Dec 1971: 73rd Mtn Bde. Served with IPKF in Sri Lanka.
20th Bn	Dec 1971: 3rd Inf Div.
21st Bn	Served with IPKF in Sri Lanka.
22nd Bn	
23rd Bn	Dec 1971: 45th Inf Bde.
24th Bn	Dec 1971: 58th Inf Bde.
25th Bn	
26th Bn	Served with IPKF in Sri Lanka.
27th Bn	
28th Bn	
29th Bn	

Three TA battalion are associated with the Punjab Regiment: 102nd Infantry Bn (TA) at Kalka, 150th Infantry Bn (TA) at Delhi and 156th Infantry Bn (TA) (H and H) at Rajouri.

Regimental Centre: Meerut; moved 1976 to Ramgarh Cantonment, Bihar.

Regimental Insignia: A Galley, an ancient Greek or Roman warship, with a bank of oars and sail.[171] Below, a scroll with the words "PUNJAB REGIMENT". (The only change from the earlier badge was elimination of "2nd" from the scroll.)

Motto: Sthal Wa Jal (By Land and Sea)

Honours: Jammu and Kashmir 1947-48 (1st Patiala [15]), Jhangar (1st Patiala [15]), Zoji La (1st Patiala [15]); Jammu and Kashmir 1965 (9, 19), Hajipir (19), Kalidhar (9); Punjab 1965 (7, 13, 16), Burki (16), Dograi (7, 13); East Pakistan 1971 (7); Jammu and Kashmir 1971 (18, 21), Nangi Tekri (21), Brachil Pass and Wali Malik (18); Punjab 1971 (9, 15, 22); Sindh 1971 (23), Longanewala (23)

The Madras Regiment

Formed as 3rd Madras Regiment from 73rd Carnatic Infantry [1st Bn], 75th Carnatic Infantry [2nd Bn], 79th Carnatic Infantry [3rd Bn], and 86th Carnatic

---

170 Battalion was mixed with other Indian classes; this may have been (as with some other regiments) a reaction to the 1984 Sikh revolt. If so, it was probably reversed after 1999.

171 Awarded originally to 69th Punjabis (later 2nd Punjab) for their readiness to serve overseas in the early 19th Century, when few units did so most were apparently reluctant to do so.

Infantry [10th Bn]. However, all of these were disbanded: 3rd Bn November 1923, 2nd and 10th Bns March 1926, and 1st Bn February 1928. Despite the lack of any Regular units, four battalions were formed in the Indian Territorial Force (ITF): 11th Madras, 12th Malabar, 13th Malabar, and 14th Coorg. The 1st to 4th Bns were reformed in the Second World War by redesignating the four ITF battalions. In 1946 the 2nd Bn was converted to the parachute role, reverting to normal infantry in 1950.

The regiment recruits from South India Communities in Andhra Pradesh, Tamil Nadu, Karnataka, Kerala, Pondicherry, Goa, Laksdweep, Andaman Islands and Nicobar Islands..

Following the war, four former State Forces battalions (1st and 2nd Travancore Infantry, Cochin Infantry, and Mysore Infantry) were added as the 9th, 16th, 17th and 18th Battalions, respectively.

1st Bn	Aug 1947: Ranchi. Served in J&K 1948. 1962: 48th Inf Bde (Bomdila); sent to NEFA Oct. Sep 1965: 80th Inf Bde [also shown with 52nd Mtn Bde]. Dec 1971: 43rd Lorried Inf Bde [mech: Topas]. *Transferred Apr 1979 as 1st Mech Inf.*
2nd (Para) Bn	Aug 1947: 50th Para Bde (Quetta). Served in Kashmir 1948 (77th Para Bde). Converted to infantry as **2nd Bn**. 1965: 29th Inf Bde. Served with IPKF in Sri Lanka.
3rd Bn	Aug 1947: existed in cadre only; disbanded 1950. Reformed later. Sep 1965: 69th Mtn Bde. Dec 1971: 65th Inf Bde.
4th Bn	Aug 1947: Delhi. Served in Kashmir 1948 (5th Inf Bde). 1962-63: 99th (I) Inf Bde in the Congo. Sep 1965: 69th Mtn Bde. Dec 1971: 340th Mtn Bde.
5th Bn	Served with IPKF in Sri Lanka (91st Inf Bde).
6th Bn	
7th Bn	Sep 1965: 93rd Inf Bde. Served with IPKF in Sri Lanka.
8th Bn	[Personnel used to raised 4th Field Regiment May 1956 and later reformed.] Dec 1971: 32nd Inf Bde.
9th Bn (Travancore)	Raised 1 Apr 1951 (ex 1st Travancore Inf). [Personnel used to raised 28th LAA Regiment May 1956 and later reformed.] Sep 1965: 65th Inf Bde. Dec 1971: 31st Inf Bde.
10th Bn	Sep 1965: 52nd Mtn Bde.
11th Bn	Served with IPKF in Sri Lanka.
12th Bn	Served with IPKF in Sri Lanka.
13th Bn	
14th Bn	
15th Bn	

16th Bn (Travancore)	Raised 1 Apr 1951 (ex 2nd Travancore Inf). Dec 1971: 47th Inf Bde.
17th Bn (Cochin)	Raised 1 Apr 1951 (ex Cochin Inf). 1965: joined 30th Inf Bde 15 Sep then to 85th Inf Bde 21 Sep. Dec 1971: 116th Inf Bde.
18th Bn (Mysore)	[1st Mysore Inf served in Hyderabad Sep 1948.] Raised 1 Apr 1951 (ex Mysore Inf). 1Sep 965: 116th Inf Bde. Dec 1971: 31st Inf Bde.
19th Bn	Dec 1971: 168th Inf Bde but under 323rd Inf Bde. Served with IPKF in Sri Lanka.
20th Bn	
21st Bn	
22nd Bn	
23rd Bn	
24th Bn	
25th Bn	Served with IPKF in Sri Lanka.
26th Bn	Dec 1971: 350th Inf Bde. Participated in Operation Blue Star Jun 1984.
27th Bn	Raised 1 Jun 1971. Dec 1971: Southern Cmd, later to Kutch Sector.
28th Bn	

Two TA battalions are associated with the Madras Regiment: 110th Infantry Bn (TA) at Coimbatore and 122nd Infantry Bn (TA)[172] at Cannonore.

Regimental Centre: Wellington (Nilgiri Hills), Tamil Nadu.

Regimental Insignia: An Assaye Elephant posed upon a shield with two crossed swords behind it. Below, a scroll reading “THE MADRAS REGIMENT”.

Before 1950, the shield was topped by a crown rather than the elephant.

Motto: Swadharme Nidhanam Shreyaha (It is a glory to die doing one’s duty)

Honours: Jammu and Kashmir 1947-48 (1, 4), Tithwal (1), Punch (4); Jammu and Kashmir 1965 (1), Kalidhar (1); Punjab 1965 (1, 3, 4, 9), Maharajke (4); East Pakistan 1971 (8, 26), Siramani (26); Punjab 1971 (6, 16), Basantar River (6, 16); Sindh 1971 (18).

---

172 Raised as 51st Light Armoured Regt in 1949; redesignated 1956 and affiliated to the regimen.

The Grenadiers Regiment

Formed as 4th Bombay Grenadiers from 101st Grenadiers [1st Bn], 102nd King Edward's Own Grenadiers [2nd Bn], 108th Infantry [3rd Bn], 109th Infantry [4th Bn], 112th Infantry [5th Bn], and 113th Infantry [10th Bn]. However, most were disbanded in the 1930s: 3rd and 4th Bns in April 1930 and 5th Bn November 1933. One ITF battalion (11th) was formed. The 3rd, 4th and 5th Bns were all reformed during World War Two. During that war the regiment was tasked to provide motorised battalions for armoured brigades. Redesignated 1945 as The Indian Grenadiers and 1950 as The Grenadiers.

The regiment recruits Rajputs, Kaimkhanis,[173] Hindustani Mussalmans,[174] Dogras, Guijars, Ahirs, Meenas, Gujeratis, Jats and other Indian classes.

Three State Forces battalions (Kutch & Saurashtra SF, Mewar Infantry, and Bikaner & Jaisalmer Risala) were incorporated as the 7th, 9th and 13th Battalions, respectively.

1st Bn	Aug 1947: 4th Div/PBF. Served in Kashmir 1948. *Transferred Aug 1949 as 2nd Guards.*
2nd Bn	Aug 1947: Madukkarai. Sep 1965: Gujarat and Maharashtra Area , then 28th Inf Bde.
3rd Bn	Aug 1947: Kohat Bde.[175] Sep 1948: 7th Inf Bde. Dec 1971: 47th Inf Bde.
4th Bn	Aug 1947: 19th Inf Bde (Iraq). 1962: 7th Inf Bde. Sep 1965: 7th Mtn Bde. Dec 1971: 115th Inf Bde.
5th Bn	Dec 1971: 9th Mtn Bde, then detached to 71st Bde.
6th Bn	
7th Bn	Raised 1 Apr 1951. (ex Kutch & Saurashtra SF).[176] Sep 1965: 7th Mtn Bde [also shown with 112th Inf Bde]. Dec 1971: 3rd Armd Bde [mech: BTR-60] but with 26th Inf Div. *Transferred Apr 1979 as 9th Mech Inf.*
8th Bn	Sep 1965: 93rd Inf Bde.

173 Khaimkhani companies are in the 5th, 6th, 8th, 13th, 16th, 17th and 21st Battalions. The word is sometimes rendered as Kayumkhanis,.

174 Hindustani Mussalman companies are in the 4th, 20th and 22nd Battalions.

175 The battalion was at Thal to June 1947; August location unknown but probably Kohat.

176 This was originally a camel-mounted battalion, primaly composed of Rajputs. After conversion to infantry with a composition of Jats and Dogras (50%) and Katchis and Saurashtrians (50%).

9th Bn (Mewar)	[1st Mewar Inf served with 9th Inf Bde, Hyderabad, Sep 1948.] Raised 1 Apr 1951. (ex Mewar Inf). Dec 1971: 164th Mtn Bde.
11th Bn	Dec 1971: 54th Inf Bde.
12th Bn	Dec 1971: 268th Inf Bde. Served with IPKF in Sri Lanka. Served in 1999 Kargil War.
13th Bn (Jaisalmer)	Raised 1 Apr 1951. (ex Bikaner & Jaisalmer Risala SF).[177] Sep 1965: D Sqn with 30th Inf Bde [camel-mounted]. Dec 1971: Kilo Sector, Southern Cmd [camel-mounted].
14th Bn	Dec 1971: 120th Inf Bde.
15th Bn	Dec 1971: 72nd Inf Bde.
16th Bn	Raised 1 Jun 1966. Dec 1971: 38th Inf Bde. Served with 121st Inf and 56th Mtn Bdes 1999 Kargil War.
17th Bn	Dec 1971: 11th Inf Div [camels].
18th Bn	Served with 56th and 192nd Mtn Bdes 1999 Kargil War.
19th Bn	Served with IPKF in Sri Lanka.
20th Bn	Served with IPKF in Sri Lanka.
21st Bn	
22nd Bn	Served in 1999 Kargil War.

Two TA battalions are associated with the Grenadiers Regiment: 118th Infantry Bn (TA) at Nagpur and 123rd Infantry Bn (TA) at Jaipur.

Regimental Centre: Nasirabad, Rajasthan; moved 1975 to Jabalpur, Madhya Pradesh.

Regimental Insignia: A brass grenade with 17 closed flames in two tiers, bearing a horse over an edge of ground. The insignia is worn on the uniform with a white hackle. The basic design remained unchanged after 1950, although the flames now rise straighter up rather than fanning out, and the horse was (formerly) explicitly the White Horse of Hanover. The badge was worn with a white pon pon from 1946, changing 1954 to the white hackle worn before 1946.

Motto: Sarvada shaktishali (Always powerful)

PVC: three (the most for a single regiment)[178]

---

[177] A camel-mounted battalion until sometime after the 1971 war. When converted to infantry, its composition was Rajputs (75%) and Kaimkhanis (25%).

[178] CQM Havildar Abdul Hamid, 4th Bn (10 Sep 1965)(P); Maj Hoshiar Singh, 3rd Bn (17 Dec 1971); Gren Yogendra Singh Yadav, 18th Bn (4 Jul 1999).

Honours: Gurais, Jammu and Kashmir 1947-48;[179] Jammu and Kashmir 1965 (8); Asal Uttar (4), Punjab 1965 (4); Rajasthan 1965 (3, 13); Chakri (8), Jarpal (3), Punjab 1971 (3, 8); Tiger Hill, Kargil 1999.

The Maratha Light Infantry

Formed as 5th Maratha Light Infantry from 103rd Mahratta[180] Light Infantry [1st Bn], 105th Mahratta Light Infantry [2nd Bn], 110th Mahratta Light Infantry [3rd Bn], 116th Mahrattas [4th Bn], 117th Mahrattas [5th Bn], and 114th Mahrattas [10th Bn]. One ITF battalion (11th) was formed. Known wartime units included the 6th, 7th and 17th Bns. In 1946 the 3rd Bn converted to the parachute role, later becoming one of the battalions of the new Parachute Regiment.

The regiment recruits Marathas and all India.[181]

Three State Forces battalions (Bajaram Rifles, Baroda Rifles, and Hyderabad Infantry) were incorporated as the 19th, 20th and 22nd Battalions, respectively.

1st Bn	Aug 1947: 268th Inf Bde (Japan); returned to India Oct 1947. Served in Kashmir 1948. Sep 1965: 163rd Inf Bde. Dec 1971: 95th Mtn Bde. Served with IPKF in Sri Lanka (91st Inf Bde).
2nd Bn	Aug 1947: 7th Inf Bde (Mahd Island, Bombay). Sep 1965: 67th (I) Inf Bde.
3rd (Para) Bn	Aug 1947: 77th Para Bde (Multan). Served in Kashmir 1947-48 (50th Para Bde). *Transferred Apr 1952 as 3rd Para.* New **3rd Bn** raised later. Dec 1971: 61st Inf Bde.
4th Bn	Aug 1947: Belgaum. Dec 1971: 322nd Inf Bde.
5th Bn	Aug 1947: demonstration bn at Small Arms/Infantry School (Saugor/Mhow). Served in Kashmir 1948 (77th Para Bde). Sep 1965: 30th Inf Bde, to 85th Inf Bde 18 Sep but left soon after. Dec 1971: 62nd Mtn Bde. Served with IPKF in Sri Lanka.
6th Bn	
7th Bn	Sep 1965: 161st Inf Bde. Dec 1971: 71st Mtn Bde.
8th Bn	Served with IPKF in Sri Lanka.
9th Bn	Dec 1971: 74th Inf Bde.
11th Bn	
12th Bn	
13th Bn	
14th Bn	

[179] Earned by 1st Bn (later 2nd Guards) but retained by the regiment.
[180] Spelling commonly used by the British.
[181] Some battalions have troops from all India, and one has South Indian Communities.

15th Bn	Dec 1971: 96th Inf Bde.
16th Bn	
17th Bn	Served with IPKF in Sri Lanka.
18th Bn	
19th Bn (Kolhapur)	Raised 1 Apr 1951 (ex Bajaram Rifles). 1962: 65th Inf Bde (Hyderabad); sent to Ladakh Oct. Dec 1971: 42nd Inf Bde.
20th Bn (Baroda)	Raised 1 Apr 1951 (ex Baroda Rifles). Sep 1965: 161st Inf Bde. Dec 1971: 165th Mtn Bde [mech: SKOTs]. *Transferred Apr 1979 as 10th Mech Inf.*
21st Bn	Raised? *Transferred Feb 1966 as 21st Para-Cdo.*
22nd Bn (Hyderabad)	Raised 1 Apr 1951 (ex Hyderabad Inf). Sep 1965: 120th Inf Bde. Dec 1971: 202nd Mtn Bde.
26th Bn	

Two TA battalions are associated with the Maratha Light Infantry: 101st Infantry Bn (TA) at Pune and 109th Infantry Bn (TA) at Kolhapur.

Regimental Centre: Belgaum, Karnataka.

Regimental Insignia: A bugle and cords with a pair of crossed swords and a shield between the bugle and cords, topped by the Ashoka Lions. The insignia is worn with a red and green hackle and with a black diamond backing to the badge.

The old badge was topped with a crown and had the numeral "5" between the cords.

Motto: Duty, Honour and Courage.

Honours: Naushera, Jhangar, Jammu and Kashmir 1947-48;[182] Punjab 1965 (2, 19), Burki (19), Hussainiwal Bridge (3); Rajasthan 1965 (4, 5); East Pakistan 1971 (1, 5, 20, 22), Suadih (5), Jamalpur (1); Punjab 1971 (15), Burj (15)

The Rajputana Rifles

Formed as 6th Rajputana Rifles from 104th Wellesley's Rifles [1st Bn], 120th Rajputana Infantry [2nd Bn], 122nd Rajputana Infantry [3rd Bn], 123rd Outram's Rifles [4th Bn], 1st Bn/125th Napier's Rifles [5th Bn], and 13th Rajputs (The Shekhawati Regiment) [10th Bn]. One ITF battalion (11th) was formed. Known wartime units included the 7th, 8th and Machine Gun Bns. In 1946 the 4th Bn converted to the parachute role, reverting to normal infantry in 1950.

---

[182] These honours were earned by 3rd (Parachute) Bn; although it took its honours with it to the new Parachute Regiment, the Maratha Light Infantry did not lose them.

The regiment recruits Jats and Rajputs (including Gujeratis).[183]

Two State Forces battalions (Sawai Man Guards [a Jaipur unit] and Saurashtra Infantry)[184] were incorporated as the 17th and 18th Battalions, respectively.

1st Bn	Aug 1947: Wana Bde (Wana). *Transferred Aug 1949 as 3rd Guards.*
2nd Bn	Aug 1947: Meerut. Served in Kashmir 1948 (19th Inf Bde). Sep 1965: 29th Inf Bde. Dec 1971: 85th Inf Bde. Served with 56th Mtn Bde 1999 Kargil War.
3rd Bn	Aug 1947: ?[185] Sep 1965: 93rd Inf Bde. Dec 1971: 45th Inf Bde.
4th (Para) Bn	Aug 1947: 14th Para Bde (Lahore).[186] Converted to inf as **4th Bn**. With 99th (I) Inf Bde in the Congo 1962-63. Sep 1965: 99th Mtn Bde. Dec 1971: 161st Inf Bde.
5th Bn	Aug 1947: 5th Inf Bde (Amritsar). Served in Kashmir 1948 (5th Inf Bde). Sent Aug 1953 to Korea to guard POW camp following armistice; returned Jan 1954(?). Sep 1965:116th Inf Bde [also shown with 112th Inf Bde]. Served with IPKF in Sri Lanka (41st Inf Bde).
6th Bn	Raised before Apr 1948. Served in Kashmir 1948 (161st Inf Bde). Dec 1971: 104th Inf Bde.
7th Bn	Raised 1 Mar 1962. Dec 1971: 61st Mtn Bde. Served with IPKF in Sri Lanka.
8th Bn	Raised 1 Jan 1963. Dec 1971: 104th Inf Bde.
9th Bn	Raised 1 Apr 1964. Dec 1971: 120th Inf Bde.
11th Bn	Raised 1 Oct 1964. Dec 1971: 80th Inf Bde. Served with IPKF in Sri Lanka. Served with 102nd Inf Bde 1999 Kargil War.
12th Bn	Raised ca. 1971 by redesignation of 31st Bn. Dec 1971: 71st Mtn Bde.
13th Bn	Raised 15 Jan 1966. Dec 1971: 95th Mtn Bde.
14th Bn	Sep 1965: 70th Inf Bde.
15th Bn	Raised 15 May 1976.
16th Bn	Raised 1 Jul 1979. Served with IPKF in Sri Lanka.
17th Bn (Sawai Man)	[As Sawai Man Guards served in Kashmir 1948 (77th Para Bde). Raised 1 Apr 1951 (ex Sawai Man Guards). Sep 1965: 31st Inf Bde. Dec 1971: 30th Inf Bde.

[183] 3rd, 6th and 8th Battalions have one company each of Kheimkhanis; 9th Battalion has one company of Gujaratis from Sauirashtra.

[184] The latter was formed by amalgamation of the Bhavnagar, Dharangadhara, Mahwan, Nawanagar and Porbander Infantry and the Bhavnagar Lancers.

[185] In Burma with 98th Inf Bde to May 1947; location on return unknown.

[186] Brigade HQ went to Pakistan.

18th Bn (Saurashtra)	Raised 1 Apr 1951 (ex Saurashtra Inf). Sep 1965: 62nd Mtn Bde. Dec 1971: 16th (I) Armd Bde [mech: Topas]. *Transferred Apr 1979 as 11th Mech Inf.*
19th Bn	Dec 1971: 73rd Mtn Bde. Served with IPKF in Sri Lanka.
20th Bn	Raised 1 Jan 1981.
21st Bn	Raised 11 Feb 1985.
31st Bn	Raised 1960s under modified establishment for CI in the NE. *Redesignated ca. 1971as 12th Bn.*

Two TA battalions are associated with the Rajputana Rifles: 105th Infantry Bn (TA) at Delhi Cantonment and 128th Ecological Bn (TA) at Bikaner.

Regimental Centre: Delhi Cantonment, Delhi.

Regimental Insignia: Bugle and Cords (with the letters "RR" between the bugle and cords), all below a pair of crossed Katars (Rajput daggers).

The prior badge had a crown above, and was blackened. When replaced in 1954, it was changed to silver and the Katars replaced the crown.

Motto: Veer Bhogya Vasundhra (The Brave Enjoy the Earth)

PVC: one[187]

Honours: Punch (2, 5), Jammu and Kashmir 1947-48 (2, 5, 6, Sawai Man Gds [17]); Jammu and Kashmir 1965 (3); Charwa (4), Asal Uttar (18), Punjab 1965 (4, 5, 18); East Pakistan 1971 (7, 12, 19); Basantar River (18), Punjab 1971 (18); Drass (2), Tololing (2), Kargil 1999 (2).

The Rajput Regiment

Formed as 7th Rajputs from 2nd Queen Victoria's Own Rajput Light Infantry [1st Bn], 4th Prince Albert Victor's Rajputs [2nd Bn], 7th Duke of Connaught's Own Rajputs [3rd Bn], 8th Rajputs [4th Bn], 11th Rajputs [5th Bn], and 16th Rajputs (The Lucknow Regiment) [10th Bn]. One ITF battalion (11th) was formed. Known wartime units included the 6th, 15th, 17th and Machine Gun Bns. In 1946 the 3rd Bn converted to the parachute role, reverting to normal infantry in 1950.

At the time of partition, battalions contained up to 50% Punjabi Muslims, who were transferred to the new Pakistan Army and replaced by Gujars (also spelled Gujjars) transferring from Punjab Regiments going to Pakistan. Bengalis and Muslims began entering the regiment in the 1950s. The regiment now recruits

---

187 Co Havildar Major Piru Singh Shekhawat, 6th Bn (17-18 Jul 1948)(P).

Rajputs (about 51%), Gujars, Brahmins and Bengalis,[188] with a small percentage of Muslims.

Two State Forces battalions (Sadul Light Infantry and Jodhpur Sirdar Infantry) were incorporated as the 19th and 20th Battalions, respectively.

1st Bn	Aug 1947: Fatehgarh. Served in Kashmir 1948 (50th Para Bde and 19th Inf Bdes). *Transferred Aug 1949 as 4th Guards.*
2nd Bn	Aug 1947: Fatehgarh. Served in J&K 1948 mainly on LofC duties. 1962: 7th Inf Bde in NEFA and largely destroyed in Chinese invasion. Sep 1965: 104th Inf Bde. Dec 1971: 83rd Mtn Bde.
3rd (Para) Bn	Aug 1947: 77th Para Bde (Multan). Served in Kashmir 1947-48 (50th Para Bde). Converted to inf as **3rd Bn**. Sep 1965:93rd Inf Bde.
4th Bn	Aug 1947: 161st Inf Bde (Ranchi). Served in Kashmir 1947-48 80th Inf and 77th Para Bdes). 1962: 65th Inf Bde (Hyderabad); sent to NEFA Oct. Aug and Sep 1965: 68th Inf Bde. Dec 1971: 9th Mtn Bde. Served with IPKF in Sri Lanka.
5th Bn	Dec 1971: 28th Inf Bde. Served with IPKF in Sri Lanka. Served in 1999 Kargil War.
6th Bn	Sep 1965: 41st Mtn Bde [also shown as leaving 163rd Inf Bde to go to 191st Inf Bde]. Dec 1971: 59th Mtn Bde. Served with IPKF in Sri Lanka.
7th Bn	
8th Bn	
9th Bn	Dec 1971: 26th Inf Div.
11th Bn	
12th Bn	
13th Bn	
14th Bn	Sep 1948: with 1st Armd Bde. 1965: 58th Inf Bde. Dec 1971: 65th Inf Bde.
15th Bn	Dec 1971: 67th Inf Bde.
16th Bn	Dec 1971: 165th Mtn Bde.
17th Bn	Served in Nagaland during 1955-56 insurgency operations. 1965: 65th Inf Bde. Dec 1971:86th Inf Bde. Served with IPKF in Sri Lanka.
18th Bn	Engaged in firefights with the Chinese on the border Sep 1967. Dec 1971: 311th Mtn Bde. *Transferred Apr 1979 as 13th Mech Inf.*

[188] 2nd Battalion has a Bengali company.

19th Bn (Bikaner)	Raised 1 Apr 1951 (ex Bikaner Sadul LI). [Personnel used to raised 5th Field Regiment May 1956 and later reformed.] Sep 1965: 7th Inf Div. Dec 1971: Juliet Sector, XI Corps.
20th Bn (Jodhpur)	Raised 1 Apr 1951 (ex Jodhpur Sirdar Infantry).Raised 1 Apr 1951 (ex Jodhpur Sardar Inf). Dec 1971: 31st Inf Bde. *Transferred ? as 24th Mech Inf.*
21st Bn	Dec 1971: 71st Mtn Bde.
22nd Bn	Dec 1971: 7th Mtn Bde.
23rd Bn	
24th Bn	
25th Bn	Served with IPKF in Sri Lanka.
26th Bn	
27th Bn	Served with 102nd Inf Bde 1999 Kargil War.

Two TA battalions are associated with the Rajput Regiment: 113th Infantry Bn (TA) at Calcutta and 131st Ecological Bn (TA) at Gwalior.

Regimental Centre: Fategarh, Uttar Pradesh.

Regimental Insignia: A pair of crossed Katars (Rajput daggers) flanked by three Ashoka leaves on either side. Above, the Ashoka Lions; below, a scroll reading "THE RAJPUT REGIMENT".

The earlier badge had "VII" within the wreath of Ashoka leaves and a crown above.

Motto: Sarvatra Vijay (Victory everywhere)

PVC: one[189]

Honours: Naushera (1),[190] Zoji La (4), Jammu and Kashmir 1947-48 (1, 3, 4); Jammu and Kashmir 1965 (4); Punjab 1965 (20); Madhumati River (22), Khansama (21), Akhaura (18), East Pakistan 1971 (2, 6, 18, 21, 22); Mynamati (7); Kinsar (20) Sindh 1971 (20).,

The Jat Regiment

Formed as 9th Jat Regiment from 1st Bn/6th Jat Light Infantry [1st Bn], 119th Infantry (The Moultan Regiment) [2nd Bn], 10th Jats [3rd Bn], 18th Infantry [4th Bn], and 2nd Bn/6th Jat Light Infantry [10th Bn]. (The Kumaon Rifles

---

[189] Naik Jadu Nath Singh, 1st Bn (Feb 1948)(P).

[190] Battalion later transferred as 4th Guards but honour retained by the regiment.

temporarily formed the 5th and 6th Bns of the regiment before being attached to the 19th Hyderabad Regiment.) The 4th Bn was disbanded before 1939. One ITF battalion (11th) was formed. The 4th Bn was reformed in World War II (but lost in Malaya and not reformed) and other known wartime units included the 5th, 6th and Machine Gun Bns.

The regiment is composed of Jats from Haryana, Rajasthan, Delhi, and Uttar Pradesh, with the exception of three battalions. 12th Bn is All India All Class; 15th Bn is a mixture of classes with a common heritage: Ahirs, Jats, Gujars and Rajputs. The 20th Bn had a mixed class composition of Jats, Dogras, Garhwalis, and Marathas on raising, but was changed to all-Jat in 1999.

1st Bn	Aug 1947: Rawalpindi and Chitral Garrisons. 1962: sent to 114th (I) Inf Bde ca Sep. Sep 1965: 38th Inf Bde. Dec 1971:43rd Lorried Inf Bde [mech: Topas]. *Transferred Apr 1979 as 2nd Mech Inf.*
2nd Bn (Mooltan)	Aug 1947: Kohat Bde (Kohat). Served in J&K 1947-48. 1961-62: 99th (I) Inf Bde in the Congo. Sep 1965: 114th Inf Bde. Dec 1971: 61st Mtn Bde.
3rd Bn (Dograi)	Aug 1947: Ranchi. Served in Kashmir 1948 (77th Para Bde). Sep 1965: 54th Inf Bde. Dec 1971: 322nd Inf Bde.
4th Bn (Asifwala)	Raised 15 Jan 1962 at Bareilly. Dec 1971: 67th Inf Bde. Served with IPKF in Sri Lanka. Served in Nagaland 1994. Served with 121st Inf Bde 1999 Kargil War..
5th Bn (Ladakh)	Aug 1947: Kohat Bde (Kohat). Sent to Ladakh Apr 1962 (114th (I) Inf Bde); given honour title in recognition of their actions during the Chinese invasion. Sep 1965: 43rd Lorried Inf Bde [mech]. Dec 1971: 7th Mtn Bde.
6th Bn	Aug 1947: Bareilly. Served in Kashmir 1948. Sep 1948: Hyderabad. Sent Aug 1953 to Korea to guard POW camp following armistice; returned Jan 1954(?). Sep 1965: 162nd Inf Bde. Dec 1971: 181st Mtn Bde. Served in Siachen 1993-94.
7th Bn	Raised 15 Nov 1962 at Bareilly. Sep 1965: 162nd Inf Bde. Kashmir CI operations 1997. May have served in 1999 Kargil War.
8th Bn (Poonch)	Raised 14 Dec 1959 at Bareilly. Dec 1971: 93rd Inf Bde.
9th Bn (Chhamb)	Raised 1 Jun 1962 at Bareilly. Dec 1971: 68th Inf Bde.
11th Bn	Raised 1972 by conversion of 31st Bn. Served in Siachen 1988-89.
12th Bn	Raised 7 Jun 1970 at Bareilly. With IPKF in Sri Lanka. Served in Siachen 1998-99.

13th Bn	
14th Bn (Comilla)	Raised 1 Oct 1963 at Bareilly. Sep 1965: 120th Inf Bde. Dec 1971: 301st Mtn Bde. Served with IPKF in Sri Lanka.
15th Bn	Raised 15 May 1976 at Bareilly.[191] Served with IPKF in Sri Lanka.
16th Bn	Raised 1 Oct 1964 at Bareilly. Served in Siachen 1990-91.
17th Bn	Raised 1 Jun 1966 at Jabalpur. Served with 79th Mtn Bde 1999 Kargil War.
18th Bn	Raised 1 Oct 1966 at Secunderabad.
19th Bn	Raised 1 Aug 1980 at Bareilly.
20th Bn	Raised on 27 Feb 1985.[192] Served in Siachen 1989-90.
21st Bn	Raised 1 Nov 1987 at Bareilly. Served in Siachen 1991-92.
31st Bn	Raised 1968.[193] Dec 1971: Mizo Hills Range, then Kilo Force, 23rd Mtn Div. *Converted 1972 as 11th Bn.*

Two TA battalions are associated with the Jat Regiment: 114th Infantry Bn (TA) at Fatehgarh and 151st Infantry Bn (TA) at Muzaffarpur.

Regimental Centre: Bareilly, Uttar Pradesh.

Regimental Insignia: The Roman numeral nine representing its former numerical designation. The insignia also has a bugle just below the "IX" indicating the Light Infantry antecedents of two of its battalions. Above, the Ashoka Lions; below, a scroll reading "THE JAT REGIMENT".

The earlier badge lacked the bugle horn and was topped by a crown.

Motto: Sanghan Va Veerta (Unity And Valour).

Honours: Rajaori (2), Zoji La (3), Jammu and Kashmir 1947-48 (2, 3, 5); Ladakh 1962 (5); Dograi (3), Phillora (5), Punjab 1965 (3, 5); East Pakistan 1971 (14); Jammu and Kashmir 1971 (8).

---

[191] Known as the AJGAR battalion from its class composition of Ahirs, Jats, Gujars and Rajputs.

[192] Raised with a mixed class company composition of Jats, Dogras, Garhwalis and Marathas. Ordered to reorganized as all-Jat in August 1998 and this was completed 31 December 1999.

[193] Raised as an "I" battalion for counterinsurgency in the North East with a special T/O, with personnel from the Grenadiers and the Jat, Sikh, Punjab and Dogra Regiments. In 1972 it was converted to a standard battalion and renumbered.

The Sikh Regiment

Formed as 11th Sikhs from 14th King George's Own Ferozopore Sikhs [1st Bn], 15th Ludhiana Sikhs [2nd Bn], 45th Pattrey's Sikhs [3rd Bn], 36th Sikhs [4th Bn], 47th Sikhs [5th Bn], and 35th Sikhs [10th Bn]. (The 5th Bn was lost in Malaya in 1942 and not reformed.) Known wartime units included the 6th, 15th and Machine Gun Bns.

The regiment only recruits Sikhs, although for a time after 1984 the 13th Bn had a class composition of Sikhs, Dogras, Garhwalis and South Indian Communities. It later (1999?) changed back to a Sikh unit.

1st Bn	Aug 1947: Delhi. Sent to Kashmir by air Oct 1947: first unit committed; served 1947-48 (161st and Z/163rd Inf Bdes).1962: 62nd Inf Bde (Ramgarh); sent to NEFA Oct. Sep 1965: 104th Inf Bde. *Transferred Apr 1979 as 4th Mech Inf.*
2nd Bn	Aug 1947: 7th Inf Bde (Jullundar). Sep 1948: 7th Inf Bde. CI operations in Nagaland 1956. Sep 1965: 25th Inf Div, then its 93rd Inf Bde. Dec 1971:54th Inf Bde.
3rd Bn	Aug 1947: Kohat Bde (Thal). Hyderabad police action Sep 1948. Dec 1961: 63rd Inf Bde. Sep 1965:268th Inf Bde.
4th Bn	Aug 1947: 25th Inf Bde (Mona).[194] Dec 1961: 63rd Inf Bde. 1962: 11th Inf Bde. Sep 1965:65th Inf Bde, detached 11 Sep to 4th Mtn Div.
5th Bn	Raised before 1963 by renumbering 7th Bn. Dec 1971: 191st Inf Bde.
6th Bn	Dec 1971: 93rd Inf Bde.
7th Bn	Aug 1947: Basra garrison to Oct 1947. Served in Kashmir 1948 (161st Inf Bde). *Redesignated before 1963 as 5th Bn.* Raised anew 1963. Sep 1965: 93rd Inf Bde. Served with IPKF in Sri Lanka.
8th Bn	Dec 1971: 161st Inf Bde. Served with 56th Mtn Bde 1999 Kargil War..
9th Bn	Dec 1971: 104th Inf Bde. Disbanded 1 Apr 1985.[195]
10th Bn	Dec 1971: 85th Inf Bde.
11th Bn	Served in 1999 Kargil War.
12th Bn	
13th Bn	

---

[194] Brigade HQ went to Pakistan.

[195] The battalion was involved in a mutiny, which began 9 June 1984 with recruits at the Regimental Centre, who killed the Centre's commander.

14th Bn	Served with 70th Inf Bde 1999 Kargil War..
15th Bn	
16th Bn	Raised ca 1947 from Sikhs formerly in regiments going to Pakistan. Served with IPKF in Sri Lanka.
17th Bn	Raised ca 1947 from Sikhs formerly in regiments going to Pakistan. Served with IPKF in Sri Lanka.
18th Bn	Raised ca 1947 from Sikhs formerly in regiments going to Pakistan.
19th Bn	
20th Bn	
21st Bn	
22nd Bn	Served with IPKF in Sri Lanka.

There are three TA battalions associated with the Sikh Regiment: 124th Infantry Bn (TA) at New Delhi, 152nd Infantry Bn (TA) at Ludhiana and 157th Infantry Bn (TA) (H and H) at (BD Bari).

Regimental Centre: Nowshera (in Pakistan), then Ambala Cantonment 1947, Meerut Cantonment 1952, and finally in 1976 Ramgarh Cantonment, Bihar.

Regimental Insignia: A sharp-edged Quoit, or Chakra, which the Khalsa Armies had used in combat. Within the Chakra rings a lion, symbolic of the name (Singh) every Sikh carries.

A variety of badges were in use before, all based on the Quoit. For example, the 1st Battalion's badge was topped with crown and motto of the Prince of Wales.

Motto: Nischey Kar Apni Jeet Karon (I Fight For Sure To Win)

PVC: two[196]

Honours: Srinagar (1), Tithwal (1), Punch, Jammu and Kashmir 1947-48 (1, 5); Raja Picquet-Chand Tekri (2), Op Hill (NL 1053) (7), Jammu and Kashmir 1965 (2, 7); Burki (4), Punjab 1965 (4); Siramani (4), East Pakistan 1971 (4); Defence of Punch (6), Jammu and Kashmir 1971 (5, 6); Punjab 1971 (2); Parbat Ali (10), Sindh 1971 (10).

---

[196] Lance Naik Karam Singh, 1st Bn (13 Oct 1948); Subedar Joginder Singh, 1st Bn (23 Oct 1962)(P).

The Sikh Light Infantry

This regiment was formed in October 1941 from Mazhabi and Ramdasia Sikhs[197] as The Mazhbi and Ramdasia Sikh Regiment, and given the designation The Sikh Light Infantry in 1944. It was later linked with three disbanded battalions of Sikh Pioneers,[198] and thus given precedence behind the Sikh Regiment. The 1st to 3rd Bns were retained after the war; the wartime 25th and 26th Bns disbanded. The regiment recruits Mazhabi Sikhs.

1st Bn	Aug 1947: Kirkee. 1962: 48th Inf Bde (Ambala); sent to NEFA Oct. Sep 1965:162nd Inf Bde. Served with IPKF in Sri Lanka.
2nd Bn	Aug 1947: Basra garrison. Dec 1961: with 50th (I) Para Bde. 1962: 62nd Inf Bde (Ramgarh); sent to NEFA Oct. Sep 1965: 31st Inf Bde. Dec 1971: 42nd Inf Bde.
3rd Bn	Aug 1947: Madras. Sep 1948: Hyderabad. Dec 1971: 72nd Inf Bde.
4th Bn	962: 48th Inf Bde (Ambala); sent to NEFA Oct and transferred to 62nd Inf Bde. Sep 1965: 161st Inf Bde. Dec 1971: 62nd Mtn Bde. Served with IPKF in Sri Lanka.
5th Bn	Sep 1965: 80th Inf Bde. Dec 1971: 80th Inf Bde.
6th Bn	Sep 1965: 191st Inf Bde. Dec 1971: 167th Mtn Bde.
7th Bn	Dec 1971: 161st Inf Bde. Served with IPKF in Sri Lanka.
8th Bn	Dec 1971: 96th Inf Bde.
9th Bn	Dec 1971: 48th Inf Bde.
10th Bn	Dec 1971: 85th Inf Bde.
11th Bn	Dec 1971: airfield defence, Western Cmd.
12th Bn	
13th Bn	Served with IPKF in Sri Lanka (72nd Inf Bde).
14th Bn	Served with IPKF in Sri Lanka. May have served in 1999 Kargil War.
15th Bn	
16th Bn	
17th Bn	
18th Bn	

There are two TA battalions associated with the Sikh Light Infantry: 103rd Infantry Bn (TA) at Ludhiana and 158th Infantry Bn (TA) (H and H) at Janlot.

---

[197] Sikhs descended from the former Hindu lower castes.

[198] The Sikh pioneer regiments were all disbanded following World War One, and absorbed into the various corps of Sappers and Miners. Certain other pioneer regiments were formed into new regiments, but they were all disbanded in the 1930s. The 1st, 2nd and 3rd Battalions are considered reconstitutions of the 23rd, 32nd and 34th Sikh Pioneers.

Regimental Centre: Ferozepore, Punjab; moved 1951 to Meerut, Utter Pradesh;[199] moved 1976 to to Fatehgarh, Uttar Pradesh.

Regimental Insignia: A sharp-edged Quoit, or Chakra, used by the Sikhs in combat, mounted with a Kirpan (the Sikh dagger) pointing upwards.

Motto: Degh Teg Fateh (Prosperity in Peace, Victory in War)

Honours: Kalidhar (6), Op Hill (NL 1053) (5), Jammu and Kashmir 1965 (5, 6); Punjab 1965 (1); East Pakistan 1971 (2, 4); Fatehpur (8), Punjab 1971 (8); Parbat Ali, Sindh 1971.

The Dogra Regiment

Formed as 17th Dogra Regiment from 37th Dogras [1st Bn], 38th Dogras [2nd Bn], 1st Bn/41st Dogras [3rd Bn], and 2nd Bn/41st Dogras [10th Bn]. One ITF battalion (11th) was formed. Known wartime units included the 4th, 5th and Machine Gun Bns. (2nd Bn was lost at Singapore 1942 and reformed April 1946 by redesignation of 6th Bn. 3rd Bn was lost at Singapore 1942 and reformed May 1946 by redesignation of 7th Bn.)

The regiment recruits Dogras.

1st Bn	Aug 1947: 123rd Inf Bde (Ramgarh). 1961-62: 99th (I) Inf Bde in the Congo. Sep 1965: 2nd (I) Armd Bde [mech] but with Rajatal, later Bharat, Force. Dec 1971: 2nd (I) Armd Bde [mech: Topas]. *Transferred Apr 1979 as 7th Mech Inf.*
2nd Bn	Aug 1947: 114th Inf Bde (Lahore). Served in Kashmir 1948 (161st Inf Bde). Sep 1965: 62nd Mtn Bde. Dec 1971: 5th Mtn Bde.
3rd Bn	Aug 1947: internal security duties Multan area. Sent Aug 1953 to Korea to guard POW camp following armistice; returned Jan 1954(?). Sep 1965: 93rd Inf Bde. Dec 1971: 83rd Mtn Bde.
4th Bn	Aug 1947: Kohat Bde (Thal). Served in Kashmir 1948 (19th Inf Bde). 1962: 11th Inf Bde. Dec 1971: 26th Inf Div.
5th Bn	Dec 1971: 7th Inf Div.
6th Bn	1965:161st Inf Bde.
7th Bn	
8th Bn	Dec 1971: 45th Inf Bde.

[199] Initially consolidated with the Punjab Regimental Centre, it was separated in April 1963.

9th Bn	Sep 1948: 1st Armd Div. 1962: 70th Inf Bde. Sep 1965: 1st Armd Bde [mech]. Dec 1971: 41st Mtn Bde. Served with IPKF in Sri Lanka.
10th Bn	Dec 1971: 86th Inf Bde. Participated in Operation Blue Star Jun 1984. Served with IPKF in Sri Lanka.
11th Bn	Dec 1971: 51st Para Bde.
12th Bn	
13th Bn	Raised 6 Apr 1948 at Jalandhar.1962: 62nd Inf Bde (Ramgarh); sent to NEFA Oct. Sep 1965: 62nd Mtn Bde. Dec 1971: 32nd Inf Bde. Served with IPKF in Sri Lanka.
14th Bn	[Personnel used to raised 14th Field Regiment May 1956 and later reformed.] 1965: 19th Inf Bde. Dec 1971: 3rd Inf Div.
15th Bn	[Personnel used to raised 15th Field Regiment May 1956 and later reformed.] Sep 1965: 54th Inf Bde. Dec 1971: 35th Inf Bde. Served with IPKF in Sri Lanka.
16th Bn	Sep 1965: 96th Inf Bde. Dec 1971: 47th Inf Bde. Served in 1999 Kargil War.
17th Bn	
18th Bn	
19th Bn	

There are three TA battalions associated with the Dogra Regiment: 112th Infantry Bn (TA) at Jalandhar, 153rd Infantry Bn (TA) at Meerut and 159th Infantry Bn (TA) (H and H) at Thalela. The Dogra Scouts are also associated with the regiment.

Regimental Centre: Jalandhar Cantonment, Punjab; moved 1952 to Meerut Cantomnent, Punjab; moved 1976 to Faziabad, Uttar Pradesh.

Regimental Insignia: A tiger, revered as the mount of Goddess Durga, who is a widely worshipped deity in the Dogra Hills. The tiger is on a straight scroll reading "THE DOGRA REGIMENT"; below all is a scroll reading "KARTAVYAM ANVATMA" (the regimental motto).[200]

The prior badge was quite different: the numerals "17" with a crown above and scroll reading "DOGRAS" below. (The 1st Battalion had a separate badge, based on the Prince of Wales's plumes and coronet.)

Motto: Kartavyam Anvatma (Duty before Death)

Honours: Jhanagar (4), Rajaori (4), Uri (2), Jammu and Kashmir 1947-48 (2, 4); Hajipir (6), Raja Picuqet-Chand Tekri (3), Op Hill (NL 1053) (2), Jammu

---

[200] However, there are illustrations showing the badge without the lower scroll.

and Kashmir 1965 (2, 3, 6); Asal Uttar (1), Dograi (15), Punjab 1965 (1, 15); Suadih (9), Siramani (13), Chauddagram (3), East Pakistan 1971 (3, 9, 13); Dera Baba Nanak (10), Punjab 1971 (1, 10, 15).

The Garhwal Rifles

Formed as 18th Royal Garhwal Rifles from the four battalions of the 39th Garhwal Rifles: the 1st, 2nd and 3rd Bns assumed the same numbers and the 4th Bn became the 10th Bn. One ITF battalion (11th) was formed. Known wartime units included the 4th and 5th Bns. (2nd Bn lost at Singapore 1942 and reformed May 1946 by redesignation of 4th Bn.)

The regiment recruits Garhwalis (any resident of Garhwal; originally only Rajputs were recruited). The exception was 18th Bn, which recruited Jats, Dogras and Marathas.[201]

1st Bn	Aug 1947: Peshawar Bde (Peshawar). Sep 1965: 30th Inf Bde. Dec 1971: 43rd Lorried Inf Bde [mech: Topas]. *Transferred Apr 1979 as 6th Mech Inf.*
2nd Bn	Aug 1947: Lansdowne. Sep 1965: 120th Inf Bde. Dec 1971: 5th Mtn Bde.
3rd Bn (Scout)	Aug 1947: Rawalpindi. Served in 1947-48 (80th and Z/163rd Inf Bdes). Sent Aug 1953 to Korea to guard POW camp following armistice; returned ca. Jan 1954. Sep 1965: 38th Inf Bde. Dec 1971: 91st Inf Bde.
4th Bn	1962: 62nd Inf Bde (Ramgarh); sent to NEFA Oct. Dec 1971: 80th Inf Bde. Served with IPKF in Sri Lanka. 163rd Inf Bde in Kashmir May 2003.
5th Bn	Sep 1965: 70th Inf Bde. Dec 1971: 202nd Mtn Bde. Served with IPKF in Sri Lanka.
6th Bn	Sep 1965: 99th Mtn Bde. Dec 1971: 162nd Inf Bde.
7th Bn	Dec 1971: 52nd Inf Bde.
8th Bn	Sep 1965: 43rd Lorried Inf Bde [mech]. Dec 1971: 38th Inf Bde.
9th Bn	Participated in Operation Blue Star Jun 1984.
10th Bn	Dec 1971: 191st Inf Bde. Served with 121st Inf Bde 1999 Kargil War.
11th Bn	Dec 1971: 99th Mtn Bde. Served with IPKF in Sri Lanka.
12th Bn	Dec 1971: 71st Mtn Bde. Served with IPKF in Sri Lanka.

[201] As with a few other regiments, this may have been in response to the 1984 Sikh uprising; if so, it was probably changed after 1999. Gautam, op.cit., always careful to show all mixed class battalions or recruiting, indicates only Garhwalis.

13th Bn	Served with IPKF in Sri Lanka.
14th Bn	
15th Bn	163rd Inf Bde in Kashmir May 2003.
16th Bn	Served with IPKF in Sri Lanka.
17th Bn	Served with 70th Inf Bde 1999 Kargil War.
18th Bn[202]	Served with 56th Mtn Bde 1999 Kargil War. Served with IPKF in Sri Lanka.
19th Bn	

Two TA battalions are associated with the Garhwal Rifles: 121st Infantry Bn (TA) at Calcutta and 127th Ecological Bn (TA) at Dehradun.
Regimental Centre: Lansdowne, Uttar Pradesh.

Regimental Insignia: The Maltese Cross, with a bugle in the centre and the Ashoka Lions above. There is a ring around the bugle reading "THE GARHWAL RIFLES". The only change after 1950 was the substitution of the Ashoka Lions for the crown.

Motto: Yudhaya Krit Nischya

Honours: Tithwal (3), Jammu and Kashmir 1947-48 (1, 3); Nuranang (4), Ladakh 1962; Buttur Dograndi (8), Punjab 1965 (6, 8); Gadra Road (1), Rajasthan 1965 (1); Hilli (5), East Pakistan 1971 (5); Tiger Hill (18?), Kargil 1999.

The Kumaon Regiment

Formed as 19th Hyderbad Regiment from 94th Russell's Infantry [1st Bn], 96th Berar Infantry [2nd Bn], 1st Bn/97th Deccan Infantry [3rd Bn], 98th Infantry [4th Bn], 99th Deccan Infantry [5th Bn], and 95th Russell's Infantry [10th Bn]. The 5th Bn was disbanded Apr 1924 and the 3rd Bn in December 1931. The Kumaon Rifles (originally 5th and 6th Bns, 9th Jat Regiment) were merged as 1st Bn Kumaon Rifles and attached to the 19th Hyderabad Regiment.[203] One ITF battalion (11th) was formed. Known wartime units included the 5th and 8th Bns. (4th Bn lost at Singapore 1942 and reformed April-May 1946 by redesignation of 8th Bn.) Redesignated 1945 as The Kumaon Regiment. In 1946 the 1st Bn converted to the parachute role, later becoming one of the battalions of the new Parachute Regiment.

---

[202] Became 18th Joint Bn 1985, adding companies of Jat, Dogra and Maratha regiments. Reverted to pure Garwhali unit December 1999 as 18th Bn.
[203] None of the 1914 regiments included "Kumaon" in their title, so I am not sure which regiments were used to form the Kumaon Rifles.

The regiment recruits Kumaonis (75%) and Ahirs (25%).

Two State Forces battalions (4th Gwalior Infantry and Indore Infantry) were incorporated as the 14th and 15th Battalions, respectively. The new Naga Regiment was affiliated with the Kumaon Regiment on formation in November 1970, and that regiment's 1st and 2nd Bns remain affiliated.

1st (Para) Bn	Aug 1947: 2nd Abn Div defence bn (Karachi or Quetta). Served in Kashmir 1947-48 (161st and 19th Inf Bdes). *Transferred Apr 1952 as 3rd Para.*
2nd Bn	Aug 1947: internal security duties Calcutta.
3rd Bn Rifles	Raised 1950 by redesignation of 1st Kumaon Rifles. Sep 1965: 114th Inf Bde. Dec 1971: 301st Mtn Bde.
4th Bn	Aug 1947: 11th Inf Bde (Deolali). Second bn into Kashmir Oct 1947; served 1947-48 (161st Inf Bde). Sep 1965: 104th Inf Bde. Dec 1971: 81st Mtn Bde. 1984 into Siachin.
5th Bn	Dec 1971: 26th Inf Div.
6th Bn	Aug 1947: internal security duties Jhansi & Allahabad. Sep 1948: Hyderabad. 1962: 11th Inf Bde. Sep 1965: 96th Inf Bde. Dec 1971: 74th Inf Bde.
7th Bn	Dec 1971: 68th Inf Bde. Served with IPKF in Sri Lanka. 2008: CI Kashmir (Poonch District).
8th Bn	Sep 1965: 104th Inf Bde.
9th Bn	Sep 1965: 69th Mtn Bde. Dec 1971: 181st Mtn Bde. Jun 1985: Participated in Operation Blue Star Jun 1984. Served with IPKF in Sri Lanka.
11th Bn	Served with IPKF in Sri Lanka.
12th Bn	Dec 1971: 61st Mtn Bde.
13th Bn	1962: sent to 114th (I) Inf Bde in Sep. Dec 1971: 322nd Inf Bde. 1994 CI in Kashmir. Served with 102nd Inf Bde in 1999 Kargil War. 2004: UN service, UNMEE Eritrea-Ethiopia.
14th Bn (Gwalior)	[4th Gwalior Inf served with 1st Armd Bde, Hyderabad Sep 1948.] Raised 1 Apr 1951. (ex 4th Gwalior Inf). Sep 1965: 62nd Mtn Bde. Dec 1971: 181st Mtn Bde. *Transferred Apr 1979 as 5th Mech Inf.*
15th Bn (Indore)	Raised 1 Apr 1951 (ex Indore Inf). Sep 1965: 191st Inf Bde, later 41st Mtn Bde. Dec 1971: 31st Inf Bde. Participated in Operation Blue Star Jun 1984. Kashmir 1990s.
16th Bn	Served with IPKF in Sri Lanka.
17th Bn	(ex 31st Bn). Dec 1971: 66th Mtn Bde.
18th Bn	Served with IPKF in Sri Lanka.
19th Bn	2008: CI in NE.

20th Bn	
21st Bn	
31st Bn	Raised ? *Redesignated ca. 1971 as 17th Bn.*
1st Kumaon Rifles	Aug 1947: internal security duties Allahabad & Aligarh. Served in J&K 1948 with 19th Inf Bde. Redesignated 1950 as 3rd Bn of regiment but designated as 3rd Kumaon Rifles rather than 3rd Kumaon Regiment.

Two TA battalions are associated with the Kumaon Regiment: 111th Infantry Bn (TA) at Allahabad and 130th Ecological Bn (TA) at Pithoragarh. The Kumaon Scouts are affiliated with the regiment.

Regimental Centre: Agra, Uttar Pradesh; moved 1948 to Ranikhet, Uttaranchal.

Regimental Insignia: A demi-rampant lion holding a cross. The demi-rampant lion is part of the arms of the Russel family, whose ancestor had started the body of troops now formed into the Kumaon Regiment. Below, a scroll reading "KUMAON". This replaced the completely different badge used by the 19th Hyderabad Regiment. Somewhat surprisingly, it was not changed after 1950.

Motto: Prakramo Vijayate (Valour Triumphs)

PVC: two[204]

Honours: Srinagar (4), Jammu and Kashmir 1947-48 (4); Rezang La (13), Ladakh 1962 (13); Sanjoi-Mirpur (4), Jammu and Kashmir 1965 (4, 14); Punjab 1965 (9); Bhaduria (17), Shamsher Nagar (4), East Pakistan 1971 (3, 4, 9, 12, 17); Jammu and Kashmir 1971 (7); Punjab 1971 (6); Gadra City (15), Sindh 1971 (13, 15).

The Assam Regiment

This regiment was raised 15 June 1941. Its three battalions (one only raised in November 1945) remained on duty. The regiment recruits from a variety of peoples from the Northeast Region (NER), especially Nagas, Kulkis, Mizos, Lushias, Assamese and Kacheri, plus others in smaller numbers. In 1984, the 12th and 14th Battalions were reorganized with a company each of personnel from the Northeast Region, South Indian Communities, Garhwalis and Dogras.

---

[204] Maj Som Nath Sharma, 4th Bn (3 Nov 1947—the first award)(P); Maj Shaitan Singh, 13th Bn (18 Nov 1962)(P).

This was reversed in 1999 and the battalions reverted back to their prior NER composition.

1st Bn	Aug 1947: Shillong. Sep 1965: 114th Inf Bde. Dec 1971: 164th Mtn Bde.
2nd Bn	Aug 1947: Nowshera Bde (Malakand, Dargai & Chakdara). Sep 1965: 70th Inf Bde. Dec 1971: 161st Inf Bde.
3rd Bn	Aug 1947: Shillong. Served in Kashmir 1948. Dec 1971: 67th Inf Bde.
4th Bn	Dec 1971: 340th Mtn Bde (or 38th Inf Bde?). Served with IPKF in Sri Lanka.
5th Bn	Dec 1971: 191st Inf Bde. Served with IPKF in Sri Lanka.
6th Bn	Dec 1971: 165th Mtn Bde.
7th Bn	Served with IPKF in Sri Lanka.
8th Bn	
9th Bn	
10th Bn	
11th Bn	
12th Bn	
13th Bn	
14th Bn	
15th Bn	

A TA battalion is associated with the Assam Regiment: 119th Infantry Bn (TA) at Shillong.

Regimental Centre: Shillong, Meghalaya.

Regimental Insignia: Uni-horned Rhinoceros of Assam. Below, a scroll reading "ASSAM REGT". The badge is in silver with the background of the scroll in black.

Motto: Assam Vikram (Unique Valour)

Honours: Jammu and Kashmir 1947-48 (3); Chamb (5), Jammu and Kashmir 1971 (5).

The Bihar Regiment

Biharis earlier served in the Hyderabad [Kumoan] Regiment; the Bihar Regiment was raised in 1942. The current 2nd Battalion was the first unit raised as part of the new regiment; the 1st Battalion was the old 11th [ITF] Bn of the

Hyderabad [later Kumoan] Regiment. A third battalion was formed November 1945 and a 25th Bn existed May-October 1945.
The regiment recruits anyone from North Bihar, as well as Adivasis from the Chottanagur Plateau (Jharkand and Orissa) and 5% from Other Indian Communities. Most battalions are evenly split between Biharis and Adivasis; one is half Biharis and a quarter each Adivasis and men from Orissa. The 16th Bn has Biharis, Adivasis and Mazhabi and Ramdasias Sikhs.

1st Bn	Aug 1947: Agra. Served with 70th Inf Bde 1999 Kargil War.
2nd Bn	Aug 1947: Madras Area. Served in Kashmir 1948. Dec 1961: 63rd Inf Bde. Sep 1965:80th Inf Bde.
3rd Bn	Aug 1947: Ranchi. Dec 1971: 104th Inf Bde.
4th Bn	Served with IPKF in Sri Lanka.
5th Bn	Dec 1971: 163rd Inf Bde.
6th Bn	Sep 1965: 114th Inf Bde [also shown with 161st Inf Bde].
7th Bn	Sep 1965:161st Inf Bde. Dec 1971: 167th Mtn Bde. Served with IPKF in Sri Lanka.
8th Bn	Dec 1971: 83rd Mtn Bde.
9th Bn	Dec 1971: 29th Inf Bde. Served with IPKF in Sri Lanka.
10th Bn	Dec 1971: 311th Mtn Bde.
11th Bn	
12th Bn	Participated in Operation Blue Star Jun 1984.
13th Bn	
14th Bn	
15th Bn	Served with IPKF in Sri Lanka.
16th Bn	Raised Feb 1985.
17th Bn	
21st Bn	

There are two TA battalions associated with the Bihar Regiment: 120th Infantry Bn (TA) at Bhubaneswar and 154th Infantry Bn (TA) at Brichgunj (Port Balair).

Regimental Centre: Ranchi from April 1946, Gaya November 1946, and then from March 1949, Danapur Cantonment, Bihar.

Regimental Insignia: The Ashoka Lions;[205].below, a scroll reading "BIHAR".

Motto: Karam Hi Dharm (Work is Worship)

---

[205] The regiment used the Ashoka Lions on their badge during the Second World War, preceding its adoption as a national emblem.

Honours: Akhaura (10), East Pakistan 1971 (10); Chamb, Jammu and Kashmir 1971.

The Mahar Regiment

This regiment was another wartime unit, raised in 1941. In 1946 it became the Mahar Machine Gun Regiment, taking over the role of providing medium machine gun support to the rest of the army.[206] Its first three wartime battalions remained on duty; a 25th Bn also existed during the war. In 1962 it became a normal infantry regiment and machine guns were integrated into infantry battalion establishments.

The regiment now recruits Mahar and all India; five battalions are solely Mahars, one has personnel from border regions, and the remainder are all India mixed class.

Three battalions of the Border Scouts, raised for manning the Punjab border, were absorbed in 1956.

1st Bn	Aug 1947: MG bn for 5th Inf Div (Ranchi). Served in Kashmir 1947-1948. Sep 1965: 31st Inf Bde. Dec 1971: 115th Inf Bde.
2nd Bn	Aug 1947: Basra Garrison. Dec 1971: 85th Inf Bde.
3rd Bn	Aug 1947: MG bn for 4th Inf Div (with PBF). Sep 1965:191st Inf Bde.
4th Bn (Borders)	Raised 1956 (ex Border Scouts bn).[207] Dec 1971: 268th Inf Bde. Served with IPKF in Sri Lanka.
5th Bn (Borders)	Raised 1956 (ex Border Scouts bn). Dec 1971: 161st Inf Bde.
6th Bn (Borders)	Raised 1956 (ex Border Scouts bn). 1962: elements with 4th Inf Div. Dec 1971: 48th Inf Bde.
7th Bn[208]	Dec 1971: 25th Inf Div.
8th Bn	Served with IPKF in Sri Lanka (91st Inf Bde).
9th Bn	Sep 1965: 41st Mtn Bde. Served with 102nd Inf Bde 1999 Kargil War.
10th Bn	Sep 1965: 120th Inf Bde. Dec 1971: 81st Mtn Bde.
11th Bn	Raised ca 1965.
12th Bn	Raised ca 1965. Served with 79th Mtn Bde 1999 Kargil War.
13th Bn	Raised 1966. Dec 1971: 33rd Inf Bde but under 93rd Inf Bde.

---

[206] This echoed British World War Two practice of having certain regiments dedicated to this role, although the British would abandon dedicated machine gun battalions after the war.

[207] Coy A, 4th Bn served with 99th (I) Infantry Brigade in the Congo 1961-62 and D Coy, 4th Bn 1962-63.

[208] The 7th to 10th Bns were raised 1959-1962 as machine gun battalions.

14th Bn	Redesignation of 31st Bn. Dec 1971: Mizo Hills Range.
15th Bn	Redesignation of 32nd Bn.
16th Bn	Raised ca. 1972 by conversion of 8th Para. *Transferred Apr 1979 as 12th Mech Inf.*
17th Bn[209]	
18th Bn	
19th Bn	Served with IPKF in Sri Lanka.
31st Bn	Raised 1968 under modified establishment for CI operations in the Northeast. *Redesignated 14th Bn by Dec 1971.*
32nd Bn	Raised under modified establishment for CI operations in the Northeast.[210] Dec 1971: Kilo Force, 23rd Mtn Div. *Redesignated 15th Bn sometime after Dec 1971.*

Two TA battalions are associated with the Mahar Regiment: 108th Infantry Bn (TA) at Saugar and 115th Infantry Bn (TA) at Belgaum.

Regimental Centre: Arangon (near Ahmednagar), Maharashtra ; moved 1948 to Saugor, Madhya Pradesh.

Regimental Insignia: A pair of crossed Vickers medium machine guns, mounted on a tripod with a dagger. The dagger was initially the Pillar of Koregaon, where the combined British and Mahar troops defeated a Maratha Army. Considered improper, the pillar was subsequently removed and was replaced with a dagger. Below, a scroll reading "THE MAHAR REGIMENT". A hackle in the cap badge was introduced in 1969.

Motto: Yash Siddhi (Success and Attainment)[211]

PVC: one[212]

Honours: Jammu and Kashmir 1947-48 (1); Ladakh 1962 (1); Jaurian Kalit (9), Kalidhar (3), Jammu and Kashmir 1965 (3, 9, 11); Asal Uttar (2), Tilakpur-Mahadipur (10), Punjab 1965 (2, 10); Shamsher Nagar (10), East Pakistan 1971 (10); Thanpir (13), Jammu and Kashmir 1971 (13); Harar Kalan (1), Shehjra (6), Punjab 1971 (1, 6); Parbat Ali (2), Sindh 1971 (2).

---

209 The 17th to 19th Bns were raised late 1970s-early 1980s.

210 According to Global Security, this was the first battalion of the regiment to be composed solely of hill tribes. www.globalsecurity.org/military/world/india/rgt-mahar.htm

211 Has also been translated as Attainment of Fame.

212 Maj Ramaswamy Parameshwara, 8th Bn (25 Nov 1987: Sri Lanka)(P).

The Jammu and Kashmir Rifles

The Jammu and Kashmir Infantry were State Forces and became the only ones taken into the Indian Army as a distinct regiment. (The 1st and 2nd Jammu and Kashmir Infantry and 3rd Jammu & Kashmir Rifles all dated from the 19th Century; the 4th and 7th Jammu & Kashmir Infantry were raised in the 1930s, and the 9th Jammu & Kashmir Infantry in 1940.) All but the 3rd Bn had service during at least part of the war and all were demobilized afterwards; the 7th Bn was disbanded in 1945 but then reformed in 1947. The 5th, 6th and 8th Bns were active in the fighting 1947-48 but apparently disbanded later.[213] (Those battalions active in 1947-48 served in defence of the state.[214]) While the Indian Army took over control of all of the State Forces in 1947, those from Jammu and Kashmir were not part of the 1 April 1951 integration of others into the Army, and the Jammu and Kashmir Infantry were only full integrated into the Army 1 January 1957. The regiment's title was changed in 1963 to The Jammu and Kashmir Rifles.

The regiment recruits Dogras, Gorkhas, Sikhs and Muslims.[215]

1st Bn	Raised 1 Jan 1957 (ex 1st J&K Inf). Dec 1971: 350th Inf Bde.
2nd Bn	Raised 1 Jan 1957 (ex 2nd J&K Inf). 1962: 5th Inf Bde. Dec 1971: 28th Inf Bde. Served with IPKF in Sri Lanka.
3rd Bn	Raised 1 Jan 1957 (ex 3rd J&K Rifles). 1962: 67th Inf Bde, to NEFA Oct. Sep 1965:268th Inf Bde. Served in 1999 Kargil War.
4th Bn	Raised 1 Jan 1957 (ex 4th J&K Inf). 1965:58th Inf Bde.
5th Bn	Dec 1971: 168th Inf Bde.
6th Bn	1965:68th Inf Bde.
7th Bn	Raised 1 Jan 1957 (ex 7th J&K Inf). Sep 1965: 114th Inf Bde.
8th Bn	Reformed ? Sep 1965: 168th Inf Bde.
9th Bn	Raised 1 Jan 1957 (ex 9th J&K Inf). Sep 1965: 7th Mtn Bde. 30th Inf Bde.
10th Bn	Dec 1971: 167th Mtn Bde.

---

[213] The Bharat Rakshak page on State Forces battalions taken into the Army show only the 1st, 2nd, 3rd, 4th, 7th and 9th J&K Infantry becoming battalions of the new regiment: www.bharat-rakshak.com/LAND-FORCES/Units/Features/221-ISF.html.

[214] Officially all of the State Force Infantry resisted heroically, and many certainly did (the stand at Uri being a notable example) and these bought time for regular units of the Indian Army to be sent in. However, not all of their Muslim personnel were willing to fight the invaders and some deserted or mutinied. That factor and the initial poor deployments of the units make the success of the remainder that much more creditable.

[215] 13th Battalion is composed solely of Dogras from Himachal Pradesh, Punjab, and Jammu and Kashmir.

11th Bn	
12th Bn	
13th Bn	1999 Kargil War: 79th Mtn Bde.
14th Bn	Dec 1971: 65th Inf Bde..
15th Bn	
16th Bn	Raised ? *Transferred Apr 1979 as 14th Mech Inf.*
17th Bn	
18th Bn	
19th Bn	
20th Bn	

Three TA battalions are associated with the Jammu and Kashmir Rifles: 126th Infantry Bn (TA), 155th Infantry Bn (TA) at Sujanpur and 160th Infantry Bn (TA) (H and H) at Kupwara.

Regimental Centre: [As State Force, Jammu to 1950, then Srinagar] Srinagar; moved 1959 to Morar Cantonment, Gwalior; moved 1975 to Jabalpur, Madhya Pradesh.

Regimental Insignia: An oval embracing the sun, the State emblem. The Sanskrit inscription around the sun translates as "Ever Victorious in War". Below, a scroll reading "JAMMU A KASHMIR RIFLES".

Motto: Prashata Ranvirta (Valour in Battle is Praiseworthy)[216]

PVC: two[217]

Honours: Punch (1, 7, 8, 9), Skardu (6), Jammu and Kashmir 1947-48 (1, 2, 3, 5, 6, 7, 8, 9); Asal Uttar (9), Punjab 1965 (9); Syamganj (1), East Pakistan 1971 (1).

The Jammu and Kashmir Light Infantry

Militia units were formed in the State beginning in 1947,[218] becoming organized into battalions and regimented in 1948 as the Jammu and Kashmir Militia. Some 12 battalions were formed: six in the Srinagar Valley, one in

---

[216] This has also been translated as Chivalry in the field is praiseworthy. It was the motto of the Jammu and Kashmir State Force.

[217] Rifleman Sanjay Kumar, 13th Bn (5 Jul 1999); Capt Vikram Batra, 13th Bn (6 Jul 1999)(P)—the only instance of two winners from the same unit in the same war.

[218] The early groups were the Border Defence Scouts [Jammu], Punch Scouts and Volunteers, National Home Guards [further up the Kashmir Valley], and Nubra Scouts and Nubra Home Guards in Ladakh.

Ladakh, and five in the Jammu area. (Officers came from the State Force and the Indian Army.) They were a permanernt force by April 1964. In 1972 these battalions were regularized, and redesignated in 1976 as the Jammu and Kashmir Light Infantry.

The regiment recruits Muslims, Hindus and Sikhs from the state; units are organized with 50% Muslims and 50% other J&K ethnic groups. One battalion is composed of Dogras, Sikhs, Buddhists, Gorkhas and others from the state.

1st Bn	Sep 1965: 121st Inf Bde Gp. Dec 1971: Gallies Sector, 19th Inf Div. Served with IPKF in Sri Lanka.
2nd Bn	Sep 1965:268th Inf Bde.
3rd Bn	Sep 1965: 191st Inf Bde Gp. Dec 1971: 25th Inf Div.
4th Bn	
5th Bn	
6th Bn	Sep 1965: 68th Inf Bde.
7th Bn	Dec 1971: 28th Inf Bde. *Used to form Ladakh Scouts Jun 1963.*
8th Bn	1960: at Leh, placed under 114th Inf Bde. Sep 1965:HQ 31 ComZ Sub Area, XV Corps. Dec 1971: 28th Inf Bde.
9th Bn	Sep 1965: 80th Inf Bde. Dec 1971: 121st (I) Inf Bde.
10th Bn	
11th Bn	Sep 1965: 62nd Mtn Bde. Dec 1971: 93rd Inf Bde. Served with IPKF in Sri Lanka.
12th Bn	Sep 1965: 121st Inf Bde. Dec 1971: 121st (I) Inf Bde. 1999 Kargil War: 70th Inf Bde.
13th Bn	Apr 1960: Moved to Ladakh and placed under 114th (I) Inf Bde; relieved ca Sep 1962. Sep 1965:268th Inf Bde.
14th Bn	Apr 1960: Moved to Ladakh and placed under 114th (I) Inf Bde; relieved ca Sep 1962. *Used to form Ladakh Scouts Jun 1963.*
15th Bn	
16th Bn	

Two TA battalions are associated with the Jammu and Kashmir Light Infantry: 129th Ecological Bn (TA) at Samba and 161st Infantry Bn (TA) (H and H) at Baramula. The Ladakh Scouts were associated with the regiment until they were made a regiment in 2000.

Regimental Centre: Srinagar, Jammu & Kashmir.

Regimental Insignia: A pair of crossed muskets. Below, a scroll in three parts reading "LIGHT" and "INFANTRY" on the left and right and "JAK" in the center.

Motto: Balidanam Veer Lakshanam (Sacrifice is a Sign of the Brave)

PVC: one[219]

Honours: Laleali-Picquet 707 (8), Gutrian (11), Shingo River Valley (9), Jammu and Kashmir 1971 (8, 9, 11).

The Naga Regiment

This regiment was raised 1 November 1970 as a single battalion, affiliated with The Kumaon Regiment. It did not form a 2nd Battalion until 11 February 1985, and these first two battalions remain affiliated with The Kumaon Regiment.

The regiment recruits 50% Nagas and 50% Kumaonis.[220]

1st Bn	Raised 1 Nov 1970 at Ranikhet.[221] Dec 1971: 7th Mtn Bde. 1999 Kargil War: 56th Mtn Bde.
2nd Bn	Raised 11 Feb 1985 at Haldwani.
3rd Bn	

Regimental Centre: The Kumaon Regimental Centre at Ranikhet, Uttar Pradesh.

Regimental Insignia: A pair of crossed Naga spears and a dah (a cutting weapon used in Nagaland), with a shield bearing a mithun (deer) head; below a scroll with non-English lettering.

Honours: Drass, Muskoh (2), Kargil 1999 (2).

The Ladakh Scouts Regiment

---

219 Naib Subedar Bana Singh, 8th Bn (23 Jun 1987: Siachen).

220 Per Gautam, op. cit. However, the entry for the regiment at the Bharat Rakshak web site indicates the other 50% has always been a mixture of equal numbers of Kumaoni, Garhwali and Gorkhas.

221 Designated as the Naga Regiment (rather than 1st Bn of the regiment) until a 2nd Bn was formed in 1985. Battalions from the Garhwal Rifles, Kumaon Regiment and 3 Gorkha Rifles contributed personnel to supplement Nagas.

The Ladakh Scouts were raised 1 June 1963 following the poor showing in the 1962 war with China; they are nicknamed "The Snow Warriors." They were formed with eight companies by merging the 7th and 14th Bns of the Jammu and Kashmir Militia.[222] The force expanded to as many as 28 companies. The companies were reorganized 1982-85 into three wings.[223]

Raised to the status of a full infantry regiment in June 2000 and so retitled, with additional battalions (four) planned. The regiment recruits Buddhists and Muslims from Ladakh.

1st Bn	Raised Jun 1963.[224] 1999 Kargil War: 70th Inf Bde.
2nd Bn	
3rd Bn	
4th Bn	
5th Bn	Raised 31 Jul 2002.

Regimental Centre: Srinagar, Jammu & Kashmir [1971].

Regimental Insignia: A Urial [wild sheep] native to the Ladakh mountains.

Honours: Turtuk, Jammu and Kashmir 1971

Note on the Gorkha Regiments

Six of the ten Gurkha regiments of the old Indian Army transferred to the new Indian Army in accordance with a November 1947 treaty signed by India, Nepal, and Great Britain. Personnel, in some cases almost entire battalions, from the four regiments going to the British Army elected to remain with the Indian Army in lieu of transfer to British service, allowing formation of additional battalions and a new regiment. All Gorkha regiments now recruit 70% Gorkhas from Nepal and 30% Gorkhas from India, a ratio likely to change to 60% and 40%. (However, only two of the regiments make explicit reference to this in their pages on the Indian Army web site.) There are about 45,000 Gorkhas all told in the Indian Army.

---

[222] However, 7th J&K Militia is often now sometimes shown as the source of the 1st Bn and 14th K&K Militia as converted as the 2nd Bn.

[223] Which would account for only nine of the companies, since each wing (battalion) had three companies. How the 28 companies became nine, or what if anything happened to the rest, is unknown. It also appears that the pre-2000 three wings became one battalion when the Scouts became a regiment.

[224] Known simply as the Ladakh Scouts or Ladakh Scouts Regiment until 2nd Bn of regiment was raised. A Company served with 70th Infantry Brigade and C and H Companies with 114th Infantry Brigade in 1965 war.

1 Gorkha Rifles

This regiment dates back to 1815, going through a number of designations until 1910 when it became 1st King George's Own Gurkha Rifles (The Malaun Regiment). In 1937 it was retitled as 1st King George V's Own Gurkha Rifles (The Malaun Regiment). The two regular battalions (1st and 2nd) were joined by wartime 3rd and 4th Bns; the latter two were disbanded in 1946. (2nd Bn was destroyed in Burma and disbanded January 1942; it was reformed August 1946 from the 3rd Bn.) In 1947 the regiment was selected for the Indian Army, and in 1950 retitled as 1 Gorkha Rifles (The Malaun Regiment).[225]

The regiment recruits from the Gurung and Magar, found largely in the central and west central hills.

1st Bn	Aug 1947: Razmak Bde (Razmak). Served in J&K 1947-48 with 268th Inf Bde. Sep 1965:28th Inf Bde. Served with IPKF in Sri Lanka.
2nd Bn	Aug 1947: Peshawar Bde (Peshawar). Sep 1948: 9th Inf Bde. Sep 1965: 168th Inf Bde. Dec 1971: 164th Mtn Bde.
3rd Bn	Raised 1959. 1961-62: 99th (I) Inf Bde in the Congo. 1965: 58th Inf Bde. Dec 1971: 91st Inf Bde.
4th Bn	Raised 1963. Dec 1971: 191st Inf Bde. Served with IPKF in Sri Lanka.
5th Bn	Raised 1965. Dec 1971: 41st Mtn Bde. Served with IPKF in Sri Lanka.

Regimental Centre: Dharamsala, Himachal Pradesh; 4 GR Regimental Centre moved there 1952 and the two combined as 14 Gurkha Training Centre; moved 1954 to Chakrata, Uttarakhand; moved 1960 to Subathu, Himachal Pradesh.

Regimental Insignia: A pair of crossed Khukris (a Gorkha dagger) facing down with the numeral 1 above and the light infantry bugle horn below.

Before 1950, the "1" was between the bugle horn and the intersection of the Khukris, and the badge was surmounted by the crown and motto of the Prince of Wales.

Motto: Kayar Hunu Bhanda Mamu Ramro (It is better to die than to be a coward)[226]

---

[225] It is not clear if 1 GR still uses the Malaun Regiment subtitle; it is shown without it on the Indian Army and Bharat Rakshak web pages, although Sharma (op.cit., p 158), published in 2000, shows it.

[226] From 1968 this also became the motto of 4 Gorkha Rifles. This is sometimes translated as "Better to die than live like a coward."

PVC: one[227]

Honours: Kalidhar (1), Jammu and Kashmir 1965 (1); Darsana (5), East Pakistan 1971 (5); Jammu and Kashmir 1971 (4)

3 Gorkha Rifles

Another regiment dating to 1815, with a number of titles until becoming the 3rd Gurkha Rifles in 1901. They were given the honor title "Queen's Own" in 1907 but this was changed (at the Queen's request) the next year to 3rd Queen Alexandra's Own Gurkha Rifles. The Regular battalions (1st and 2nd) were joined by two more during the war; the 4th Bn was disbanded in 1947. The regiment transferred that year to the Indian Army with three battalions, and was retitled 1950 as 3 Gorkha Rifles.

The regiment recruits from the Gurung, Thapa, Magar and Pun of central Nepal. This is one of two regiments making explicit reference to Indian domiciled Gorkhas.

1st Bn	Aug 1947: Calcutta. Sep 1965: 38th Inf Bde. Dec 1971: Bengal Area, then Romeo Force XXXIII Corps. 1999 Kargil War: 56th Mtn Bde.
2nd Bn	Aug 1947: Wahu, Murree & Rawalpindi. Served in Kashmir 1948 (77th Para Bde). Sep 1965: 114th Inf Bde.
3rd Bn	Aug 1947: 48th Inf Bde (Dhond). 1962: 11th Inf Bde. Dec 1971: 162nd Inf Bde.
4th Bn	Raised 1964. Sep 1965:80th Inf Bde.
5th Bn	Raised 1963. Dec 1971: 121st (I) Inf Bde.

Regimental Centre: Ghangora, Uttarakhand; 3 GR Regimental Centre moved there in 1952 and the two combined as 39 Gorkha Training Centre; moved 1976 to Varanasi Cantonment, Uttar Pradesh.

Regimental Insignia: A pair of crossed khukris (a Gorkha dagger) pointing upwards, with a design (similar in appearance to an angled Star of David) in-between and the numeral 3 within the design.

The prior badge had the cipher of Queen Alexandra (two interleaved A's) with a crown above and the "3" between the cipher and Khukris.

Motto: Kayar Hunu Bhanda Mamu Ramro (It is better to die than to be a coward)

---

227 Capt Gurbachan Singh Salaria, 3rd Bn (5 Dec 1961: Congo)(P).

Honours: Uri (2), Jammu and Kashmir 1947-48 (2); Shingo River Valley (5), Jammu and Kashmir 1971 (5).

4 Gorkha Rifles

Raised in 1857, going through several designations until it became the 4th Gurkha Rifles in 1901 and 4th Prince of Wales's Own Gurkha Rifles in 1924. Its Regular battalions (1st and 2nd) were joined by two more during World War II, with the 4th Bn disbanded in 1946. The three existing battalions transferred to the Indian Army in 1947, becoming 4 Gorkha Rifles in 1950.

The regiment recruits from the Magar and Gurung.

1st Bn	Aug 1947: Gardai Bde (Gardai). Served in Kashmir 1948 (5th Inf Bde). 1962: 5th Inf Bde. Dec 1971: 93rd Inf Bde.
2nd Bn	Aug 1947: Lahore and Amritsar. Sent to Ladakh 1948. Sep 1965: 168th Inf Bde. Dec 1971: 168th Inf Bde. 163rd Inf Bde in Kashmir May 2003.
3rd Bn	Aug 1947: in Burma. 1962: 70th Inf Bde. Dec 1971: 52nd Inf Bde but with 68th Inf Bde.
4th Bn	Raised 1962. 1965: 168th Inf Bde. Dec 1971: 3rd Inf Div.
5th Bn	Raised 1963. 1965:168th Inf Bde.
6th Bn	Raised 1970.

Regimental Centre: Bakloh, Himachal Pradesh; moved 1952 to Dharamsala, Himachal Pradesh and combined with 1 GR Regimental Centre to form 14 Gorkha Training Centre, which is currentluy at Sabathu, Himachal Pradesh.

Regimental Insignia: A pair of crossed Khukris (a Gorkha dagger), one pointing down and one pointing up (both hilts to the right), with the Ashoka Lions above and the Roman numeral "IV" below. (This has also been shown without the Ashoka Lions.) The former badge was surmounted by the crown and motto of the Prince of Wales but otherwise the same.

Motto: Kafar Hunu Bhanda Mamu Ramro (It is better to die than to be a coward)[228]

Honours: Punch (1), Gurais (2), Jammu and Kashmir 1947-48 (1, 2); Punjab 1965 (4); Jammu and Kashmir 1971 (3).

---

[228] The motto of 1 Gorkha Rifles, from 1968 this also became the motto of 4 Gorkha Rifles.

5 Gorkha Rifles (Frontier Force)

Raised 1858 in the Punjab Irregular Force, later the Punjab Frontier Force. Following some redesignations, the regiment became 5th Gurkha Rifles (Frontier Force) in 1901 and 5th Royal Gurkha Rifles (Frontier Force) in 1921. Similar to others, its two Regular battalions (1st and 2nd) were joined by two more, with the 4th Bn disbanded in 1946. The regiment transferred to the Indian Army in 1947, becoming 5 Gorkha Rifles (Frontier Force) in 1950.[229]

The source of this regiment's recruits is not known to the authors.

1st Bn	Aug 1947: Nagpur. Served in Kashmir 1948 (77th Para Bde). Sep 1965: 29th Inf Bde. Dec 1971: 48th Inf Bde. Served with IPKF in Sri Lanka.
2nd Bn	Aug 1947: returning from Japan. Sep 1948: Hyderabad. 1962-63: 99th (I) Inf Bde in the Congo. Sep 1965: 99th Mtn Bde. Dec 1971: 340th Mtn Bde.
3rd Bn	Aug 1947: Calcutta. Sep 1948: Hyderabad. Dec 1971: 19th Inf Bde. Served with IPKF in Sri Lanka.
4th Bn	Raised 1962. Sep 1965: 62nd Mtn Bde. Dec 1971: 59th Mtn Bde. Served with IPKF in Sri Lanka (72nd Inf Bde).
5th Bn	3/6th GR at Avadi Aug 1947; became 5th Bn ca 1948. Sep 1948: Hyderabad. 1962: 67th Inf Bde, to NEFA Oct. Sep 1965: 116th Inf Bde. Dec 1971: 95th Mtn Bde but with Echo Sector, 8th Mtn Div.
6th Bn	Sep 1965: joined 191st Inf Bde. Dec 1971: 30th Inf Bde.

Regimental Centre: Dehra Dun, Uttarakhand 1947; amalgamated with 8 GR Regimental Centre there in 1952 to form 58 Gurkha Training Centre; moved 1975 to Shillong, Meghalaya.

Regimental Insignia: A pair of crossed Khukris (a Gorkha dagger) points upward, with the numeral "5" resting on the crossing point; atop the "5" is the Ashoka Lions. The Lions replaced the royal crest (lion atop a crown) on the former design.

Motto: Shaurya Evam Nistha (Courage and Determination)

---

[229] The regiment has clung resolutely to the Frontier Force parenthetical, even though the Frontier in question is now northwest Pakistan and all other Frontier Force regiments transferred to the Pakistani Army in 1947.

Honours: Zoji La (1), Kargil (1), Jammu and Kashmir 1947-48 (1); Charwa (2), Punjab 1965 (2); Sylhet (4), East Pakistan 1971 (2, 4, 5); Jammu and Kashmir 1971 (3); Shehjra (1), Punjab 1971 (1).

8 Gorkha Rifles

This regiment traces its lineage to two different units (raised in 1824 and 1835), which became the 44th Gurkha Rifles in 1901 (the 1824 unit) and the 43rd Gurkha Rifles the same year (the 1835 unit). The two regiments then became the 8th [ex 44th] and 7th [ex 43rd] Gurkha Rifles in 1903 and finally were consolidated 1907 as the 1st and 2nd Bns of the 8th Gurkha Rifles. Like others, the regiment raised two more battalions for the Second World War; the 3rd Bn was disbanded in 1946. The regiment transferred to the Indian Army in 1947, becoming 8 Gorkha Rifles.

Another regiment whose recruitments sources are not known to the authors.

1st Bn	Aug 1947: Zhob Bde (Loralai). Apr 1961 moved to Ladakh and placed under 114th (I) Inf Bde. Sep Sep 1965: 41st Mtn Bde. Dec 1971: 14th (I) Armd Bde [mech: Topas]. *Transferred Apr 1979 as 3rd Mech Inf.*
2nd Bn	Aug 1947: 43rd Lorried Bde (Ferozepore). Sent to Ladakh 1948. Dec 1971: 163rd Inf Bde.
3rd Bn	Raised 1963. Sep 1965:104th Inf Bde.
4th Bn	Aug 1947: Kuala Lumpur, Malaya. Sep 1965: 80th Inf Bde. Dec 1971: 86th Inf Bde.
5th Bn	4th/2nd GR Sep 1947 at Calcutta; transferred 1948 as 5th Bn. Sep 1965: 28th Inf Bde. Dec 1971: 68th Inf Bde.
6th Bn	Raised 1948. Served in Kashmir 1948. 1962: 67th Inf Bde, to NEFA Oct. Sep 1965: 48th Inf Bde. Dec 1971: 323rd Inf Bde. Served with IPKF in Sri Lanka.
7th Bn	Raised 1 Jul 1979 [to replace 1/8]. Served with IPKF in Sri Lanka.

Regimental Centre: Dehra Dun, Uttarakhand 1947; amalgamated with 5 GR Regimental Centre there in 1952 to form 58 Gurkha Training Centre; moved 1975 to Shillong, Meghalaya.

Regimental Insignia: A pair of crossed khukris (a Gorkha dagger) points upward with the numeral “8” above. This did not require change after 1950.

Motto: Kafar Hunu Bhanda Mamu Niko (It is better to die than be a coward)

PVC: one[230]

Honours: Punch (6), Jammu and Kashmir 1947-48 (6); Chushul (1), Ladakh 1962 (1); Sanjoi-Mirpur (3), Jammu and Kashmir 1965 (3); Punjab 1965 (6).

9 Gorkha Rifles

The lineage of the 9th goes back to 1817, and it has had the number "9" since 1861 (the same time it began to recruit Gurkha personnel). It was wholly Gurkha from 1893, and designated the 9th Gurkha Rifles in 1901. The two Regular battalions (1st and 2nd) were joined by three more in World War II. The 2nd Bn was lost at Singapore, the 4th Bn was disbanded in 1947, and the 5th Bn redesignated as the 2nd Bn in 1946. The regiment transferred to the Indian Army in 1947, becoming 9 Gorkha Rifles.

The regiment recruits from the Chhetry, Khattry, and Thakury. This regiment's web page also made explicit reference to recruitment of Gorkhas domiciled in India.

1st Bn	Aug 1947: 5th Inf Bde. Served in Kashmir 1947-48 (80th Inf Bde). 1962: 7th Inf Bde. Sep 1965: 62nd Mtn Bde. Dec 1971: 86th Inf Bde.
2nd Bn	Aug 1947: Wana Bde. Sep 1965: 163rd Inf Bde. Dec 1971: 62nd Mtn Bde.
3rd Bn	Aug 1947: in Malaya. Served in Kashmir 1948. Sep 1965: 67th Inf Bde. Dec 1971: 87th Inf Bde.
4th Bn	Raised 1961. Dec 1971: 80th Inf Bde.
5th Bn	Raised 1963. Sep 1965:43rd Lorried Inf Bde [mech].
6th Bn	

Regimental Centre: Dehra Dun, Uttarakhand; moved 1952 to Ghangora, Uttarakhand and combined with 3 GR Regimental Centre to form 39 Gorkha Training Centre; moved 1976 to Varanasi Cantonment, Uttar Pradesh.

Regimental Insignia: A pair of crossed khukris (a Gorkha dagger) blades downsward with the numeral "9" below and the Lions of Ashoka above. As with many other regiments, the Lions replaced a crown.

Motto: Kafar Hunu Bhanda Mamu Niko (It is better to die than be a coward)

---

[230] Maj Dhan Singh Thapa, 1st Bn (20 Oct 1962).

Honours: Phillora (5), Punjab 1965 (5); Khumarkali (2), East Pakistan 1971 (2); Jammu and Kashmir 1971 (4); Dera Baba Nanak (1), Punjab 1971 (1, 3).

11 Gorkha Rifles

This regiment was raised 1 January 1948 (an 11th Gurkha Rifles had been formed in World War One and then disbanded), taking over personnel from regiments transferred to the British Army.[231]

The regiment recruits mainly Rai and Limbu from the east central hills of Nepal.

1st Bn	Raised 1 Sep 1960. Dec 1971: 301st Mtn Bde. 1999 Kargil War: 70th Inf Bde. Served with IPKF in Sri Lanka.
2nd Bn	Raised 11 Jan 1963. Dec 1971: 121st (I) Inf Bde.
3rd Bn	Raised 1 Jan 1948 at Santa Cruz, Bombay from 2nd/7th GR.[232] Sep 1965: 62nd Mtn Bde. Dec 1971: 116th Inf Bde, later with 67th Inf Bde. Served with IPKF in Sri Lanka.
4th Bn	Raised 1 Jan 1948. Disbanded 1952 following a mutiny.
5th Bn	Raised 8 May 1948. Sep 1965: 52nd Mtn Bde. Dec 1971: 340th Mtn Bde.
6th Bn	Raised 1 Oct 1963. Dec 1971: 120th Inf Bde.
7th Bn	Raised 1 Jan 1965. Dec 1971: 19th Inf Bde.

A TA battalion is associated with 11 Gorkha Rifles: 107th Infantry Bn (TA) at Darjeeling.

Regimental Centre: Palampur and Santa Cruz, Mumbai; moved 1951 to Ghangora, Darjeeling; moved 1976 to Jalapahar, West Bengal; moved 1982 to Lucknow, Uttar Pradesh.

Regimental Insignia: A pair of crossed Khukris (a Gorkha dagger) points upwards with the Roman numeral XI in-between.

Motto: Yatraham Vijayastatra (The Metaphor for Victory); the former motto was Nisswarth Kartavyam (Selfless Duty)

---

[231] The regiment was formed mainly with men from the 7th and 10th Gurkha Rifles, which recruited in eastern Nepal.

[232] Under the November 1947 treaty, transfer to the British Army was voluntary, and this battalion as a whole declined to transfer. The 4th Bn was formed entirely from 7th and 10th GR personnel not opting for British service, while the 5th Bn was partly veterans and partly new recruits.

PVC: one[233]

Honours: Bogra (5), East Pakistan 1971 (5); Shingo River Valley (2), Jammu and Kashmir 1971 (2, 7); Batalik (1), Kargil 1999 (1).[234]

The Rashtriya Rifles

This regiment (whose designation may be translated as National Rifles) was formed for counterinsurgency operations in Jammu and Kashmir. The initial approval in 1990 was for six battalions, controlled by two sector HQs. Approval was given in 1994 for ten more sector HQs and another 30 battalions. Given their CI role, battalions of the regiment have a war establishment distinct from regular infantry battalions. Existing units were tasked to man the new regiment (50% from the infantry, 40% from other arms, and 10% from services) in order to expedite their creation and expansion. Given the obvious problems of ad hoc units, a later decision made two Rashtriya Rifles battalions integral to each infantry regiment and other arms. Thus, the majority of the troops (generally 60% of other ranks) are drawn from the associated regiment and rotate back to their regiment after service.

The initial 36 battalions (50,000 personnel) began an expansion in February 2001 with the raising of four more battalions. Ultimately the regiment is to have a strength of 66 battalions (85,000 troops). The intent of the expansion was to free the Army from further CI duties in Jammu and Kashmir. By 2004 there were 57 operational battalions, and the next six were being formed. The final three were raised after that date. Battalions generally remain in one area, with personnel rotating every two years.

Given their organization and role, Rashtriya Rifles battalions do not form part of any division. Instead, there were four Counter Insurgency Force (CIF) HQs at the top, each headed by a major general. XV Corps has operational control of Victor Force (Anantnag, Badgam and Pulwana districts) and Kilo Force (Kupwara and Baramulla districts). XVI Corps has operational control of Delta Force (Doda district) and Romeo Force (Poonch and Rajouri districts). In 2002 (2003-4?), Uniform Force was established under XVI Corps (Udhampur and Raisi districts). Numbered sectors (originally 12; 17 by 2005, and 20 currently) are subordinated to the Force HQs.

---

233 Capt Manoj Kumar Pandey, 1st Bn (3 Jul 1999)(P).

234 Per the Bharat Rakshak page on the regiment; this and the Parachute Regiment are the only two instances of this theatre honour the authors have found. It also shows the battle honour Batalik, which was a battle during that war and 1/11 GR were involved.

Bn	Affiliated to	Notes
1st Bn	Mahar	Sector 2: Pulwana.
2nd Bn	Sikh LI	Sector 3: Srinagar.
3rd Bn		Sector 1:Anantnag.
4th Bn	Bihar	Sector 4: Doda.
5th Bn		Sector 3:Ganderbal.
6th Bn	Sikh	Sector 8: Kupwara.
7th Bn	Punjab	Sector 1: Anantnag [Kukanarg town].
8th Bn	Madras	Sector 11: Doda.
9th Bn		Sector 2: Anantnag. Served in 1999 Kargil War.
10th Bn	Rajput	Sector 11: Doda.
11th Bn	Dogra	Sector 9: Doda.
12th Bn	Grenadiers	Sector 11: Doda.
13th Bn	Kumaon	Sector 5: Pattan.
14th Bn	Garhwal Rifles	Sector 5: Bandipore. Served in 1999 Kargil War.
15th Bn	1/4 GR	Sector 5: Bandipore.
16th Bn	Sikh	Sector 6: Poonch.
17th Bn	Maratha LI	Sector 6: Poonch. Served in 1999 Kargil War.
18th Bn		Sector 8: Kupwara.
19th Bn		Sector 8: Kupwara.
20th Bn	Grenadiers	Sector 2: Banihal.
21st Bn	Guards	Sector 6: Kupwara.
22nd Bn	Punjab	Sector 5: Sopore.
23rd Bn	Rajput	Sector 7: Kupwara.
24th Bn		Sector 7: Kupwara.
25th Bn	Madras	Sector 6: Surankote.
26th Bn	Mech Inf	Sector 9: Kishwar.
27th Bn	Maratha LI	Sector 6: Doda.
28th Bn	J&K Rifles	Sector 10: Baramulla. 1999 Kargil War: 79th Mtn Bde.
29th Bn	Grenadiers	Sector 10: Baramulla.
30th Bn	Mahar	Sector 10: Sopore.
31st Bn	Parachute	Sector 9: Kishtwar.
32nd Bn	3/9 GR	Sector 7: Kupwara.
33rd Bn	5/8 GR	Sector 10: Bandipore.
34th Bn		Sector 12: Badgam.
35th Bn	Assam	Sector 12: Badgam.
36th Bn	Garhwal Rifles	Sector 1: Antantnag.
37th Bn	Punjab	Raised 1 Feb 2001.
38th Bn	Madras	Raised 1 Feb 2001.
39th Bn	Grenadiers	Raised 1 Feb 2001.
40th Bn	Dogra	Raised 1 Feb 2001.

Bn	Affiliated to	Notes
41st Bn		Raised by Sep 2001.
42nd Bn		Raised by Sep 2001.
43rd Bn	Raj Rifles	
44th Bn		
45th Bn	Jat	
46th Bn		
47th Bn		
48th Bn		
49th Bn		
50th Bn		Raised 2003.
51st Bn		Raised 2003.
52nd Bn		Raised 2003.
53rd Bn		Raised 2003.
54th Bn		Raised 2003.
55th Bn		Raised by 2004.
56th Bn		Raised by 2004.
57th Bn		Raised by 2004.
58th Bn		Raised in 2004.
59th Bn		Raised in 2004.
60th Bn		Raised in 2004.
61st Bn		Raised in 2004.
62nd Bn		Raised in 2004.
63rd Bn		Raised in 2004.
64th Bn		
65th Bn		
66th Bn		

Regimental Insignia: Crossed AK-47 rifles with fixed bayonets; above, the Ashoka Chakra; below, a three-part scroll with the motto “ridhta aur virta”.

Selected Infantry Regiment Badges

Brigade of the Guards

Mechanised Infantry Regiment

Punjab Regiment

Madras Regiment

Maratha Light Infantry

Rajput Regiment

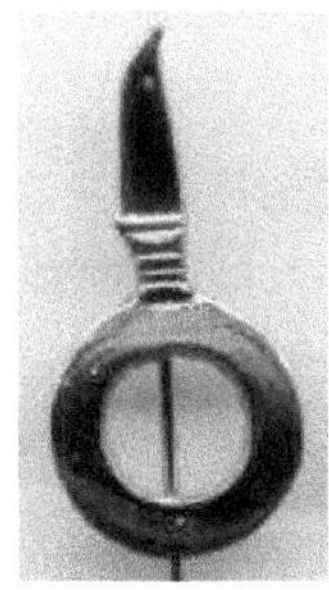

Sikh Light Infantry

Dogra Regiment

Kumaon Regiment

Assam Regiment

Bihar Regiment

Mahar Regiment

Jammu and Kashmir Rifles

Jammu and Kashmir Light Infantry

8th Gorkha Rifles

Airborne and Special Forces

In October 1946, the wartime Indian Parachute Regiment was disbanded. Its three surviving battalions were redesignated as battalions in existing infantry regiments, and eight infantry battalions were redesignated as parachute, giving the 2nd Airborne Division three parachute brigades (nine battalions) and two divisional battalions. The division was disbanded on partition, with two parachute brigade headquarters and six parachute battalions going to India, along with some of the division's other units (artillery, engineers, services, etc.).

The parachute battalions of the new Indian Army were:

1st (Para) Bn Punjab Regiment
2nd (Para) Bn Madras Regiment
3rd (Para) Bn Maratha Light Infantry
4th (Para) Bn Rajputana Rifles
3rd (Para) Bn Rajput Regiment
1st (Para) Bn Kumaon Regiment

The original parachute school at Chaklala had gone to Pakistan, and India opened a new one at Agra in November 1949. The next year, one parachute brigade and its battalions were converted to infantry. The three remaining battalions were 1st (Para) Bn Punjab Regiment, 3rd (Para) Bn Maratha Light Infantry, and 1st (Para) Bn Kumaon Regiment.

A new Indian parachute regiment was formed 15 April 1952, designated the Parachute Regiment and ranked second in order of precedence behind the Brigade of The Guards. The three remaining parachute battalions were renumbered as 1st Bn (former 1st Punjab), 2nd Bn (former 3rd Maratha Light Infantry), and 3rd Bn (former 1st Kumaon).[235] On the same date, the Parachute Regiment Depot and Records was established at the Agra parachute training center. This was expanded and redesignated 22 June 1963 as The Parachute Regiment Training Centre, at Agra Fort.[236] The Centre moved to Morar Cantonment, Gwalior, on 5 February 1965, returning to Agra 2 October 1975. Finally, on 15 January 1992 the Parachute Regiment Training Centre and other

[235] Following practice in the Indian Army for newly formed regiments, the battalions retained their former regimental titles in parentheses: e.g., 2nd Para (3rd Maratha) and brought all of their existing battle honours with them.

[236] A training wing of the Parachute Regiment was established 1 May 1962 at Kota, under the Brigade of The Guards Training Center, for direct recruitment and training of recruits for the regiment. This moved to Agra on 26 September 1963.

administrative elements relocated to Bangalore, Karnataka. However, actual parachute training remained at Agra.

In 1957, the Parachute Regiment established geographic and ethnic quotas for its battalions. 1st Parachute had Dogras, Sikhs, and others from the plains; 2nd Parachute had Marathas, South Indian Communities, and Bengalis; 3rd Parachute had Kumaons and other hill peoples. When 4th Parachute was raised in 1960 it had Gorkhas, Dogras, Garhwalis, and South Indian Communities. Following the 1971 war all battalions were given mixed (All India All Classes) companies in place of the prior companies organized on geographic or class identification.

The regiment raised its first new battalion (4th) in August 1960; a parachute pathfinder squadron had been raised (outside the regiment) the prior June, created from the President's Bodyguard. The regiment formed four further battalions between 1963 and 1965 and a second parachute brigade was raised.

A raiding unit (Meghdoot Force) had been formed in August 1965 under Major Megh Singh, from his regiment (3rd Rajput) and other sources, and these conducted operations behind Pakistani lines in Kashmir during September. Meghdoot Force became the source of the next unit raised in the Parachute Regiment, 9th Para-Commando Battalion July 1966, and it was followed by 10th Para-Commando Battalion June 1967.[237]

In 1972, the new parachute brigade and one of its battalions converted to infantry. The two para-commando battalions developed specialized roles, with 9th specializing in mountain warfare and 10th desert-specialized in Southern Command. 1st Parachute converted to the commando role in 1977, becoming a GHQ unit directly under Army command. According to some sources, it took over the mountain warfare role, and 9th Para-Commando shifted to specializing in jungle warfare. In common with other armies, the Army's special forces (the para-commando battalions) could also assume internal security roles.

There was a move in the 1980s to create a distinct Special Forces regiment. Although this failed and the battalions remained part of the Parachute Regiment, special forces did succeed in establishing a separate training center at Nahan, Himachal Pradesh in 1995.[238] By that point the para-commando battalions were redesignated as parachute (special forces). On 1 February 1996

---

[237] These were first designated as parachute battalions, taking the designation para-commando in July 1967 (although at least one source suggests the new designation came as late as 1969).

[238] One source suggests that the special forces had a training wing at Belgaum and a headquarters at Nahan in 1992.

the regiment gained another battalion when 21st Maratha Light Infantry converted as 21st Parachute (Special Forces). In 2001 the existing 2nd Parachute also converted, as 2nd Parachute (Special Forces). By this point—if not even earlier—it appears that the special forces battalions were all cross-trained, abandoning the earlier specialized roles. Elements of the regiment have served in a counterinsurgency role, both in the North East and in Jammu and Kashmir

By the end of the century, the Parachute Regiment was essentially two regiments. One part was the traditional parachute force, with the 3rd, 4th, 5th, 6th and 7th Parachute. The other part was the special forces, with the 1st , 2nd, 9th, 10th and 21st Parachute (Special Forces). The government announced the intended creation in 2003 of four new special forces battalions, to be trained in cooperation with Israel.[239] The intended role for these units was to stop cross-border infiltration in Kashmir, although they were to be trained for cross-border raids as well. 4th Parachute converted to the special forces role; there are no open source indications that the remaining battalions were ever actually formed: the Regiment's official web site shows no additional battalions. Nor is there any indication that the 4th was other than a normal special forces battalion.

The following are the battalions of the regiment:

1st Para (Punjab)	Formed 15 Apr 1952 from 1st (Para) Punjab. Replaced 3rd Para in Middle East ca Nov 1957; served a year? 1965: 68th Inf Bde. Dec 1971: 116th Inf Bde. Converted 1977 as **1st Para-Cdo**. Participated in Operation Blue Star Jun 1984. Served with IPKF in Sri Lanka. 1999 Kargil War: 50th (I) Para Bde. Later **1st Para (SF)**.
2nd Para (Maratha)	Formed 15 Apr 1952 from 3rd (Para) Maratha LI. Korea Sep 1953-Feb 1954 to oversee POW camps after armistice. 1965: 50th (I) Para Bde. Dec 1971: 50th Para Bde. Converted 2001 as **2nd Para (SF)**.
3rd Para (Kumaon)	Formed 15 Apr 1952 from 1st (Para) Kumaon. Nov 1956: to Middle East after 1956 war; left ca Nov 1957. 1965: 50th (I) Para Bde. Dec 1971: 51st Para Bde. Served with IPKF in Sri Lanka. Converted after 2001 as **3rd Para (SF)**.
4th Para	Formed Aug 1960. Dec 1971: 51st Para Bde. Served with IPKF in Sri Lanka. Converted ca. 2004 as **4th Para (SF)**.

[239] Creation of such units was proposed as early as spring 2000.

5th Para	Formed Jan 1963. Served with IPKF in Sri Lanka (18th Inf Bde). 1999 Kargil War: 70th Inf Bde.
6th Para	Formed Feb 1963. 1965: 50th (I) Para Bde. 1999 Kargil War: 50th (I) Para Bde.
7th Para	Formed Oct 1964. Dec 1971: 50th Para Bde. Served with IPKF in Sri Lanka. 1999 Kargil War: 50th (I) Para Bde.
8th Para	Formed Jan 1965. Dec 1971: 50th Para Bde. *Converted to infantry ca. 1972 as 16th Mahar.*
9th Para-Cdo	Formed 1 Jul 1966. Dec 1971: XV Corps. Served with IPKF in Sri Lanka. 1999 Kargil War: 79th and 192nd Mtn Bdes. Later **9th Para (SF)**.
10th Para-Cdo	Formed 1 Jun 1967. Dec 1971: Southern Cmd. Served with IPKF in Sri Lanka. 1999 Kargil War: 70th Inf Bde. Later **10th Para (SF)**.
21st Para (SF)	Formed 1 Feb 1966 by conversion of 21st Maratha LI.

There are two affiliated Territorial Army battalions: 106th Infantry Bn (TA) at Bangalore and 116th Infantry Bn (TA) at Deolali. It does not appear that either of these are organized or intended to operate as other than standard infantry battalions.

Regimental Badge: An open parachute with wings; in front of the wings and parachute a circle with the word "PARACHUTE" at the top; across the bottom of the circle a scroll with the word "REGIMENT"; a dagger point upwards with the hilt behind the scroll and the point in front of the upper part of the circle; all in silver.

Motto: Shatrujeet

Honours: Srinagar (1st Kumaon [3]), Naushera (3rd Maratha LI [2]), Jhangar (3rd Maratha LI [2]), Punch (1st Punjab [1], 1st Kumaon [3]), Jammu and Kashmir 1947-48 (1st Punjab [1], 3rd Maratha LI [2], 1st Kumaon [3]); Hajipir (1), Jammu and Kashmir 1965 (1); Poongli Bridge (2), East Pakistan 1971 (2); Defence of Punch (9), Jammu and Kashmir 1971 (9); Chachro (10), Sindh 1971 (10); Kargil 1999 (5, 9, 10)[240].

---

[240] From the Parachute Regiment's web site; one of the few references to this theatre honour discovered.

Other Arms and Services

There is often little information on unit designations for other combat arms or supporting arms and services of the Indian Army, especially in more recent periods. The published history of the Artillery consulted is fairly complete but ends with the 1965 war; that for the Engineers is somewhat more episodic but goes through the 1971 war. In some cases few or no designations at all are known.

The Regiment of Artillery

The Regiment of Artillery initially included all artillery types: field, air defence and coast defence. Coast artillery was handed over to the Navy in 1964. AOP squadrons, operated in cooperation with the Air Force, were transferred in November 1986 to form the new Army Aviation Corps. Air defence was separated in October 1993.

The new Army inherited 18 and a half regiments of artillery in 1947. The bulk of these were for the ground role.[241] The new Army had the following regiments, grouped by type:

1st Field Regiment (SP) [Sexton SP 25pdr]
2nd Field Regiment (SP) [Sexton SP 25pdr]
7th Field Regiment [towed 25pdr]
8th Field Regiment [towed 25pdr]
11th Field Regiment [towed 25pdr]
13th Field Regiment [towed 25pdr]
16th Field Regiment [towed 25pdr]
9th Parachute Field Regiment [75mm howitzer]
17th Parachute Field Regiment [75mm howitzer]
22nd Mountain Regiment [3.7" howitzer]
24th Mountain Regiment [3.7" howitzer]
40th Medium Regiment [5.5" gun]
20th Survey Regiment (less one battery to Pakistan)
34th Mahratta Anti-tank Regiment (SP)
35th Lingayat Anti-tank Regiment [towed 6pdr AT gun and 3" mortars]
36th Mahratta Anti-tank Regiment [towed 6pdr AT gun and 3" mortars]

---

[241] As with the Royal Artillery, regiments were numbered in a single sequence in January 1947, instead of each type of regiment numbered in its own sequence. Pakistan received nine regiments and a battery, accounting for some of the missing numbers. (A full 15 regiments were disbanded between January and August 1947.) The designations do not reflect the seniority of the regiments involved.

37th Coorg Anti-tank Regiment [towed 6pdr AT gun and 3" mortars]
26th Light AA Regiment [40mm L/60 AA gun]
27th Light AA Regiment [40mm L/60 AA gun]

In addition, there was a single coast battery (5th) and one non-divisional HQ, 11th Army Group RIA (AA), to control the various AA regiments. Ten of the regiments had been cadre-ized during demobilization, giving them the regimental HQ, one full-strength battery, and two cadre batteries. Attempts to refill cadre units took months after independence. There was also a shortage of officers: only one regimental CO and about a third of the battery commanders had been Indians in spring 1947.

The first expansion came in April 1948, with seven new regiments. One was composed of State Force batteries taken into the Army, the others were organized on a regional rather than class basis:

41st Field Regiment (new RHQ and batteries from Patiala, Bikaner and Gwalior)
42nd Field Regiment (North Indian Classes)
43rd Field Regiment (Western region, Mahattas predominant)
44th Anti-tank Regiment (South Indian Classes)
45th Light AA Regiment (South Indian Classes)
46th Light AA Regiment (North Indian Classes)
Unknown heavy AA regiment

At the same time, the Army planned to convert 24th Mountain to a medium regiment (this happened in 1949), and the anti-tank regiments were to be equipped with the 4.2" mortar. Regiments continued to be raised in the 1950s, some by converting infantry battalions and Border Scouts battalions; details are in the table below or the Corps of Air Defence Artillery section. (The infantry battalions were all reformed.) HQ 45th Artillery Brigade was raised in 1956. In 1963-64, mountain regiments were reorganized as mountain composite regiments (three mountain howitzer batteries and one heavy mortar battery). The Army also decided to raise light regiments (4.2" mortars, operating by animal transport or manpack). Three field regiments were raised at Belgaum during this period, one composed of Gorkhas and one of Jats.

Information on the Artillery is sparse; even the three official war histories rarely include artillery regiments in their details. There do not even appear to be any figures on the numbers or types of regiments at various dates, although one source indicates that there are now 200 artillery regiments.[242] The list below, clearly incomplete, contains all identified artillery regiments.[243]

1st (SP) Field Regiment	1947 regiment. Hyderabad 1948. 2nd Armd Bde Sep 1965 [Sextons].
2nd (SP) Field Regiment	1947 regiment. 1st Armd Div Sep 1965.
3rd Field Regiment, later 3rd Medium Regiment	Raised 1956 at Ambala. Med regt: XV Corps Dec 1971.
4th Field Regiment	Raised May 1956 from 8th Madras. Served in 1999 Kargil War.[244]
5th Field Regiment	Raised May 1956 from 19th Rajput. 4th Inf Div 1962 war; elements involved. 29th Inf Bde, XI Corps Sep 1965.
6th Field Regiment	Raised 1955 from disbanded Depot Field Regt. 4th Inf Div 1962 war; elements involved. 9th Inf Div Dec 1971 [25pdr]
7th Field Regiment	1947 regiment. In J&K area Aug 1965. 4th Mtn Div Dec 1971 [25pdr]
8th Field Regiment	1947 regiment.
9th (Parachute) Field Regiment	1947 regiment. Hyderabad 1948.
10th Field Regiment	Raised 1954 from Border Scouts personnel.
11th Field Regiment	1947 regiment. Committed by elements in J&K Nov 1947-May 1948. Rann of Kutch Apr 1965 [under Gujarat and Maharashtra Area].
12th Field Regiment	Raised 1954 from Border Scouts personnel. [fixed class regiment]
13th Field Regiment	1947 regiment. (Detachment sent as infantry used to form 17th Mtn Bty in J&K Nov 1947.) Sent one bty to 114th Inf Bde in 1962 war.
14th Field Regiment	Raised May 1956 from 14th Dogra. 191st Inf Bde Gp Aug 1965. 9th Inf Div Dec 1971 [25pdr].
15th Field Regiment	Raised May 1956 from 15th Dogra. 20th Inf Div Sikkim 1962. In XV Corps sector with some division Dec 1971. Served in 1999 Kargil War.

---

[242] Indian Military website, Indian Army entry, www.indian-military.org/army.html.
[243] Regiments with no service or other information shown are from a brief list in Sharma, op. cit., pp 62-63. AA and air defence regiments are shown in brackets since they were numbered in the same sequence.
[244] As indicated in Appendix J, the exact assignment of the artillery units among XV Corps, 3rd Infantry Division and 8th Mountain Division is not known.

16th Field Regiment	1947 regiment. RHQ in J&K by Dec 1947 and some or all of its batteries as well. With 5th Inf Div in 1962.
17th Parachute Field Regiment	1947 regiment. Part of 50th (I) Para Bde, probably from 1947.[245]
18th Field Regiment	20th Inf Div Sikkim 1962.
[19th Air Defence Regiment]	
20th Survey Regiment, later 20th Locating Regiment	1947 regiment. XI Corps 1965.
22nd Mountain Regiment	1947 regiment. Committed by elements in J&K Dec 1947-Jan 1948. 4th Inf Div 1962 war: committed by elements. 4th Mtn Div Dec 1971 [76mm].
23rd Composite Mountain Regiment; later 23rd Field Regiment	Raised 1953 from Gwalior, Patiala and J&K SF Mtn Btys. Mtn: XV Corps Art Bde but detached to 25th Inf Div Sep 1965. Field: [fixed class regiment]
24th Mountain Regiment, in 1949 24th Medium Regiment.	1947 regiment. I Corps Art Bde Sep 1965 (ex XXXIII Corps).
[25th Light AA Regiment	Raised 1957]
[26th LAA Regiment	1947 regiment]
[27th LAA Regiment	1947 regiment]
[28th LAA Regiment	Raised 1956]
[28th LAA Regiment	Raised Jan 1957]
30th Heavy Mortar Regiment	Formed 5 Dec 1959.
31st Heavy Mortar Regiment, later 31st Light Regiment	Raised 1956 at Ranchi from Border Scouts personnel. Lt regt: 25th Inf Div Sep 1965.
32nd Heavy Mortar Regiment, later 32nd Light Regiment	Raised 1956 at Ranchi from Border Scouts personnel. Lt regt: 3rd Inf Div Sep 1965 but sent to 121st (I) Inf Bde.
33rd Heavy Mortar Regiment	Raised 1956 at Ranchi from Border Scouts personnel. Served by elements in 1962 war.
34th Mahratta Anti-tank Regiment; later 34th Medium Regiment.	1947 regiment. Hyderabad 1948 as AT.

245 One battery served in the 1962 war.

35th Lingayat Anti-tank Regiment.	1947 regiment. Apparently disbanded later.
35th Heavy Mortar Regiment	Raised 1956 at Ranchi from Border Scouts personnel. Sent to Northeast 1962 after Chinese attack.
36th Mahratta Anti-tank Regiment; later 36th Heavy Mortar Regiment.[246]	1947 regiment. Served by elements in 1962 war.
37th Coorg Anti-tank Regiment.	1947 regiment.
38th Medium Regiment	Raised 1956 at Clement Town, Dehra Dun. XV Corps Art Bde Sep 1965, then I Corps.
39th Medium Regiment	Raised 1956 at Clement Town, Dehra Dun. XV Corps Art Bde Sep 1965.
40th Medium Regiment	1947 regiment. Hyderabad 1948 (one battery). With XI Corps 1965.
41st Field Regiment	Raised Apr 1948 from Patiala, Bikaner and Gwalior SF batteries. Served in 1999 Kargil War.
42nd Field Regiment	Raised Apr 1948 [North Indian Classes]. (25th Inf Div Sep 1965.
43rd Field Regiment	Raised Apr 1948 [Western region]. 3rd Inf Div Sep 1965.
44th Anti-tank Regiment, later 44th Heavy Mortar Regiment.[247]	Raised Apr 1948 [South Indian Classes]. Served by elements in 1962 war.
[45th Light AA Regiment	Raised 1948]
[46th Light AA Regiment	Raised 1948]
[50th Air Defence]	
52nd Composite Mountain Regiment; later 52nd Mountain Regiment	XV Corps Art Bde Sep 1965.
56th Field Regiment	
57th Field Regiment	[fixed class regiment]
59th Mountain Regiment	57th Mtn Div Dec 1971.
60th Heavy Regiment	Raised 1 Jan 1957 at Secunderabad from part of 8th and 9th Border Scouts Bns. With XI Corps 1965.
62nd Field Regiment	3rd Inf Div Sep 1965.

[246] Also referred to in the 1962 official history as 36th Light Regiment.

[247] Also referred to in the 1962 official history as 44th Light Regiment.

63rd Field Regiment	3rd Inf Div Sep 1965.
65th Mountain Regiment	57th Mtn Div Dec 1971.
67th Light Regiment	9th Inf Div Dec 1971 [120mm Mortar]
71st Medium Regiment	I Corps Art Bde Sep 1965.
75th Medium Regiment	
76th Medium Regiment	[fixed class regiment]
78th Medium Regiment	II Corps Dec 1971 [130mm]
81st Field Regiment	
82nd Heavy Mortar Regiment; later 82nd Light Regiment	As 82nd Hy Mortar: 20th Inf Div in Sikkim 1962. As 82nd Light: 57th Mtn Div Dec 1971.
85th Light Regiment	121st (I) Inf Bde Sep 1965. Also with brigade in Dec 1971.
86th Light Regiment	6th Mtn Div 1965. 10th Inf Div Dec 1971 (?).
91st Medium Regiment	
93rd Mountain Composite Regiment	6th Mtn Div 1965.
95th Mountain Composite Regiment	30th Inf Bde to mid Sep 1965.
99th Field Regiment	
101st (SP) Field Regiment	1st Armd Div Sep 1965.
[104th Air Defence Regiment	TA in 1965 war]
[105th Air Defence Regiment	TA in 1965 war]
108th Medium Regiment	Served in 1999 Kargil War.
123rd Medium Regiment	XV Corps Sep 1965.
[127th Air Defence Regiment	TA in 1965 war]
[128th Air Defence Regiment	TA in 1965 war]
139th Medium Regiment	Served in 1999 Kargil War.
141st Field Regiment	Served in 1999 Kargil War.
144th Field Regiment (TA)	67th Inf Bde Gp Sep 1965.
[151st Air Defence Regiment]	
153rd Medium Regiment	Served in 1999 Kargil War.
158th Medium Regiment	Served in 1999 Kargil War.
161st Field Regiment	41st Mtn Bde Sep 1965.
163rd Field Regiment	26th Inf Div Sep 1965 but detached to 25th Inf Div.

164th Field Regiment	"Newly raised" at time of 1965 war. 3rd Inf Div in Aug 1965 (supported 68th Inf Bde in Haji Pir Pass battle).
166th Field Regiment	Supported 35th Inf Bde in I Corps 1965 war.
168th Field Regiment	26th Inf Div, under 168th Inf Bde, Sep 1965.
169th Field Regiment	25th Inf Div Sep 1965.
174th Field Regiment	
181st Light Regiment	4th Mtn Div Dec 1971 [120mm Mortar]
194th Mountain Regiment	4th Mtn Div Dec 1971 [76mm]
195th Mountain Regiment	
197th Mountain Regiment, later 197th Field Regiment	57th Mtn Div Dec 1971 <mtn regt>. Served in 1999 Kargil War <field regt>.
212th Rocket Regiment	Served in 1999 Kargil War.
216th Medium Regiment	XV Corps Dec 1971.
244th Heavy Mortar Regiment	Served in 1999 Kargil War.
253rd Medium Regiment	Served in 1999 Kargil War.
255th Field Regiment	Served in 1999 Kargil War.
286th Medium Regiment	Served in 1999 Kargil War.
305th Medium Regiment	Served in 1999 Kargil War.
307th Medium Regiment	Served in 1999 Kargil War.
315th Field Regiment	Served in 1999 Kargil War.
871st Light Regiment	
1861st Light Regiment	Served in 1999 Kargil War.
1889th Light Regiment	Served in 1999 Kargil War.

In addition, the first regiment with the Brahmos cruise missile is numbered as 861. The Army wants to raise two more regiments, with 862 and 863 as likely numbers.[248]

The Regiment of Artillery is primarily a mixed class force, but it does have units with a class basis or batteries of a single class.[249]

The Artillery School and Centre is at Deolali, Maharashtra.

---

[248] Wikipedia article on the Brahmos missile, en.wikipedia.org/wiki/BrahMos.

[249] Gautam, op.cit., pp 39 and 53, lists 12th, 23rd and 57th Field Regiments and 76th Medium Regiment as examples of regiments with fixed-class gun batteries and all classes mixed at Regimental HQ. Former State Force units—such as 74th (Gwalior), 75th (Patiala) and 76th (Jammu and Kashmir) Mountain Batteries—are also fixed class.

Regimental insignia: An old-fashioned muzzle-loading gun; above, a scroll reading "SARVATRA" [Everywhere] crowned by the Star of India; below, the motto "IZZAT O IQBAL" [Honour and Glory] on a three-part scroll. Sarvatra, the Sanskrit for "everywhere", is thus similar to the Ubique (Everywhere) used by the British Royal Regiment of Artillery, from which regiment's badge the cannon and ramrod were copied.

The prior badge had the word "INDIA" in the top scroll but was otherwise identical.

Motto: Sarvatra-Izzat-o-Iqbal (Everywhere with honour and glory)

Honours: The artillery does not have colours, the guns serving as their colours. Individual batteries with distinguished service at a battle for which a battle honour is awarded can be awarded that battle's designation as an honour title.[250]

Corps of Army Air Defence

In October 1993 air defence units were transferred as the new **Corps of Air Defence Artillery**, and the air defence wing of the School of Artillery was separated 10 January 1994. It became the Air Defence Guided Missile Centre 15 November 1994. On 1 December 1999 it was redesignated as the Air Defence Artillery Centre. On 18 April 2005 it was redesignated again as the Army Air Defence Centre and the regimental designation was changed the same date to the **Corps of Army Air Defence**. In October 2008 the Army Air Defence Centre shifted to Gopalpur, Orissa.

The new Army began with only two regiments: 26th and 27th Light AA. These (and later-raised regiments) were equipped with the 40mm L/60 Bofors AA gun. The 45th and 46th Light AA Regiments were raised in April 1948, along with a heavy AA regiment (designation unknown). 28th LAA Regiment was formed at Hyderabad in May 1956 from 9th Madras. 29th LAA Regiment was raised 1 January 1957 at Secunderabad. 25th LAA Regiment was raised in 1957 at Deolali.

Anti-Aircraft was changed to Air Defence in 1964. At the time of the 1965 war, 19th Air Defence Regiment (raising date unknown) had a battery and a half of the new radar-directed 40mm L/70. (The remaining regular regiment, the 50th, is another one whose raising date is unknown.) Altogether the Army had 12 air defence regiments, including those of the Territorial Army (104th, 105th, 127th

---

[250] Sharma, op. cit., p 61, lists pre- and post-1947 battle honours for the Artillery, but this seems inconsistent with the information on the Indian Army's web site.

and 128th). The old 11th Army Group (AA) RIA of 1947 had survived, or been reformed, as 11th Independent Air Defence Brigade.

By 1971 there were 13 regiments equipped with the 40mm Bofors: eight L/70 and five L/60. Following the war, Territorial Army air defence units were converted to Regular, a process completed in 1975. The only other known air defence regiment is the 151st. The first SAM was the Tiger Cat, introduced in 1973, and the first mechanised weapon was the ZSU-23 Schilka. Additional gun and missile equipments came over the years, although the Army still has a large number of the 40mm L/70 towed guns.

Sources differ on what the current strength might be. One shows 52 air defence regiments overall.[251] However, the Bharat-Rakshak site indicates 12+ regiments in two SA-6 SAM groups and 50+ other regiments (35 'flak' and 15 'point defence').[252]

Regimental insignia: a silver surface-to-air missile pointing upwards, with gold flames; on either side radar emitting antennas facing outwards; toward the base of the missile a scroll with non-English lettering in gold.

Motto: Akashey shatrun jahi (Destroy the enemy in the air)

Honours: as for the Regiment of Artillery above.[253]

Army Aviation Corps

In 1947, Air Observation Post (AOP) squadrons—used to help direct artillery fire—were Royal Air Force units with Army personnel (mainly artillery officers) as pilots. India inherited part of the RAF's No 659 AOP Squadron. This was the basis for No 1 AOP Flight of the new Indian Air Force; a No 2 AOP Flight was raised at some later date. The first squadron was formed at Deolali 1 June 1958 as No 659 AOP Squadron, with a new squadron HQ and No 3 AOP Flight raised. By inference, the two existing AOP flights were incorporated into the new squadron. We have been unable to locate details on the expansion of this force, but there may have been eight squadrons by the 1980s.

---

[251] Indian Army at Indian Military website, www.indian-military.org/army.html. The Wikipedia article on the Indian Army is similar, showing 50 regiments.
[252] www.bharat-rakshak.com/LAND-FORCES/Today/22-Army-Orbat.htm.
[253] However, Sharma, op. cit., p 65, also lists some post-1947 battle honours for the Air Defence Artillery.

The Army Aviation Corps was formed 1 November 1986 when the AOP units transferred from the Air Force. There is now an independent Combat Army Aviation Training School at Nashik Road. The eight recce and observation (formerly AOP) squadrons generally consist of two to three recce & observation flights, which are separately designated and can be shifted among the squadrons. A 2005 Army Aviation Plan envisaged establishment of aviation brigades at corps and command levels. In addition to the helicopters, the Corps operates a variety of unmanned aerial vehicles.

The original AOP squadrons transferred from the Air Force are now known as army aviation squadrons (recce and observation). The probable designations for these squadrons are:

No.659 Army Aviation Squadron
No.660 Army Aviation Squadron
No.661 Army Aviation Squadron
No.662 Army Aviation Squadron
No.663 Army Aviation Squadron: served in 1999 Kargil War
No.664 Army Aviation Squadron
No.665 Army Aviation Squadron[254]
No.666 Army Aviation Squadron
No.667 Army Aviation Squadron
No.668 Army Aviation Squadron: served in 1999 Kargil War

While one source indicates that there are only eight of these squadrons, there are ten squadrons listed above. Therefore, some might be other kinds of units. By 2010, there were three utility squadrons with the new Dhruv Advanced Light Helicopter (ALH), with additional squadrons to form. There is also a special operations helicopter squadron.

Each squadron consists of two or three recce and observation flights. These flights are numbered in their own series, and retain their designations regardless of which squadron they might be assigned to. A few are independent flights, with "(Independent)" in their designation:

No.1 (I) R&O Flight
No.2 R&O Flight
No.3 R&O Flight
No.4 R&O Flight
No.5 R&O Flight: served with the UN Mission in Congo 1999 or later

---

[254] Served as the training unit at the School of Artillery, Deolali, until the Combat Army Aviation Training School was established.

No.6 R&O Flight: served in Somalia 1993-94
No.7 R&O Flight
No.8 R&O Flight: served with the UN Mission in Congo 1999 or later
No.9 R&O Flight: served with the UN Mission in Congo 1999 or later
No.10 R&O Flight
No.11 R&O Flight
No.12 (I) R&O Flight
No.13 R&O Flight
No.14 R&O Flight
No.15 R&O Flight
No.16 R&O Flight
No.17 R&O Flight
No.18 R&O Flight
No.19 R&O Flight
No.20 R&O Flight
No.21 R&O Flight
No.22 (I) R&O Flight
No.23 (I) R&O Flight
No.24 R&O Flight
No.25 R&O Flight
No.26 R&O Flight
No.27 (I) R&O Flight
No.28 R&O Flight
No.29 R&O Flight
No.30 (I) R&O Flight
No.31 R&O Flight
No.32 R&O Flight
No.33 R&O Flight
No.34 R&O Flight
No.35 R&O Flight

Taking out the six independent flights, the remaining 29 are more than sufficient to provide two-three flights to each of ten squadrons. There are (or have been) Nos 1 and 2 (Independent) Utility Helicopter Flights.

No. 201 Army Aviation Squadron is equipped with the new Dhruv Advanced Light Helicopter. It is not clear if this squadron also includes, or consists solely of, the armed version, the Light Combat Helicopter.

The 114th to 116th Helicopter Units are sometimes shown as belonging to the Army, but are in fact part of the Indian Air Force.[255]

---

[255] Bharat Rakshak web site on the Indian Air Force, www.bharat-rakshak.com/

Regimental insignia: A diving eagle, claws extended, in front of crossed sabers, above a three-part scroll with non-English lettering.

Motto: Swift and Sure

Corps of Engineers

The Corps of Engineers includes combat engineers as well as the Military Engineering Service (MES)—the works organization (construction and maintenance for the services and a secondary role in nation building), and the Border Roads Organisation (BRO), which constructs highways, airfields, buildings and bridges, generally in once inaccessible areas. The Corps also provides officers to the Military Survey and Defence Research and Development Organisation.

Indian Engineers belong to one of three groups, an inheritance of the old Indian Army, and known unofficially as the Madras, Bombay and Bengal Sappers. The Madras Sappers date back to 1780, the Bengal and Bombay Sappers to 1820. Each was a distinct corps (known officially as sappers and miners), and only in 1941 were they redesignated as groups, adding "Royal Indian Engineers" as a suffix. As with other regiments, the "Royal" was dropped in 1950. Each group has regimental colours upon which pre- and post-independence battle honours can be displayed. The new Army inherited around 35 Engineer companies in 1947, with a total of 68 units of all types.

The **Madras Engineering Group and Centre** is at Bangalore, Karnataka. The Madras Engineering Group recruits from South India Communities (from Kerala, Tamil Nadu, Andhra Pradesh and Karnataka). The Centre had a training battalion, reorganized with three companies in 1958, another sometime later, and two more in 1961. In June 1962 it became Training Battalion I and a new Training Battalion II was established. By 1965 there was a third training battalion as well as a Depot Battalion. (Training Battalion III was disbanded in April 1968.)

Honours: Zoji La (13, 433 Coys), Jammu and Kashmir 1947-48 (13, 14, 32, 36,433 Coys); Jammu and Kashmir 1965 (13 Coy); Punjab 1965 (14, 65, 428 Coys); Jammu and Kashmir 1971 (14 Regt); Basantar River 5, 9 Regts), Punjab 1971 (5, 7, 9, 201 Regts); East Pakistan 1971 (3, 4, 13 Regts).

The **Bombay Engineering Group and Centre** is at Kirkee (now Khadki), Maharashtra. (About one-third of the Group was Muslim at the time of partition

---

IAF/Units/Squadrons/292-Squadrons.html.

and went to Pakistan.) The Bombay Engineering Group recruits Marathas (40%) and Mazhabi and Ramdasiya Sikhs (40%) besides various other Indian classes and a small percentage of Muslims (20%). In 1949, separate units of Sikhs and Marathas were ended,with the two classes mixed. While the three groups provide all types of units, the Bombay Engineer Group is the sole source of Inland Water Transport (IWT) units.

Honours: Rajaoir (37 Coy), Jammu and Kashmir 1947-48 (19, 21, 22, 37, 99, 411 Coys); Jammu and Kashmir 1965 (305 Coy); Sylhet (108 Regt), East Pakistan 1971 (102, 108 Regts); Jammu and Kashmir 1971 (105 Regt); Drass, Kargill 1999.

The **Bengal Engineering Group and Centre** is at Rorkee, Uttar Pradesh. The Bengal Engineering Group recruits Sikhs (20%), Rajputs (20%), personnel from Bihar, West Bengal, Orissa and Ahirs (20%), and personnel from the Northeast (20%). This group was especially hard hit by partition, with many of the officers and other ranks going to Pakistan along with records and equipment. Field companies from five State Forces (Tehri Garhwal, Sirmoor, Faridkot, Malerkotla and Mandi) joined the Group between 1950 and 1952. A second training battalion was established in 1963, with a third as well as a Depot Battalion raised by 1966. The training battalions were later reduced to two (Nos 1 and 2).

Honours: Jammu and Kashmir 1947-48 (39 Coy); Jammu and Kashmir 1965 68, 73, 89, 369, 374 Coys); Rajasthan 1965 (78, 85 Coys); Punjab 1965 (100 Coy); Jammu and Kashmir 1971 (61 Regt); Sindh 1971 (57 Regt); East Pakistan 1971 (52, 58, 59, 62, 63 Regts).

Combat Engineers. Until 1965, the basic unit was the company. These either formed division engineers (three field companies and a field park company in infantry, two assault field and one assault field park companies in the 1st Armoured Division) or non-divisional equivalents, such as army engineer groups (later army troops engineers) or corps troops engineers. These GHQ units were often similar to divisional engineers but could be organized with a variety of numbers and types of companies under command depending on their assigned role. Following the 1965 war, the basic unit became the regiment, which seem to have been standardized over time at four field companies.[256] There have always been a variety of specialist companies: e.g., construction, construction equipment, plant, tipper, and workshop and park. Engineer

---

[256] At least some divisions were in the process of reorganizing their divisional engineers into regiments in September 1965 when they went to war. Divisions still had field park companies at the time.

brigades existed as early as independence, and were basically a HQ that could be placed in command of various Engineer units. At one time there was a plan to have one engineer brigade for each corps, but that was abandoned as the number of corps increased.

Except for the Corps history, virtually no Corps of Engineers units are identified in any source. This part will provide as much information as possible for units above company level, drawing from the official history, newspaper references, and a few other sources.

Engineer Brigades

416: raised March 1961, with 641 and 642 Corps Troops Engineers,[257] and in Ladakh by mid 1962. In the Punjab (I Corps area) during 1971 war.

417: Raised in December 1961 for Goa operations, with 643 Corps Troops Engineers and control of 17th and 20th Divisional Engineers.

471: raised 1963 at Hebbal and sent to Nagaland that year. With XXXIII Corps in 1971 war (13th, 52nd, 111th and 235th Regiments). Currently with X Corps in Punjab.

474: part of the Punjab Boundary Force August-September 1947; apparently disbanded later and reformed by 1965. Sent to Jullundar early September 1965. Operated with XI Corps in the 1971 war. Currently with II Corps in Haryana.

475: currently with XXI Corps in Madhya Pradesh.

Army Engineer Groups[258]

620: served in Jammu and Kashmir and withdrawn 1948 after LOC work.

623: served in Hyderabad action 1948 (operating in support of 1st Armoured Division, whose engineers were in Jammu and Kashmir).

624: served in Hyderabad action 1948.

629: sent to Jammu and Kashmir in February 1948.

631: sent to Jammu and Kashmir in January 1948.

Army Troops Engineers[259]

465: sent from Kirkee to Nagaland November 1962.

467: joined 416 Engineer Brigade 1964.

468: raised at Hebbal in 1963.

624: worked in Damodar Valley ca. 1953-54. On Border Roads duty in NEFA ca. 1962.

625: worked on bridging and other projects around Allahabad 1953. In Nepal on road building 1953-55. On Border Roads duty in NEFA ca. 1962.

---

[257] By 1963, 641 was gone; 467 Army Troops Engineers joined in 1964.

[258] Redesignated later as Army Troops Engineers.

[259] Those active in 1965 would have been redesignated as regiments.

Corps Troops Engineers[260]

451: in Rann of Kutch area April-July 1965. Supported 11th Infantry Division, Southern Command, in 1965 war.

624: sent to NEFA July 1960 (road building). Sent from Kirkee to Nagaland 1963.

632: sent from Allahabad to Kohima September 1956 and redesignated 20th Division Engineers. Reformed later; on Border Roads duty in Jamma ca. 1962.

640: raised 1960 at Hebbal; with 417 Engineer Brigade in Goa operation 1961. Sent from Kirkee to XI Corps in 1965 war.

641: raised 1960 at Hebbal;joined 416 Engineer Brigade March 1961; gone by 1963.

642: joined 416 Engineer Brigade March 1961.

643: with 417 Engineer Brigade in Goa operation 1961. In Bhutan 1962 (border roads).

644: first Border Roads operations, Nagaland, 1962.

Airfield Engineers[261]

623 Forward: sent to Nepal for road-building 1959.

625: sent to NEFA July 1960 for road building.

Bomb Disposal Groups:

191: raised 1965 at Madras Centre.

197: raised 1965 at Bombay Centre.

IWT Engineers:

457: raised 1965 at Bombay Centre.

The following are the known Engineer regiments:[262]

1	(Madras Group)
2	(Madras Group) Served in East Pakistan 1971.
3	(Madras Group) 1971: 23rd Mtn Div. Served with IPKF in Sri Lanka. *Honours*: East Pakistan 1971.
4	(Madras Group) Served with IPKF in Sri Lanka. *Honours*: East Pakistan 1971.

---

260 Those active in 1965 would have been redesignated as regiments.

261 Those active in 1965 would have been redesignated as regiments.

262 Because of the way the Engineers official history volume is written, some 1971 divisional assignments are inferred. A regiment with no information beyond group is from the lists of Madras and Bengal Engineer Group units in Sharma, op. cit. It appears that he was unable to compile a list of units in the Bombay Engineer Group. The group is shown only where known for sure, but it can often be inferred from the affiliation of regiments on either side of it.

5	(Madras Group) 1971: I Corps or 54th Inf Div. *Honours*: Basantar River, Punjab 1971.
6	(Madras Group)
7	(Madras Group) 1971: I Corps. *Honours*: Basantar River, Punjab 1971.
8	(Madras Group) 1971: 14th Inf Div. Served with IPKF in Sri Lanka.
9	(Madras Group) 1971: I Corps or 54th Inf Div. *Honours*: Punjab 1971.
10	(Madras Group) 1971: Abohar Fortress, XI Corps.
11	(Madras Group)
12	(Madras Group)
13	(Madras Group) 1971: under 471 Engr Bde in XXXIII Corps. *Honours*: East Pakistan 1971.
14	(Madras Group) *Honours*: Jammu and Kashmir 1971.
15	(Madras Group) 1971: 57th Mtn Div.
16	(Madras Group) Served with IPKF in Sri Lanka.
17	(Madras Group)
18	(Madras Group)
38	(Madras Group)
51	(Bengal Group) Served with IPKF in Sri Lanka.
52	(Bengal Group) 1971: under 471 Engr Bde in XXXIII Corps. *Honours*: East Pakistan 1971.
53	(Bengal Group) Served with IPKF in Sri Lanka.
54	(Bengal Group)
55	(Bengal Group) 1971: I Corps or 15th Inf Div.
56	(Bengal Group) 1971: 12th Inf Div. Currently a Rapid engineer regiment.
57	(Bengal Group) 1971: 11th Inf Div. Honours: Sindh 1971.
58 Corps	(Bengal Group) 1971: II Corps. *Honours*: East Pakistan 1971.
59	(Bengal Group) *Honours*: East Pakistan 1971.
60	(Bengal Group) 1971: Abohar Fortress, XI Corps.
61	(Bengal Group) 10th Inf Div 1971 war. *Honours*: Jammu and Kashmir 1971.
62	(Bengal Group) 1971: IV Corps. *Honours*: East Pakistan 1971.
63	(Bengal Group) 1971: 4th Mtn Div. *Honours*: East Pakistan 1971.
64	(Bengal Group)
65	(Bengal Group)
66	(Bengal Group) Currently stationed at Ambala.
67	(Bengal Group)
68	(Bengal Group)
69	Raised 2005; current stationed at Chandigarh.

102	(Bombay Group) 1971: 9th Inf Div. *Honours*: East Pakistan 1971.
103	1971: I Corps or 15th Inf Div.
104	(Bombay Group) 1971: 36th Inf Div. *Honours*: Punjab 1971.
105	(Bombay Group) XV Corps sector 1971 war. *Honours*: Jammu and Kashmir 1971.
106	1971: in Jammu and Kashmir.
107	1971: in Jammu and Kashmir. Currently stationed at Mumbai.
108	(Bombay Group) 1971: 8th Mtn Div. *Honours*: Sylhet, East Pakistan 1971.
109	1971: Abohar Fortress, XI Corps. (Normally 7th Inf Div?)
110	(Bombay Group) Served with IPKF in Sri Lanka. *Honours*: Punjab 1971.
111	1971: under 471 Engr Bde in XXXIII Corps.
113	(Bombay Group) 1971:39th Inf Div. *Honours*: Punjab 1971.
115	Served with IPKF in Sri Lanka.
201 Army	(Madras Group) 1971: I Corps. *Honours*: Punjab 1971.
202	(Madras Group) [presumptively an army regiment]
203 Army	(Madras Group) 1971: II Corps.
234 Armoured	(Bengal Group)
235 Army	(Bengal Group) 1971: under 471 Engr Bde in XXXIII Corps.
236	(Bengal Group) [presumptively an army regiment]
237 Army	(Bengal Group) 1971: I Corps.
267 Army	1971: I Corps.
268 Army	Raised in 1964. 1971: II Corps.
270 Army	1971: Southern Cmnd. Served with IPKF in Sri Lanka.

Companies can be rotated among regiments, and independent brigades can have an assigned company. As before, specialist companies can be found outside of the regiments.[263] Appendix F lists all identified Engineer companies.

The **Military Engineering Service** handles the design, construction and maintenance of the buildings, airfields, installations, military roads, etc., required by the Armed Forces. Work is generally handled by contracts and utilizes Corps of Engineers personnel and the civilian Indian Defense Service Engineers for oversight and control. Each command (including those of the other services) has a Chief Engineer. In the Army, each Chief Engineer has MES districts generally aligning with areas, and divisions which generally align with sub-areas of the commands.

---

[263] Notable examples being bomb disposal companies and bridging units.

Notable early projects for the MES included the National Defence Academy at Kharakvasla (begun in 1949) and the Corps' own College of Military Engineering at Kirkee (the first parts of which were completed in 1949).[264] The first ever roads in NEFA were begun in 1952, under HQ 640 Northern Troops Engineers. (Five field companies were committed by the next year, along with a special works company and other resources.)

By the late 1950s the MES began to turn to accommodations for the Army itself. Since the Indian Army of the Raj had been oriented to the Northwest Frontier, many of the large cantonments went to Pakistan, and troops of the new Army found themselves lodged in tents.[265] A notable example was the construction of a divisional cantonment at Ambala, involving the MES, troops of the 4th Infantry Division, and civilian tradesmen. Similar projects occurred at Jammu (26th Infantry Division) and Ferozepur (5th Infantry Division). This work continued as divisions were shifted to different locations and as the number of divisions increased.

In 1959, the MES was transferred from the Engineer-in-Chief to the Quartermaster General, and a new Director General of Works (a major general's post) was created under the QMG. Following the 1962 war with China, this decision was reversed. Each command was then divided into zones, with Chief Engineers (brigadier or colonel). The MES, as might be imagined, was continuously busy on roads, bridges, cantonments and other projects. In addition to the zones, the MES had formations known as HQ Works Engineers, such as 134 sent into Nagaland in 1963. Works units and personnel operated in conjunction with combat Engineer units along the border areas. The 1971 war necessitated creation of internment camps for the large numbers of Pakistani troops captured in East Pakistan. HQ 136 Works Engineers went into Bangladesh to help rebuild that country.[266]

As noted earlier, the MES also provided works support to the other armed services and the Ministry of National Defence. Another responsibility involved construction or improvement of ordnance factories, e.g., the new Tank Factory at Avadi (near Madras), begun in late 1961. In 1963, this led to creation of a Directorate of Works (Defence Production) in the Engineer-in-Chief's office.

The **Border Roads Organisation** (BRO) was formally established 7 May 1960 in order to develop communications in remote areas of the north and northeast

[264] Now known as Khadki, Kirkee is just north of Poona (now Pune), and Pune is now generally given as the College of Military Engineering's location.
[265] Praval, op. cit., pp 25-26.
[266] HQ 133 and 137 Works Engineers have also been identified. It appears that works sections (numbered in the 800s and 900s) rather than works companies are the norm.

States. It has some Corps of Engineers personnel, but also personnel directly recruited into the BRO, known as the General Reserve Engineer Force (GREF).[267] There is a Director General Border Roads. The organization comes under the Ministry of Highways for general administration.

While some work had been done using MES and combat engineer resources, many areas along the border (from Punjab to NEFA) had few or no all weather roads to key areas. GREF Centres were established at Roorkee and Allahabad for training new recruits. The basic formation is the Border Roads Task Force (BRTF), a lieutenant colonel's command: three construction companies with heavy equipment, a workshop and supply company and medical elements. Ten were in process of raising by May 1960, drawing on existing Corps of Engineers units and new recruiting, especially of ex servicement.[268] Over time, the BRO has progressed from a largely road- and bridge-building force to responsibility for other works activities in remote areas and—in wintertime—snow removal.

The **Military Survey Organisation** began with a Surveyor General (Delhi), 3rd Field Survey Company (at Dehradun), and miscellaneous elements including 14 survey parties (mixed Engineers and civilians). Regional organisations were the Eastern Circle (Calcutta) and Southern Circle (Bangalore), although a Northern Circle was formed 1 November 1948 by converting the Geodetic Branch at Dehradun. In addition to survey work, the MSO provides all required maps for the Army. In 1963, 3rd Field Survey Company was expanded and reorganized as 501st Field Survey Engineer Group and the Army Headquarters Survey Company became the 502nd Photo Mapping Engineer Group. In addition to purely military work, MSO is responsible for the Survey of India (i.e., mapping the entire country), with nine regional circles headed by colonels or their civilian equivalent.

The Corps of Engineers has some **transportation** responsibilities. The new Army had 6th Docks and IWT [Inland Water Transportation] Group (possibly raised in 1948)[269] and 137th Railway Engineer Group. The Bombay Engineer

---

[267] GREF personnel are uniformed and subject to the Army Act but distinct from the Corps of Engineers.

[268] The following BRTFs have been identified: 1st to 15th, 17th, 19th, 21st, 22nd and 29th. Not all have been active at one time, and some were disbanded following completion of a particular project. Especially in the early years, units from the Corps of Engineers continued to be used in projects. In addition, there are maintenance task forces which also have some construction capability; 31st, 32nd, 35th, 36th, 37th, and 43rd are known, along with 41st Signals Task Force which handled telephone poles and lines.

[269] At least through 1972, this group appears never to have exceeded three operating companies and a river survey company; the latter was disbanded in 1967 by which year

Group was given responsibility for docks and IWT and the Madras Engineer Group for railway units. 137th Railway Engineer Group was disbanded in 1955, the Army retaining only a composite company (with operating, workshops, construction and maintenance elements) at the College of Military Engineering. That company was disbanded in 1967, leaving no Regular railway element.[270]

The equipment and supplies necessary for successful engineering are held at depots or other organizations and known as **Engineer Stores**. Stores were overseen by the Engineer Stores and Plant Directorate of the Engineer-in-Chief. The largest elements are the Engineer Stores Depots, while the field is supported by Engineer Parks or Sub Parks. Only a few designations are known: 571 Engineer Park was established April 1948 in Jammu and Kashmir, supported later by 572 Engineeer Sub Park in the area of the Valley and Ladakh. 583 Engineer Sub Park was raised at Pandu in 1959 to support the Army's move into Assam. 585 Engineer Park, at Siliguri moved to Bengdubi in anticipation of the 1971 war.

The **College of Military Engineering** is at Pune. It was established in 1943 at Roorkee as the School of Military Engineering. It moved to Poona (now Pune) in 1948, and was upgraded November 1951 as the College of Military Engineering. It covers all four major responsibilities of the Corps: combat engineering, the Military Engineering Service, the Border Roads Organisation, and Survey.

Motto:
Bengal Engineers Group: Ekta – sewa – ilan –drirhta - shoorvirta

PVC: one[271]

Regimental Badge: A Chakra, inscribed "Sarvatra [everywhere]" on the bottom, containing a fort based on the design of Purana Qila of Delhi and surrounded by a wreath of lotus buds; above, the Ashoka Lions; below, a scroll reading "CORPS OF ENGINEERS." This badge came into use for officers in 1957 and for all ranks in 1960.

The old badge had been the Star of India surrounded by a wreath of lotus buds, with a scroll across the bottom of the wreath reading "INDIAN ENGINEERS." The authors do not know if there was an interim badge used until 1957 and 1960.

---

the group had two operating companies and a workshop company, along with an IWT unit at Calcutta. Initially at Bombay, the group moved in 1965 to Gauhati on the Brahmaputra River.

[270] However, the Territorial Army has always had a strong railway engineer element.

[271] 2/Lt Rama Raghoba Rane (8 Apr 1948).

Corps of Signals

The Corps of Signals provides communications services to the Army. It is organized into regiments and companies. There are now two Army HQ Signal Regiments (1st and 2nd), both at New Delhi. There is also a Rapid Signal Regiment, the 14th . Each corps has two regiments, both bearing the corps number: a Corps Operating Signals Regiment and a Corps Engineering Signals Regiment. Each division has its own Signal Regiment and each independent brigade has a Signal Company. The Corps of Signals is also responsible for electronic warfare.

Following partition, the Signal Training Centre was established at Jabalpur, Madhya Pradesh: one of two in the old Indian Army, the other went to Pakistan. Following the 1962 war with China, two more centres were established, one at Goa and an additional one at Jabalpur. 3 Signal Training Centre, the new one at Jabalpur, was disbanded in 1967. The current 1 and 2 Signal Training Centres (Jabalpur and Goa, respectively) each have one military training regiment and three technical training regiments. 1 Signals Training Centre also includes a depot regiment. The School of Signals at Mhow was redesignated 1 October 1967 as the Military College of Telecommunication Engineering.

Motto: Teevra Chaukas (Swift and Secure)

Badge: The figure of Mercury on a globe, both in silver; below the globe, twelve laurel leaves (six on each side) in gold and a scroll bearing the motto "Teevra Chaukas"; the whole surmounted by the Star of India in gold.

The former badge was the figure of Mercury in silver, within a gold oval containing a globe and laurel leaves at the bottom and the inscription "INDIAN SIGNAL CORPS" around the top, the whole surmounted by a small Star of India.

Army Service Corps [Sena Seva Corps]

The Army Service Corps (Royal Indian Army Service Corps until 1950) provides all mechanical transport (except first-line transport) and is responsible for procurement and distribution of supplies throughout the Army. The Corps is primarily divided into Supply, Mechanical Transport, FOL [Fuel Oil and Lubricant], Air Despatch, and Animal Trahnsport wings. The Indian Catering Corps (military cooks) was merged into the Corps in 1948, followed by the Indian Army Corps of Clerks.The Army Postal Service was part of the Corps from 1950 until 1972 when it became a separate corps. The corps is now known as the Sena Seva Corps.

Division ASC elements were reorganized in 1963 as a battalion. The basic transport unit is the ASC battalion(motor transport); these were created in 1976 by merging the various independent transport companies and platoons. That same year, ASC battalions (air maintenance) for the air dispatch role were established in place of the earlier Army Air Transport Organisation (AATO) and Rear Airfield Supply Organisation (RASO) organizations.

The corps had two main centres: ASC Centre (North) at Meerut and ASC Centre (South) at Bangalore, both established in 1947. The northern centre moved to Gaya in February 1976. The ASC School was at Bareilly. On 1 May 1999 it moved to Bangalore, where it was consolidated with the ASC Centre (South) and the Army School of Mechanical Transport to form the ASC Centre and College.

Badge: Wheeled chakra within a wreath of laurel leaves; above, the Ashoka Lions, with the motto "Satyameva Jayate" from Mundaka Upanishad' (Truth Alone Triumphs) in the Devanagari script curved below the Lions and laurel wreath.[272] Across the bottom of the laurel wreaths and wheel a three-part scroll reading "ARMY" "SERVICE" "CORPS", all in gold.[273]

The prior badge, in gold, was an eight-pointed star with the topmost point replaced by a crown; centered on the star the garter and motto of the Order of the Garter; within the garter the Royal Cypher; around the garter a belt with the words "Royal Indian Army Service Corps."

Motto: Seva Asmakam Dharma (Service is our Creed)[274]

Army Medical Corps

The Army Medical Corps Centre and School at Lucknow was formed in 1957 by amalgamation of the former AMC Centre (North) and AMC Centre (South). However, in December 1962 a new AMC Centre (South) was established at Hyderabad and Lucknow again became AMC Centre (North). Each had a training battalion, split in 1963 into military training and technical training battalions. However, the centres were merged again in 1967 as the AMC Centre Lucknow, with the Hyderabad centre closed down. The officer training wing became an officer training school in August 1969, leading to the current designation as Army Medical Corps Centre and School.

---

[272] This may be the only badge to incorporate the motto of the National Emblem.
[273] From the design shown on the ASC portion of the Indian Army web site, the scroll is no longer in English and also written in the Devanagari script.
[274] Adopted in 1950; before that, the motto was from the British Order of the Garter: Honi Soit Qui Mal y Pense (Evil to him who evil thinks).

The Armed Forces Medical College (AFMC) was formed 1 May 1948 at Poona (Pune). It is responsible for graduate training of doctors and, from 1962, has an undergraduate wing as well. Nursing officer training is conducted by the College of Nursing, Pune, as well as by various nursing schools. Training for paraprofessionals is done by the Armed Forces Medical College, the Army Medical Corps Centre and School at Lucknow, and at various military hospitals. The Officers Training School at Lucknow provides training in such subjects as military science, military medicine and general administration to medical officers, nursing officers, and non-technical officers.

There is an **Army Dental Corps** and and an **Army Nursing Service**. A Dental Wing at the AFMC was reestablished in 1955; from May 1947 training was the reposnibility of the Command Dental Centres. There were (as of 1980) five Command Dental Centres and 42 one-chair centres. In 1958 each corps was authorized a dental unit and more field units were authorized in 1961 and 1963. In companies, dental personnel are found within the field ambulance (the basic field medical unit).

Army Ordnance Corps

The Army Ordnance Corps procures all of the types of stores needed by the Army, including inventory management. There are seven central ordnance depots (Agra, Kanpur, Cheoki, Jabalpur, Delhi Cantonment, Dehu Road near Pune, and Malad near Mumbai); three central vehicle depots (Delhi Cantonment, Panagar and Avadi); a special vehicle depot for the Armoured Corps (Kirkee); and six central ammunition depots (Pulagaon, Dehu Road, Panagar, Bhrarartpur, Lalru, and Bhatinda). There are a few smaller depots as well.

The AOC School and Depot was at Jabalpur, moving to Secunderabad in 1953.

Motto: Shastaro se shakti (Strength through arms)

Corps of Electrical and Mechanical Engineers

The Corps of Electrical and Mechanical Engineers is responsible for the repairs, inspections and recovery of Army equipment. It can also be involved in trials, manufacturing, and design and development. It was split from the Army Ordnance Corps during World War II.

There are eight army base workshops, under the control of HQ, Base Workshop Group in Meerut. Those known include:

- 505 Army Base Workshop, in New Delhi, which specializes in armoured fighting vehicles
- 507 Army Base Workshop specializes in “B” vehicles (support vehicles)
- 509 Army Base Workshop specializes in radar systems, optical and other fire control instruments, and electronic testing
- 510 Army Base Workshop, Meerut, specializes in air defence and guided missile systems
- 512 Army Base Workshop handles the overhaul of tanks
- 515 Army Base Workshop also handles “B” vehicles, along with small arms and engineering equipment
- 3 Advance Base Workshop supports Northern Command, including overhaul of guns and engines, and now also handles thermal imaging and electronics equipment.

The eight base workshops are at Delhi, Agra, Meerut, Kirkee, Jabalpur, Kankinara, Allahabad and Bangalore.

An EME Centre was established at Katni, moving later toBangalore, along with an EME School at Poona. These were consolidated at Secunderabad in 1953, later designated No 1 EME Centre. No 3 EME Centre was established at Bhopal in 1962. Training centres are at Kamptee, Bhopal and Allahabad, with an additional school and an advance base workshop at Baroda.

Motto: Karam hi dharam (Work is [the] supreme duty)

Pioneer Corps

The Pioneer Corps provides units and personnel to work with engineers; these are generally considered as semi-skilled labour, as opposed to the Engineers with their various trades. They are mainly utilized in forward or operational areas where civilian labour is not available or security reasons prevent their use. They can also be used for guard and escort duty of installations and convoys.

The Corps began in 1940 as the Labour Corps, becoming the Auxiliary Pioneer Corps in 1941 and then the Indian Auxiliary Pioneer Corps in 1942. Finally, in November 1943, it was designated the Indian Pioneer Corps and labourers were redesignated as pioneers (non combatant). Its role was to provide semi-skilled labour to work with Engineer units and unskilled labour at various depots.

The Corps was reduced in strength in 1950,[275] but increased commitments along the northern border, especially from 1959, led to expansion. In addition to their military duties, the Pioneers have also been committed for flood and earthquake relief work and other aid to civil authorities.

Only a small number of pioneer companies are known, taken from the official history of the Corps of Engineers:

1232nd Pioneer Coy: in Nagaland 1956.
1452nd Pioneer Coy: roadbuilding in Kashmir 1965.
1588th Pioneer Coy: with 632nd CTE roadbuilding in Ladakh 1962.
1592nd Pioneer Coy: roadbuilding in Uttar Pradesh 1962.
1596th Pioneer Coy: with 643rd CTE roadbuilding in Bhutan 1961.
1610th Pioneer Coy: in Southern Command during 1965 war.
1627th Pioneer Coy: in Southern Command during 1965 war.

Local porter companies were established in northern areas ca. 1959, becoming labour companies in 1961, pioneer companies (Northern Command) in 1963, and finally reorganized and redesignated as pioneer companies in 1964.

The Training Centre moved from Jalna to Mathura on 28 March 1948. It later made a number of other moves—Nainital 1950, Alwar (Rajasthan) 1965, Bangalore (Hebbal) 1975—and from 1992 has been at Bangalore (Agram). (From August 1950 to August 1954, due to reductions in strength, the Centre was known as the Pioneer Corps Records and Depot.)

Motto: Shram Sarva Vijayee (With Labour, everything can be won)

Corps of Military Police

The Corps of Military Police provide the many services associated with MP forces in armies. The CMP Centre and School was at Secunderabad from 1944 to October 1947. It then moved twice (to Deolali 13 October 1947 and Faizabad 3 May 1948) and since 22 December 1975 has been at Bangalore. Until 1963, personnel for provost units were drafted from other regiments. Direct recruitment for the Corps began in that year.

Defence Security Corps

The Defence Security Corps—sixth largest in the Indian Army, with 31,000 personnel—is responsible for providing security for the installations of all three services and Ministry of Defence civil establishments. The Defence

---

[275] There had only been some 5,700 personnel in March 1948.

Department Constabulary was raised in April 1947, becoming the Ministry of Defence Security Corps on independence. On 16 August 1958 it was transferred from the Ministry of Defence to the Army and renamed the Defence Security Corps. The motto is Raksha Tatha Suraksha.

Other Branches

The **Intelligence Corps** handles intelligence activity and field security (i.e., counteringelligence) training for all three services as well as handling intelligence and security for the Army. The Training School and Depot was at Muiree, moving to Mhow in November 1947 and Pune in September 1952. Their motto is Sada Satark. Badge: The Star of India within two branches of laurel above a scroll inscribed "INTELLIGENCE CORPS."

The **Remounts and Veterinary Corps** is responsible for the provision and care of Army animals. Their Centre and School (from 1 January 2005, Centre and College) is at Meerut Cantonment. (From May 1947 to April 1948 it was at Sabathu.) The Corps is also responsible for the training of military dogs. There is a training regiment and a technical training squadron, along with the veterinary and dog training faculties. Until 1960 this and the military farms system were combined as one corps, initially designated the Indian Remount, Veterinary and Farms Corps and from 1950 as the Veterinary, Remounts and Farms Corps. The Corps motto is Pashu Seva Asmakam Dharma (Service to Animals is Out Duty).

Military farms—many of which went to Pakistan on partition—were initially grouped with the remount and veterinary service. In 1960 there were separated as the **Corps of Military Farms**. In addition to research, their main role is to provide milk and other products for the soldiers and baled hay for pack animals. There is a Military Farms School at Meerut.

The **Army Educational Corps** provides educational services, including university-level courses. (The Indian Army Educational Corps—its designation to 1950—only came into existence on 1 June 1947.) Its officers are posted at district or division level and above and various defence and military academies. Army schools for the soldiers' children are also supervised by Corps officers. The AEC Training College and Centre is at Pachmarhi. This was at first designated the Army School of Education, then (1949) as the AEC Centre and School, and finally (in 1961) as the AEC Training College and Centre. From 1995 the College has been affiliated to Barkatullah Universities, Bhopal. The motto is Vidhaiv Balam (Knowledge is Strength).

The **Army Postal Service** was only formed in 1972. Before that, postal services were under the Army Service Corps. Postal facilities (generally Field Post Offices [FPOs]) exist at various organizational and territorial levels. There are two major centres: 1 Central Base Post Office—56 APO (New Delhi), and 2 Central Base Post Office—99 APO (Kolkata). There is also an APS Centre at Kamptee, Nagpur. The motto is Service before self.

Territorial Army

The post-independence Territorial Army (TA) dates to 9 October 1949. It originally consisted of a variety of units, including armoured regiments, artillery, engineers, signals, and various support arms. However, by 1975 all of those units had been converted to Regular or disbanded, and only infantry battalions remained in the TA. Subsequently, some support units were formed in the TA, such as railway, general hospital, and telecommunications units. The TA's role is "to relieve the Regular Army from static duties and assist civil administration in dealing with natural calamities and maintenance of essential services in situations where life of the communities is affected or the Security of the Country is threatened and to provide units for Regulars Army as and when required."[276] There is a TA group HQ at each command except the newest, South West, which has a director.

Infantry and ecological battalions (intended for reforestation) are numbered in a single series and each is affiliated with a regular infantry regiment. The six new "Home and Hearth" (H and H) battalions are intended for local defense in Jammu and Kashmir.[277]

Battalion	**Affiliation (home station) and notes**
101st Inf	Maratha LI (Pune). Dec 1971: at Jodhpur, Southern Cmd.
102nd Inf	Punjab (Kalka).
103rd Inf	Sikh LI (Ludhiana). Dec 1971: airfield defence, Western Cmd.
105th Inf	Raj Rifles (Delhi Cantonment). Dec 1971: 67th Inf Bde.
106th Inf	Parachute (Bangalore)
107th Inf	11 Gorkha Rifles; raised 1 Oct 1960 (Darjeeling). Dec 1971: 71st Mtn Bde.
108th Inf	Mahar (Saugar).
109th Inf	Maratha LI (Kolhapur). Dec 1971: Bhuj, Southern Cmd.
110th Inf	Madras (Coimbatore).
111th Inf	Kumaon (Allahabad).
112th Inf	Dogra (Jalandhar). Dec 1971: Abohar Fortress, XI Corps.
113th Inf	Rajput (Calcutta).
114th Inf	Jat (Fatehgarh). Raised 1 October 1960 at Dehra Doon..
115th Inf	Mahar (Belgaum). Dec 1971: Foxtrot Sector.

---

276 Indian Army website.

277 The plan to raise these battalions was announced in 2003; see *Times of India*, 7 May 2003, timesofindia.indiatimes.com/india/6-Territorial-Army-battalions-to-be-raised-in-JK/articleshow/45683992.cms. The locations differ from those announced in the news article.

Battalion	Affiliation (home station) and notes
116th Inf	Parachute (Deolali). Dec 1971: Kutch Sector, Southern Cmd.
117th Inf	Guards (Tiruchi). Dec 1971: at Barmer, Southern Cmd.
118th Inf	Grenadiers (Nagpur). Dec 1971: various duties Delhi Area, Western Cmd.
119th Inf	Assam (Shillong).
120th Inf	Bihar (Bhubaneswar).
121st Inf	Garhwal Rifles (Calcutta).
122nd Inf	Madras (Cannonore).
123rd Inf	Grenadiers (Jaipur). Dec 1971: airfield defence, Rajasthan, Southern Cmd.
124th Inf	Sikh (New Delhi). Dec 1971: airfield defence Western Cmd.
125th Inf	Guards (Secunderabad).
126th Inf	J&K Rifles (c/o 56 APO). Dec 1971: at Pathankot, Western Cmd.
127th Eco	Garhwal Rifles (Dehradun).
128th Eco	Rajputana Rifles (Bikaner).
129th Eco	J&K LI (J&K).
130th Eco	Kumaon (Pithoragarh)
131st Eco	Rajput (Gwalior).
132nd Eco	(Bhatti Mines, Delhi).*
150th Inf	Pun jab (Delhi).
151st Inf	Jat (Muzaffarpur).
152nd Inf	Sikh (Ludhiana).
153rd Inf	Dogra (Meerut).
154th Inf	Bihar (Brichgunj [Port Balair]).
155th Inf	J&K Rifles (Sujanpur).
156th Inf (H&H)	Punjab (Rajouri).
157th Inf (H&H)	Sikh (BD Bari).
158th Inf (H&H)	Sikh LI (Janlot).
159th Inf (H&H)	Dogra (Thalela).
160th Inf (H&H)	J&K Rifles (Kupwara).
161st Inf (H&H)	J&K LI (Baramula).

* This battalion does not have a known regimental affiliation.

So-called departmental units include:

- 13 railway engineer regiments:[278] 968th (Ludhiana), 969th (Jamalpur), 970th (Jhansi), 971st (Delhi), 972nd (Muzaffarpur), 1031st (Kota), 1032nd (Adra), 1034th (Bangalore), 1101st (Chandigarh), 1103rd (Kota), 1105th (Secunderabad), 1051st (Ludhiana) and 1052nd (Adra);
- two special engineer regiments: 801st R&P[279] (Agra) and 811th ONGC[280] (Baroda);
- seven general hospitals, at Kolkata, Allahabad, Jaipur, Patiala, Gauhati, Ahamadabad and Rothak;
- 777th Telecom Signal Regiment (Mhow); and
- 414th ASC Battalion (Kamptee)

The railway engineer regiments were originally designated as railway engineer groups. (The 968th to 971st were all in existence by 1950.) During the 1971 war there was a 472nd Railway Engineer Brigade (TA) mobilized to support operations against East Paklistan. There was also a 1033rd Railway Engineer Group (TA) mobilized in the west.

The ASC battalion was formed after 1981 from personnel of nationalized oil companies to provide the capability for uninterrupted fuel supplies in the case of internal disturbances. It was earlier at Nagpur.[281] This suggests a similar role for the two special engineer regiments.

---

[278] The railway units are have the role of maintaining train operations in times of emergency. See the article, "NCR to set up Territorial Army training centre", *The Times of India*, 25 Jun 2009timesofindia.indiatimes.com/city/allahabad/NCR-to-set-up-Territorial-Army-training-centre/articleshow/4702559.cms, on a plan by North Central Railway (NCR) to establish a new regiment at the Jhansi TA training centre.

[279] Refinery and Pipeline.

[280] Oil and Natural Gas Corporation.

[281] Sharma, op. cit., p 182.

Scouts

Scouts units were raised along the border with Tibet. They are recruited from local personnel, and are intended to screen their relatively inhospitable areas.

The Ladakh Scouts can be found in the section above on Infantry, since they were ultimately regularized as an infantry regiment.

There are three remaining units: Himachal Scouts, also known as 1st Scouts; Kumaon Scouts, also known as 2nd Scouts; and Garhwal Scouts, also known as 3rd Scouts. The Himachal Scouts have two wings, each the rough equivalent of a battalion. The other two are approximately battalion-strength. The Kumaon Scouts operate as part of the Kumaon Regiment for training and administrative purposes. The Garhwal Scouts have a similar relationship to the Garhwal Rifles.

In 2004, permission had been granted to raise a battalion-sized scouts unit from the Gujjar and Bakrawal tribes in the Poonch-Rajouri region of southwest Jammu and Kashmir. This would be the first Scouts unit not formed along the border with Tibet. Further details, such as the designation or actual raising of the unit, are unknown.

There have been political requests to raise other Scouts units, but until recently none were approved. However, published reports indicated that an Army commanders' conference, chaired by General V K Singh (then COAS) "discussed raising of battalions of 'Arunachal and Sikkim Scouts" on the lines of the Ladakh Scouts" and that a proposal to this effect was expected to be sent to the government for final approval.[282]

---

[282] *The Times of India*, 18 May 2010, timesofindia.indiatimes.com/articleshow/5941569.cms. Figures of up to 5,000 personnel for the Arunachal Scouts have appeared in various unofficial sources, e.g., "Army open to 'Arunachal Scouts' plan", StratPost, 28 June 2009, www.stratpost.com/army-open-to-arunachal-scouts-plan.

Assam Rifles

The Assam Rifles are a paramilitary organization officially part of the Ministry of Home Affairs.[283] However, they come under the operational and administrative control of the Army. The Assam Rifles had five battalions in 1947, and the force has grown steadily since then: 17 battalions in 1960, 21 in 1968, and 46 currently. It originally recruited from the North East, the area in which it was deployed. However, it was later changed to recruit personnel on an all-India basis. One writer felt that this change cost its rapport with the local populations, and noted that a former Chief of the Army Staff felt that it should recruit at least 60-70% of its personnel from the North East.[284]

The Assam Rifles are deployed all over the North East, including Sikkim. However, it has operated in Sri Lanka (three battalions with the IPKF) and Jammu and Kashmir (eight battalions). Most officers are seconded from the Army, but some are promoted from within the force. With expansion, the rank of the Director General increased, and it is currently a lieutenant general.

The Directorate General is at Shillong. The regimental insignia consists of crossed khukris, with the Lions of Ashok above and a scroll below reading "ASSAM RRIFLES."

---

[283] The force originated in 1870 as the Assam Military Police, renamed Assam Rifles in 1917 due to the wartime service of many of their personnel with Gorkha regiments. Following independence, India separated them from the control of the Assam Police Inspector General and gave them their own Director General.

[284] Brig S. P. Sinha, "CI Operations in the Northeast," *Indian Defence Review* 21.2 (Jan 2007).

Appendix A: Chiefs of the Army Staff

This position was originally known as Commander-in-Chief, and the first two were British officers from the old Indian Army. The first Indian Commander-in-Chief was appointed January 1949.[285] The new title Chief of the Army Staff (COAS) was used from 1 April 1955.

Gen Sir Robert Lockhart	15 Aug 1947 – 31 Dec 1947
Gen Sir Roy Bucher	1 Jan 1948 – 15 Jan 1949
Fd Marshal KM Cariappa	16 Jan 1949 – 14 Jan 1953[286]
Gen KS Rajendra Sinhji	15 Jan 1953 – 14 May 1955
Gen SM Shrinagesh	15 May 1955 – 7 May 1957
Gen KS Thimayya	8 May 1957 – 7 May 1961
Gen PN Thapar	8 May 1961 – 19 Nov 1962
Gen JN Chaudhuri	20 Nov 1962 – 7 Jun 1966
Gen PP Kumaramangalam	8 Jun 1966 – 7 Jun 1969[287]
Fd Marshal SHFJ Manekshaw	8 Jun 1969 – 15 Jan 1973[288]
Gen GG Bewoor	16 Jan 1973 – 31 May 1975
Gen TN Raina	1 Jun 1975 – 31 May 1978
Gen OP Malhotra	1 Jun 1978 – 31 May 1981
Gen KV Krishna Rao	1 Jun 1981 – 31 Jul 1983
Gen AS Vaidya	1 Aug 1983 – 31 Jan 1985
Gen K Sundarji	1 Feb 1985 – 31 May 1988
Gen VN Sharma	1 Jun 1988 – 30 Jun 1990
Gen SF Rodrigues	1 Jul 1990 – 30 Jun 1993
Gen BC Joshi	1 Jul 1993 – 19 Nov 1994
Gen S Roy Chowdhury	20 Nov 1994 – 30 Sep 1997
Gen VP Malik	1 Oct 1997 – 30 Sep 2000
Gen S Padmanabhan	1 Oct 2000 – 30 Dec 2002
Gen NC Vij	31 Dec 2002 – 31 Jan 2005
Gen JJ Singh	1 Feb 2005 – 30 Sep 2007
Gen Deepak Kapoor	30 Sep 2007 – 30 Mar 2010
Gen VK Singh	31 Mar 2010 –

---

[285] Army Day, 15 January, is based on General Cariappa's appointment.

[286] Promoted to field marshal only in 1986.

[287] In 1966, the normal tenure for all Service Chiefs was reduced from four to three years.

[288] Promoted to field marshal two weeks before the retirement date shown.

Appendix B: Identified Brigades

Armoured Brigades

1st Armd	Aug 1947: 1st Armd Div (Secunderabad). Participated in securing Hyderabad Sep 1948. The brigade has always been part of 1st Armd Div, at Jullundar to 1954-55, then at Jhansi-Babina, and around 1972 to Nabha.
2nd (I) Armd	Aug 1947: Ahmednagar, an indep bde. Oct 1962 at Babina. 1965: XI Corps. Dec 1971 placed under 39th Inf Div. Assigned new 31st Armd Div 1972. An indep bde again in 1992. Currently assigned to IX Corps.
3rd (I) Armd	Raised 1970 in Eastern Command.[289] Dec 1971: placed under 10th Inf Div. Shifted to Jammu after the war. Currently assigned to IX Corps.
4th (I) Armd	Raised shortly after 1971 war. 2004: XII Corps.
....	
6th (I) Armd	Mike Force, raised ad hoc in 1971, became 6th (I) Armd Bde. Currently assigned to X Corps.
....	
14th (I) Armd	Dec 1971: XI Corps.
....	
16th (I) Armd	Dec 1971 placed under 54th Inf Div. Currently assigned to IX Corps.
....	
18th Armd	2004: 36th Inf Div.
....	
23rd (I) Armd	Raised shortly after 1971 war. Currently assigned to XI Corps.
....	
27th Armd	2004: 18th Inf Div.
31st Armd	2004: 11th Inf Div.
....	
34th Armd	2004: 31st Armd Div.
....	
39th Armd	2004: 33rd Armd Div.
.....	

---

[289] The original brigade commander asked for it to be given the lineage of the 255th Indian Independent Tank Brigade of the Second World War. This despite the fact that the current 1st Armoured Brigade was actually formed in 1946 by redesignation of the 255th Indian Independent Tank Brigade.

43rd Armd	Formed ca. 1972 by reorganization of 43rd Lorried Inf Bde, remaining part of 1st Armd Div.
....	
57th Armd	2004: 33rd Armd Div.
58th Armd	2004: 14th Inf Div.
.....	
88th Armd	2004: 33rd Armd Div.
....	
94th Armd	Currently assigned 31st Armd Div.
....	
98th Armd	Raised 1984 for 1st Armd Div.
....	
140th (I) Armd	Reported as the first formation to receive the Arjun tank; no other information available.[290]
...	
180th Armd	24th Inf Div.
....	
224th (I) Armd	Raised in the 1980s. In 1992 became **224th Armd Bde** and assigned 31st Armd Div in place of 2nd Armd Bde.

Parachute Brigades

50th Para	Aug 1947: Quetta. Served in Kashmir from Nov 1947 (second brigade sent in, having been at Gurdaspur on internal security duties). From 1950 **50th (I) Para Bde**. Served under 17th Inf Div Dec 1961 for occupation of Goa. Oct 1962 at Agra. Apr-Jun 1965 under Southern Command for fighting Rann of Kutch and then in Kashmir Aug-Sep 1965 (XI Corps, under 15th Inf Div). Committed in East Pakistan Dec 1971 and then shifted to Punjab. Nov 1988 sent to Maldives in response to a coup there. 1999 Kargil War, Army then XV Corps reserve then committed under 8th Mtn Div.
51st (I) Para	Formed 1965 and deployed to Himachel Pradesh area on border with China (Sugar sector); in Punjab Dec 1971 (Foxtrot Sector). *Converted 1972 as 51st Inf Bde.*

[290] Strategy Page, "India and the Homemade Headache," 1 April 2010; www.strategypage.com/htmw/htarm/20100401.aspx. See also the discussion thread at a Bharat Rakshak forum on armoured vehicles, forums.bharat-rakshak.com/ viewtopic.php?f=3&t=5530&start=120.

77th Para	Aug 1947: Multan (Baleli was its normal station).Sent into Kashmir 1948. Placed under Sri [19th] Division May 1948. *Converted 1950 as 77th Inf Bde.*

Infantry, Mechanised and Mountain Brigades

5th Inf	Aug 1947: Punjab Boundary Force (Amritsar), then 4th Inf Div. Sent into Kashmir Oct 1948. Oct 1962: 4th Inf Div (Along) but then to new 2nd Inf Div (later Mtn Div). **5th Mtn Bde**. Dec 1971: 2nd Mtn Div but under 101 Comm Zone then XXXIII Corps.
6th (I) Inf	Oct 1962: Secunderabad, Southern Cmnd [Army HQ Reserve]
7th Inf	Aug 1947: Madh Island, Bombay. Later came under 4th Inf Div. Participated in securing Hyderabad Sep 1948. Oct 1962: 4th Inf Div (Tawang; largely destroyed at Namkachu during war with China). 1963 **7th Mtn Bde** under 4th Mtn Div (Ambala). 1965: 4th Mtn Div but sent to XI Corps to cover sector between 7th and 15th Infantry Divisions. Dec 1971: 4th Mtn Div. 1972 **7th Inf Bde** in 4th Inf Div. Currently under 7th Inf Div.
…	
9th Inf	Participated in securing Hyderabad Sep 1948. Oct 1962: 20th Inf Div but detached along Nepal-Tibet border. 1963 **9th Mtn Bde** and assigned 6th Mtn Div. Detached by 1965 as indep bde at Joshimath UP. Dec 1971: 6th Mtn Div.
…	
11th Inf	Aug 1947: Punjab Boundary Force (Amritsar), then 4th Inf Div. Oct 1962: 4th Inf Div (Darjeeling, but in Nagaland); at front Nov 1962 and passed to new 2nd Inf Div.
…	
18th Inf	Dec 1971: 36th Inf Div. Served with IPKF as indep bde 1988-90.
19th Inf	Aug 1947: Lucknow. Sent into Kashmir Feb 1948 (sixth brigade sent). Oct 1962: 26th Inf Div. 1965: 26th Inf Div. Dec 1971: 26th Inf Div.
…	
25th Inf	Currently under 24th RAPID.
…	
28th Inf	1965: Western Cmd Reserve, later to XV Corps; quickly sent to new 10th Inf Div Sep 1965. Dec 1971: 10th Inf Div.

29th Inf	1965: 15th Infantry Division but detached to XI Corps to cover Dera Baba Nanak sector. Dec 1971: 7th Inf Div.
30th Inf	1965: 11th Inf Div; gave some bns to new 85th Inf Bde. Dec 1971: 12th Inf Div.
31st Inf	1965: Kilo Sector, Rann of Kutch Apr 1965. Dec 1971: 11th Inf Div.
32nd Inf	Dec 1971: 9th Inf Div.
33rd Mtn	Newly raised 1963 (Sugar Section) and assigned 4th Mtn Div. Remained in Sugar Section during 1965 war and passed to 39th Inf Div. Later **33rd Inf Bde**. Dec 1971: 39th Inf Div but under 25th Inf Div. Sent to Ladakh during 1999 Kargil War.
…	
35th Inf	1965: 14th Inf Div but u/c 1st Armd Div and then 6th Mtn Div. Dec 1971: 14th Inf Div but placed under 15th Inf Div. Currently under 14th RAPID.
36th Inf	Oct 1962: 26th Inf Div. Dec 1971: 26th Inf Div.
…	
38th Inf	1965: 15th Inf Div. Dec 1971: 15th Inf Div.
39th Mech	Possible initial designation for what later became the 39th Armd Bde of 33rd Armd (ex Mech) Div.
40th (I) Inf	In 1965 in IV Corps.
41st Mtn	1965: XV Corps reserve; sent to to 10th Inf Div early Sep 1965. Assigned ca 1966 to 4th Mtn Div. Dec 1971: 4th Mtn Div. 1972 **41st Inf Bde** in 4th Inf Div. With 36th Inf Div in IPKF 1987-90. Currently under XXI Corps (?) (Jaffna?).
42nd Inf	Dec 1971: 9th Inf Div.
43rd Lorried Inf	Aug 1947: Punjab Boundary Force (Ferozepore); later returned to 1st Armd Div: has been assigned continuously to 1st Armd Div. *Reorganized ca. 1972 as 43rd Armd Bde.*
44th Mtn	Currently under 18th RAPID.
45th Inf	Dec 1971: 12th Inf Div.
…	
47th Inf	Dec 1971: 54th Inf Div. With 54th Inf Div in IPKF 1987-1990. Currently under XXI Corps (54th Inf Div?).
48th Inf	Aug 1947: Dondh. 15 Nov 1960 assigned new 17th Inf Div at Ambala. Goa occupation Dec 1961. Oct 1962: 17th Inf Div. Came under command 4th Inf Div during 1962 war with China. 1965: 7th Inf Div. Dec 1971: 7th Inf Div.
…	
51st Inf	Formed 1972 in 16th Inf Div by conversion of 51st Para Bde.

52nd Mtn	1965: XI Corps but sent to XV Corps and joined new 10th Inf Div Sep 1965. **52nd Inf Bde** Dec 1971: 10th Inf Div.
53rd Mtn	Raised 1984 as part of 28th Mtn Div. Sent to Ladakh during the 1999 Kargil War.
54th Inf	1965: 15th Inf Div. Dec 1971: 15th Inf Div.
55th (I) Mech	Raised in the 1980s. Currently under XI Corps.
56th Mtn	1986: 8th Mtn Div. Dec 1971: 8th Mtn Div but on CI duty Nagaland. 1999 Kargil War (8th Mtn Div).
57th Inf	1965: XI Corps.[291] **57th Mech**. Possible initial designation for what later became the 57th Armd Bde of 33rd Armd (ex Mech) Div.
58th Inf	1965: 14th Inf Div but u/c 1st Armd Div Sep 1965. Dec 1971: 14th Inf Div but placed under 15th Inf Div. Currently under 14th RAPID.
59th Mtn	Dec 1971: 8th Mtn Div. 1986: 8th Mtn Div.
…	
61st Inf	Taken over by 57th Inf Div. Later **61st Mtn Bde**. Dec 1971: 57th Mtn Div but under 23rd Mtn Div.
62nd Inf	Raised Ramgarh 1959 as part of new 20th Inf Div. 1962: 20th Inf Div. Came under command 4th Inf Div during 1962 war with China. 1963 **62nd Mtn Bde** (Kasauli-Dagshai-Solan) assigned 4th Mtn Div. 1965: 4th Mtn Div but sent to 25th Inf Div. Dec 1971: 4th Mtn Div. 1972 **62nd Inf Bde** in 4th Inf Div.
63rd Inf	Raised 15 Nov 1960 at Ambala for new 17th Inf Div. Dec 1961 occupation of Goa. Oct 1962: 17th Inf Div.
64th Inf	Oct 1962: 27th Inf Div.
65th Inf	Oct 1962 indep bde at Hyderabad (Southern Cmd). Came under command 4th Inf Div during 1962 war with China. 1965: 7th Inf Div. Dec 1971: 7th Inf Div.
66th Inf	Raised Dinapur Aug 1962. Oct 1962: 20th Inf Div. **66th Mtn Bde**. Dec 1971: 20th Mtn Div. **66th Inf Bde**. Sent to Somalia 1992 as indep bde for duty under UNOSOM II; withdrew beginning Dec 1994.
67th Inf	Came under command 4th Inf Div during war 1962 with China. 1965: XI Corps, Fazilka Sector. Dec 1971: XI Corps. Currently under 16th Inf Div.

[291] It is possible that this is a typographic error in a source, since it is the only reference, and that the 67th Infantry Brigade was intended.

68th Inf	1965: 3rd Inf Div in Aug, then XV Corps reserve (indep bde) then under 19th Inf Div. Dec 1971: 10th Inf Div. Later **68th (I) Inf Bde**. Sent to Ladakh 1999 during Kargil War.
69th Mtn	1965: 6th Mtn Div.
70th Inf	26 Oct 1962 (Demchok) assigned new 3rd Inf Div; not involved in war with China. 1965: 3rd Inf Div. From 3rd Inf Div to 8th Mtn Div 1989. Kargil conflict (3rd Inf Div). Currently under 8th Mtn Div.
71st Mtn	Dec 1971: 8th Mtn Div but under XXXIII Corps and then 6th Mtn Div.
72nd Inf	Dec 1971: 36th Inf Div but placed under 39th Inf Div. With 36th Inf Div in IPKF 1987-90. Currently under 36th RAPID (Jaffna?).
73rd Inf	Oct 1962: 23rd Inf Div. **73rd Mtn Bde**. Dec 1971: 57th Mtn Div. Currently under 57th Mtn Div.
74th Inf	Dec 1971: 54th Inf Div.
…	
76th Inf	With 54th Inf Div in IPKF 1987-1990. Currently under XXI Corps (54th Inf Div?).
77th Inf	Raised 1950 by conversion of 77th Para.
79th Mtn	1999 Kargil War (8th Mtn Div).
80th Inf	Aug 1947: Muttra. Fourth brigade sent intoKashmir, Dec 1947. Oct 1962 25th Inf Div. 1965: 25th Inf Div (Naoshera?). Dec 1971: 25th Inf Div. Currently under 25th Inf Div.
81st Mtn	Dec 1971: 8th Mtn Div. 1986: 8th Mtn Div.
82nd Inf	Oct 1962: indep bde at Jodhpur (XI Corps). Came under command 4th Inf Div during war with China.
83rd Mtn	Dec 1971: 23rd Mtn Div.
…	
85th Inf	1965: new bde HQ joined 11th Inf Div Sep, taking some bns from 30th Inf Bde. Dec 1971: 11th Inf Div.
86th Inf	Dec 1971: 15th Inf Div.
87th Inf	Dec 1971: 39th Inf Div but placed under 36th Inf Div.
88th Mech	Possible initial designation for what later became the 88th Armd Bde of 33rd Armd (ex Mech) Div.
91st Inf	Dec 1971: 54th Inf Div. With 54th Inf Div in IPKF 1987-1990. Apparently disbanded later. Re-raised Feb 2009 as an amphibious bde; located at Kerala.[292] Under XXI Corps.

[292] However, the Navy did not have the capability to transport more than two battalions, and only in 2010 did it seek to increase that so that it could carry an entire brigade. See

93rd Inf	Oct 1962 25th Inf Div. 1965: 25th Inf Div (Poonch). Dec 1971: 25th Inf Div.
…	
95th Mtn	Dec 1971: 8th Mtn Div but under 101 Comm Zone.
96th Inf	1965: XI Corps reserve, then returned to 15th Inf Div. Dec 1971: 15th Inf Div.
…	
99th Inf	Raised 15 Nov 1960 at Ambala for 17th Inf Div. Detached and served in the Congo 1961 to Mar 1963. Converted as **99th Mtn Bde** and assigned 6th Mtn Div 1963. 1965: 6th Mtn Div. Dec 1971: 6th Mtn Div.
…	
101st Inf	Formed by renumbering 161st Inf Bde, but then later reverted to former designation.
102nd Inf	Raised at Thoise sometime 1972-87. 1999 Kargil War under 3rd Inf Div. Currently under 3rd Inf Div.
…	
104th Inf	Oct 1962 19th Inf Div (Tithwal). 1965: 19th Inf Div. Dec 1971: 19th Inf Div.
105th (I) Inf	1965: XI Corps, Fazilka Sector.
…	
112th Inf	1965: Rann of Kutch Apr 1965; permanent station Dhrangadhra.
…	
114th Inf	Aug 1947: Punjab Boundary Force (Lahore). Mar 1960 established in Ladakh (Udhampur) as 114th (I) Inf Bde. 26 Oct 1962 indep bde at Leh assigned new 3rd Inf Div as 114th Inf Bde. Destroyed Oct 1962 at Chushul and later reformed. 1965: 3rd Inf Div (Chushul).
115th Inf	Dec 1971: 36th Inf Div. With 36th Inf Div in IPKF 1987-90. Currently under 36th RAPID (Jaffna?).
116th Inf	Joined 14th Inf Div Aug 1965. Dec 1971: 14th Inf Div. Currently under 14th RAPID.
…	
120th Inf	Oct 1962 25th Inf Div. 1965: 25th Inf Div (Rajouri). Dec 1971: 25th Inf Div.
121st (I) Inf	Responsible for Ladakh up to Mar 1960 as extension of Kargil sector. 1965: indep bde gp XV Corps. Dec 1971: indep bde under 3rd Inf Div. Under 8th Mtn Div for Kargil conflict 1999.

(9 Jun 2010) indiatoday.intoday.in/site/Story/100770/India/army-and-navy-plan-to-set-up-a-marine-brigade.html.

123rd Inf	Aug 1947: 5th Inf Div (Ramgarh). Oct 1962: 27th Inf Div. **123rd Mtn Bde**. Dec 1971: sent from Eastern Cmnd to Western Comd. Currently under 27th Mtn Div.
…	
161st Inf	Aug 1947: 5th Inf Div (Ranchi). First brigade sent into J&K very early Nov 1947. Placed under Sri [19th] Division May 1948. (Sometime after the war, renumbered as 101st Inf Bde but that bde later reverted to original designation as 161st.) 1965: 19th Inf Div. Dec 1971: 19th Inf Div.
162nd Inf	1965: 26th Inf Div. Dec 1971: 26th Inf Div.
163rd Inf	Raised 1948 at Srinager as ad hoc "Z" Bde; placed under Sri [19th] Division May 1948. Later numbered, remaining in Kashmir but then apparently inactivated. Re-raised ca. Oct 1962 when moved to Leh and assigned new 3rd Inf Div; not involved in war with China. 1965: 3rd Inf Div but detached to SRI Force, XV Corps in West Kashmir. Dec 1971: XI Corps, coming under Foxtrot Sector (moved there Jul 1971).
164th Inf	Oct 1962: 17th Inf Div. Dec 1971: **164th Mtn Bde**. XXXIII Corps.
165th Inf	Sent into J&K ca. 1948. Oct 1962: 20th Inf Div (Ramgarh?). **165th Mtn Bde**. Dec 1971: 20th Mtn Div.
…	
167th Mtn	Dec 1971: 8th Mtn Div but under 101 Comm Zone then XXXIII Corps.
168th Inf	Oct 1962: 26th Inf Div. 1965: 26th Inf Div. Dec 1971: 26th Inf Div but under I Corps.
…	
181st Inf	Sent to Nagaland Apr 1956 (first Army formation sent there) as indep bde gp. Oct 1962 assigned to new 2nd Inf Div. Later **181st Mtn Bde**. Dec 1971: 23rd Mtn Div.
…	
191st Inf	1965: indep bde gp XV Corps; before the war on CI duty in the Chaamb-Jaurian area against Pakistan infiltrators; placed under new 10th Inf Div early Sep 1965. Dec 1971: 10th Inf Div.
192nd Inf	Was in Nagaland by Oct 1956. Tentative designation for brigade in 23rd Inf Div Oct 1962. **192nd Mtn Bde**. 1999 Kargil War (8th Mtn Div).
…	
201st Inf	In Nagaland by late 1956; first brigade sent there.

202nd Inf	Oct 1962: indep bde at Calcutta, Eastern Cmd reserve. **202nd Mtn Bde**. Dec 1971: 20th Mtn Div.

…

268th Inf	Aug 1947: Japan; to India Aug-Oct 1947. Sent into J&K Nov 1947 (third brigade to enter). Oct 1962 19th Inf Div (Baramula). 1965: 19th Inf Div. Dec 1971: 19th Inf Div.

…

301st Inf	In Nagaland by 1958. Oct 1962: 23rd Inf Div. **301st Mtn Bde**. Dec 1971: 23rd Mtn Div. Later **301st Inf Bde**. In charge of troops in UN Congo Mission Dec 2004 to date.

…

303rd Mtn	Dec 1971: 8th Mtn Div but left on border under Rear HQ XXXIII Corps.

…

311th Mtn	Dec 1971: 57th Mtn Div.

…

322nd Inf	Dec 1971: 12th Inf Div.

323rd Inf	Dec 1971: 39th Inf Div. Sent to Baramulah in Kashmir during 1999 Kargil War.

…

330th Inf	Dec 1971: 11th Inf Div.

…

340th Mtn	Dec 1971: bde gp under 20th Mtn Div. Then moved to Kutch for an offensive. Later **340th Inf Bde** and trained for amphib role from 1983. Served with IPKF 1987-90. Later **340th (I) Mech Bde**. 2004, currently under XII Corps.

…

350th Inf	Dec 1971: 9th Inf Div. Currently under 15th Inf Div.

Note: The following brigades were active 14 August 1947 and transferred directly to the new Indian Army. (The word "Indian" had been dropped from designations in 1946.)

1st Armoured Brigade: The original 1st Armoured Brigade was disbanded in 1943 as 251st Indian Tank Brigade. The wartime 255th Indian Tank Brigade was redesignated in June 1946 as 1st Armoured Brigade and assigned to 1st Armoured Division; at Secunderabad with the division in August 1947.[293]

---

[293] Raised Jun 1941 as 5th, later 255th, Indian Armoured Brigade, coming under 2nd (later 32nd) Indian Armoured Division, and then 44th Indian Armoured Division. Relieved Apr 1944 and redesignated Aug 1944 as 255th Indian Tank Brigade. Served in eastern India and Burma from Oct 1944, returning to India Feb-May 1946. Despite

2nd Armoured Brigade: Began forming at Meerut February 1940; numbered as 2nd Indian Armoured Brigade 1 July 1940 and assigned to 1st Indian Armoured Division. Relieved July 1941 and sent to Iraq as an independent brigade group. Renumbered October 1940 as 252nd Indian Armoured Brigade. Came under command of 31st (formerly 1st) Indian Armoured Division June 1942, continuing to serve in Iraq. Division and brigade renumbered October 1945 as 1st and 2nd. Returned to India January 1946 and relieved by June 1946 when designated 2nd Armoured Brigade (Independent). At Ahmednager in Aug 1947.

50th Parachute Brigade: Raised October 1941 at Delhi. The bulk of it served at Kohima and Imphal in 1944, then it was withdrawn and later recommitted. It was withdrawn to India August 1944 and assigned to 44th (later 2nd) Indian Airborne Division the next month. The brigade was at Quetta in August 1947.

77th Parachute Brigade: Formed June 1942 as 77th Indian Infantry Brigade and trained for deep penetration behind Japanese lines. It operated there April-June 1943. It was reorganized and became part of Special Force/3rd Indian Infantry Division (the Chindits). Its second long range penetration role was March-June 1944. The remnants withdrew to India the next month. In March 1945 it was reorganized as 77th Indian Parachute Brigade and assigned to 44th (later 2nd) Indian Airborne Division. Its station in August 1947 was Baleli but it was temporarily at Multan.

5th Infantry Brigade: Formed September 1939 by redesignating 9th [Jhansi] Brigade and assigned 4th Indian Infantry Division. Served in North Africa with the division, Syria 1941 as an independent brigade group, then back to North Africa and the 4th Division. Following duty in Palestine it went back to North Africa, then Italy and Greece. It returned to India with the division January-February 1946 and stationed at Poona from August. However, in August 1947 it was at Amritsar as part of the Punjab Boundary Force.

7th Infantry Brigade: Began forming June 1940 in the Poona [Independent] Brigade area, intended for 5th Indian Infantry Division. However, served with 4th Indian Infantry Division in Eritrea, North Africa and Greece. Returned to India with the division January-February 1946 and stationed at Madh Island, Bombay. Detached from 4th Infantry Division when the latter moved to Jullundur.

11th Infantry Brigade: Began existence as Force Heron (formed from 11th [Ahmednagar] Infantry Brigade) August 1939 and sent to Egypt. Joined 4th

---

being used to form 1st Armoured Brigade in 1946, its lineage was claimed by 3rd Armoured Brigade when it formed in 1970.

Indian Infantry Division in North Africa, Etitrea, and North Africa again. Lost at Tobruk June 1942. Reformed in Egypt October-November 1943, rejoining 4th Indian Infantry Division in Italy February 1944, later moving to Greece with the division. Returned to India with the division February 1946 and stationed at Deolali. However, in August 1947 it was at Jullundur as part of the Punjab Boundary Force.

19th Infantry Brigade: Formed October 1940 as part of 8th Indian Infantry Division, serving with it in the Middle East and Italy. After returning to India it was detached mid 1946 as an independent brigade group, moving to Iraq August 1946-June 1947 to secure the Abadan refineries. It was stationed at Lucknow upon its return.

43rd Infantry Brigade (Lorried), also known as 43rd (Gurkha) Lorried Infantry Brigade: Formed in Persia January 1943 by reconstituting the destroyed 3rd Motor Brigade[294] and assigned to 31st Indian Armoured Division. It was detached in July 1944 and sent to Italy, serving under a variety of divisions throughout the war. Following post-war garrison and POW duties, it moved to Syria until returned to India February 1946. It was assigned to 1st Armoured Division that April. However in July 1947 it moved to Ferozepore and came under the Punjab Boundary Force.

48th Infantry Brigade: Formed October 1941 for 19th Indian Infantry Division, going to Burma January 1942. It came under 17th Indian Infantry Division the next month, serving with that division until it was disbanded January 1947 in Burma. The brigade then returned to India as an independent brigade; located at Dhond in August 1947.

80th Infantry Brigade: Formed in May 1942 and joined 20th Indian Infantry Division that July. Fought in eastern India and Burma from January 1944. Moved with the division to Saigon September 1945, then detached to Celebes and other islands. Returned to India August 1946 as an independent brigade; stationed at Muttra in August 1947.

114th Infantry Brigade: Formed as 14th Indian Infantry Brigade October 1940 under 7th Indian Infantry Division on the NW Frontier. Redesignated May 1942 as 114th Indian Infantry Brigade. Detached May 1943 and with the 26th Indian Infantry Division in the Arakan August to mid September 1943 before

---

294 3rd Motor Brigade had been formed in July 1940 from truck-mounted cavalry regiments. Sent to North Africa, it was twice destroyed in combat. The remnants went to Persia in August 1942 and came under 31st Indian Armoured Division. When reconstituted as 43rd Indian Infantry Brigade (Lorried) it had three Gurkha Rifles battalions.

returning to 7th Indian Infantry Division. Returned to combat November 1943. Detached and moved to Bangkok September 1945, rejoining the division May 1946 in Malaya. Returned to India October 1946, moving to Nowshera. Detached July 1947 to the Punjab Boundary Force and moved to Lahore.

123rd Infantry Brigade: Formed February 1941 as 23rd Indian Infantry Brigade under command of 14th Indian Infantry Division until March 1942 when it transferred to 23rd Indian Infantry Division and was renumbered that May as 123rd. Returned to 14th Indian Infantry Division July 1943 when committed to combat. Withdrawn to India April 1943, it joined 5th Indian Infantry Division July 1943 and was back in combat that November. Moved with division to Singapore in September 1945 and then in the Dutch East Indies November 1945 to April 1946 when brigade and division returned to India; stationed at Ramgarh in August 1947.

161st Infantry Brigade: Formed November 1941 in Cyprus by reconstitution of the British 161st Infantry Brigade under 5th Indian Infantry Division. Served as a motor brigade in Egypt for a period 1942 before rejoining 5th Indian Infantry Division December 1942 and moving to Iraq. Moved to India with division May 1943 and entered combat that November. Moved with division to Singapore in September 1945 and then to Java in November, going later to Batavia. (Under other commands then to April 1946 when it rejoined 5th Infantry Division.) Returned to India with the division May 1946 and located at Ranchi in August 1947.

268th Infantry Brigade: Formed August 1942 as a lorried brigade under 43rd Indian Armoured Division, going to the new 44th Indian Armoured Division April 1943. Later in GHQ Reserve as a conventional infantry brigade, moving to the front in May 1944.[295] Returned to India July 1945 and gave up its remaining battalions. However, it then reorganized to form the Indian component of Brindiv [British-Indian Division], part of the British Commonwealth Occupation Force (Japan). The division moved by sea to Japan 1 March-19 May 1946, stopping at Singapore and Hong Kong en route. Brindiv was disbanded 1 May 1947 in Japan, at which time 268th Infantry Brigade was reorganized as a brigade group. It left Japan August-October 1947 for India.

[295] Officially it was a lorried brigade until March 1945 but that was an administrative formality.

Appendix C: Unit Organization

Armoured Division

Until after the 1971 war, the sole armoured division followed the 1945 British pattern: an armoured brigade (four regiments) and a lorried infantry brigade (three battalions, later [1971] in APCs despite retention of "lorried" in the brigade designation). There was no assigned reconnaissance unit and the division artillery brigade had a variety of towed and SP weapons over the years. There were the normal supporting arms and services, such as engineer and signals regiments, supply units, repair units, etc. The armoured regiment had 45 tanks, three in regimental HQ troop and 14 in each of three squadrons.

In 1965, the 1st Armoured Division had a somewhat modified organization, with a mechanised battalion joining the four armoured regiments in the armoured brigade [equipped with Centurions], and the lorried infantry brigade included an attached armoured regiment [with Shermans]. The artillery brigade had one medium and two field regiments, along with a light AA regiment assigned later.

There was little change between then and the 1971 war, with four armoured regiments and four mechanised battalions, and the armoured and lorried infantry brigade HQs. Following the war, the division reorganized with two armoured brigades, each with two armoured regiments and two mechanised battalions. The new 31st Armoured Division adopted this new organization from its formation in 1972. In 1984, armoured divisions were changed to three armoured brigades, with six armoured regiments (an increase of two) and four mechanised infantry battalions.

The current Indian armoured division is organized as follows:[296]

- Division HQ
  - Staff
  - HQ Squadron

---

[296] The only known source of current Indian division TOEs is at Global Security, www.globalsecurity.org/military/world/india/divisions-toe.htm. This has been supplemented by other material, in particular Indian Armored Division (2001); Independent Armored and Mechanized Brigades (2001); Mandeep Singh Bajwa, Armored Regiments (2001); Mandeep Singh Bajwa and Ravi Rikhye , Indian Army RAPID Divisions (2001); India Army: Infantry Battalion TOE (2002); and Ravi Rikhye, Indian Armor TOES (2008).

Three Brigade HQs[297]
- 6 Tank Regiments [45 tanks each][298]
- 4 BMP Battalions [1050 personnel, 58 BMP; three companies]

Reconnaissance and Support Battalion[299]
Aerial Reccc Flight [5 x Helicopters]
Artillery Brigade[300]
- 3 (4?) x 155mm Medium Regiments [18 guns each]
- Medium MLRS Battery
- SATA Battery

Air Defense Artillery Group[301]
- SP Medium SAM Regiment
- SP Light (SA-13/16) Regiment
- SP Tunguska Gun/Missile Regiment

Signal Regiment
Armoured/Assault Engineer Regiment
Electrical and Mechanical Engineers Regiment [Maintenance]
Army Supply Corps Battalion
- Supply Company
- 3 x Transport Companies
- Tank Transporter Company

Divisional Ordnance Unit
Provost Unit [Military Police]

Independent Armoured and Mechanised Brigades

The standard organization for an Independent armored brigade is:
- 3 tank regiments
- 1 BMP battalion
- 1 artillery regiment
- 1 reconnaissance squadron
- Bridge Layer Tank (BLT) Troop [8 x Bridge Layer tanks]

---

[297] Each brigade includes a troop of eight bridge-layer tanks.
[298] However, see discussion below on armoured regiments.
[299] Recce and support battalions are provided by infantry regiments. They use the BRDM APC, and have three companies. Each company has three platoons: ATGM, mortar, and medium MG.
[300] Artillery had been varied, with the 105mm SP Abbott, a 130mm mounted on a Vijayanta chassis without a turret, and the Bofors 155mm towed howitzer. The Global Security page shows four medium regiments instead of three.
[301] The ADA Group used to have 12 SAM-6(SP SAM regiment) and 20 ZSU-23-4 (SP AA regiment).

These brigades are normally assigned as corps troops on a scale of one per plains corps. The exception is XVI Corps (Nagrota, near Jammu). This corps, for various operational reasons, has three independent armored brigades.

The mechanised brigades are smaller. India for a long time had only 55th (I) Mechanised Brigade (Beas, Punjab), and only in 2000 added a second one, converting 340th (I) Infantry Brigade (XII Corps) to mechanised configuration. These brigades have one tank regiment and two BMP battalions. (And, presumably, an artillery regiment.)

Armoured Regiments

Regimental HQ
- RHQ Tank Troop [3 x command tanks]

HQ Squadron
- Reconnaissance Troop [7 4x4 jeep type vehicles, MMGs and radios]
- Administrative Troop
- Inter-Communication Troop [8 4x4 jeep type vehicles with radios to serve as stations to link RHQ and outlying/detached Squadrons/Troops]

3 Sabre Squadrons, each:
- HQ Troop [2 x Control tanks]
- Administrative Troop
- 4 X Tank Troops [3 tanks each]

Depending on the type of equipment, tank regiments constitute a "brick" of 55 to 70 tanks. The brick is composed of:
- 30 operational tanks
- 15 training tanks (operational in wartime)
- 10 maintenance reserve tanks

T-72 regiments had 55 tanks; newer ones have 62. The maintenance reserve is small because India does not expect a war with Pakistan to last for more than a few weeks.

AFVs in the tank regiment are known as the F echelon. A Sabre squadron's administrative troop is responsible for providing the fuel, ammunition, rations, and other supplies for 24-hours of combat, and vehicles in it are termed the A1 echelon. Additional supplies are the responsibility of the regiment's administrative troop, and vehicles in it are known as the A2 echelon. All other supporting/supply vehicles are known as B echelon vehicles.

The tank squadron has a small maintenance capability: fitters and armoured recovery vehicles are part of the Administrative Troop. The maintenance capacity at regimental level comes under the Technical Adjutant/Officer. A

Light Repair Workshop from the EME is attached to each armored regiment. The independent armored brigade and the armored division have a considerable EME (Corps of Electrical and Mechanical Engineers) contingent for maintenance support, equivalent to a large company for every armored brigade.

.

At the time of the 1965 War, there were basically two types of armoured regiments. The standard regiment:

- RHQ [3 tanks}
- Recce Troop [9 light tanks]
- 3 Sabre Squadrons, each
  - HQ [2 tanks; dozer tank; ARV]
  - 4 Tank Troops [each 3 tanks]

The regiment had 490 personnel, 45 medium tanks, and 9 light tanks. At the time a regiment was authorized 27 additional medium tanks as attrition/maintenance reserve. The figure was nominal insofar as only 250 Centurions (62 per regiment) were purchased for the armoured division. By 1974 (or possibly even the late 1960s) the light tanks in the recce troop were gone, replaced by nine jeeps.

There were also four light armoured regiments, two equipped with the French AMX-13 and two with the Russian PT-76:

- RHQ [2 tanks]
- HQ Squadron, including Mortar and Pioneer Troops
- 3 Sabre Squadrons, each
- HQ [2 tanks]
  - 3 Tank Troops [3 tanks each]
  - 2 Rifle Troops

Thus the regiment had only 35 tanks, although it also included some organic infantry and support weapons. There were some independent light armoured squadrons, identical to the regimental squadrons above.

In 1971, there were a number of independent squadrons intended for the recce role, each with 18 tanks. For the five where the equipment is known, one had the PT-76, one a mixture of PT-76 and Ferret scout cars, one AMX-13, one T-55, and one an upgunned Sherman.

Mechanised Infantry Battalions

In 1971 most battalions used the Topas, a tracked amphibious APC, one was in the BTR-60, an 8x8 amphibious wheeled APC. In either case the battalion had around 850 personnel and 32-35 APCs:

- HQ [3 APCs]
- Aid Post [2 APCs]

Mortars [6 APCs]
3 Rifle Companies, each
HQ [1 APC]
3 Rifle Platoons [each 2 APCs]

Battalions later converted to the BMP, a tracked infantry fighting vehicle.[302] These are somewhat larger in personnel (1,050) and have more combat vehicles (58 BMP), in part because each vehicle hold fewer infantry than the old APCs. The new battalion organization (ca 1984 but probably still current):

HQ [3 BMPs]
Signals [3 BMPs]
Pioneers [2 BMPs]
Aid Post [2 BMPs]
Mortars [6 BMPs]
3 Rifle Companies, each
HQ [2 BMPs]
3 Rifle Platoons, each [4 BMPs]

The Rifle Platoon has the HQ in one BMP and each of three rifle sections in their own BMP.

Infantry Division

Long the most common type of division, these generally have three brigades, each of three infantry battalions. (At times, divisions have had more than three brigades under command, and brigades have likewise been larger.)

The current infantry division is organized as follows:

Division HQ
3 Infantry Brigade HQs
3 Brigade Signal Companies (1 per brigade)
9 Infantry Battalions (3 per brigade)
Field Artillery Brigade
Four towed 155mm howitzer regiments
Engineer Regiment
Army Service Corps Battalion
Signals Regiment
Medical Battalion
Ordnance Battalion

[302] APCs have sometimes been referred to as "battlefield taxis": they get the infantry to the scene of combat, but they then dismount to fight. IFVs have gun and/or ATGM weapons mounted and (originally) ports from which weapons could be fired. In practice, the infantry still usually needs to dismount to fight.

Provost Unit [Military Police]

It is believed that infantry divisions normally have an assigned tank regiment, although that is not shown in the main source. The division artillery used to be three field and one light regiments.

Reorganized Plains Infantry Division [RAPID]

Developed during the mid to late 1980s, basically, an armoured brigade (two tank regiments and one, later two, mechanized infantry battalions) wase added to an infantry division in place of an infantry brigade. The divisions gained a reconnaissance and support battalion, and there were some changes to division artillery. There are two types of RAPID divisions: offensive and defensive, although it is unclear what the difference is.

The division includes an EME Regiment and an Aviation Platoon, similar to the armoured division, and lacks the medical and ordnance battalions found in the infantry division. The division artillery brigade substitutes a Medium MLRS Battery in place of the Mortar Light Battery, and also includes an SATA Battery. There may also be an AA Battery. Reviewing these "relatively small changes," two authors felt that they "greatly enhanced the plains division's firepower, mobility, and surveillance capability, but at an affordable cost for a resource strapped army."[303]

Mountain Division

These are very similar to the infantry division, with the biggest difference in the division artillery. The artillery brigade has three field regiments with the 105mm howitzer, a regiment with towed 155mm howitzers, and a light mortar battery (120mm). The division does have an Aviation Platoon, and lacks the medical and ordnance battalions found in the infantry division.

---

[303] Mandeep Singh Bajwa and Ravi Rikhye , Indian Army RAPID Divisions (2001).

Infantry Battalion

The basic infantry battalion, ca. 2001-2002, had a total strength of 909 personnel.[304] It was organized as follows:

Bn HQ	74	
Admin Company	146	
Coy HQ		7
QM Platoon		22
Medical Platoon		22
Trans Platoon		39
?		59
Support Company	193	
Coy HQ		7
MMG Platoon		42
Mortar Platoon		48
RL Platoon		21
Signals Platoon		38
Pioneer Platoon		37
4 x Rifle Company, each	124	
Coy HQ		13
3 x Rifle Platoon		37

The Admin Company has 59 personnel not accounted for in the details. These may be mess or additional administrative personnel.

The battalion total of 909 includes 23 Army Medical Corps (one officer and 22 other ranks), six Army Education Corps other ranks, eight EME other ranks; and two "Others" other ranks, in addition to 40 Non-Combatants (Enrolled), or NC(E) personnel. NC(E) is a category unique to the Indian Army. This includes cooks, barbers, sweepers, some types of clerk, etc. This economizes on trained personnel but can create operational problems if the flow of combat reaches these individuals.

The infantry portion of the battalion comprises 19 officers, 24 junior commissioned officers, and 787 other ranks.

---

[304] Bharat Rakshak, www.bharat-rakshak.com/LAND-FORCES/OrBat/Misc/4-B.pdf; this is the ultimate source for India Army: Infantry Battalion TOE (2002).

Appendix D: The Original Cavalry Regiments.

Unlike the Infantry, which are multi-battalion units, cavalry and armoured regiments are each a distinct regiment. This made it awkward to try and include their origins in the Indian Armoured Corps section, similar to the introductions to each of the infantry regiments.

The **Governor General's Bodyguard** dates back to 1773. Formally restyled as the Viceroy's Bodyguard in 1858 when the Crown replaced the East India Company, it seems to have retrained the old name in practice. By the Second World War it was mainly composed of Sikhs, and retained a mounted (horsed) squadron. From 1 November 1944 to 31 March 1946 the bulk of the personnel manned jeeps and light truacks as 44th Airborne Divisional Reconnaissance Squadron (Governor General's Bodyguyard). It then returned to its prior role as a mounted ceremonial unit, with the ability to function as a small mechanised unit as well. On independence, its official designation became Governor General's Bodyguyard. In January 1950 it was restyled as The President's Bodyguard.

Regimental Badge: A parachute and wings in silver at the center, with the Ashoka Lions above and "PBG" below, all in front of crossed lances. The badge (except the parachute and wings) is in gold.

The prior badge had crossed lances, points upward; at the intersection a crown above the script letters "GGBG". In 1950 this probably saw the crown replaced by the Ashoka Lions and the letters to "PBG".

Skinner's Horse (1st Duke of York's Own) was formed 1921 from 1st Duke of York's Own Lancers and 3rd Skinner's Horse (and known at first as 1st/3rd Horse). On partition, its Punjabi Muslim squadron when to Pakistan's 19th King George V's Own Lancers in return for that regiment's Sikh squadron. Redesignated 1950 as 1st Horse, although "Skinner's Horse" continued to be used unofficially.

Regimental Badge: Crossed lances with a crown between the pennants and across the bottom of the lances a scroll with non-English lettering, all in gold; at the intersection of the lances the white rose of York in silver. After1950, the crown was replaced by a rider on a rearing horse and the entire badge is in silver.

2nd Lancers (Gardner's Horse) was amalgamated 1921 with the 4th Cavalry as 2nd/4th Cavalry but redesignated 1922 as 2nd Lancers (Gardner's Horse); redesignated 1935 as **2nd Royal Lancers (Gardner's Horse)** in recognition of

Great War service. On partition, a Hindustani Muslim squadron went to Pakistan and the regiment received a Rajput squadron from 18th King Edward VII's Own Cavalry. Redesignated 1950 as 2nd Lancers, although "Gardner's Horse" continued to be used unofficially.

Regimental Badge: Two pairs of crossed lances behind the ribbon and motto (Honi Soit Qui Mal y Pense) of the Order of the Garter; within the Garter a stylized lion; at the top of the Garter a crown; all in gold.

The badge was redesigned after 1950, retaining the two pairs of crossed lances. However, they were now fronted by a circle with the legend "SECOND LANCERS" on the top left and right, and "G.H." on the base; in the center is the stylized lion; at the top of the circle is the Ashoka Lions, all in silver.

3rd Cavalry was formed in 1922 by amalgamation of the 5th Cavalry and 8th Lancers as the 5th/8th Cavalry; it was redesignated later that year as 3rd Cavalry. (The regiment was lost at Singapore in 1942 and reformed 1946 in India.) Around January 1948 it received a Sikh squadron that had belong to 11th Prince Albert Victor's Own Cavalry, which went to Pakistan on partition.

Regimental Badge: The Roman numeral III, with a crown above and a scroll reading "CAVALRY" below, all in gold. After1950, the Ashoka Lions replaced the crown.

Hodson's Horse (4th Duke of Cambridge's Own Lancers) was created September 1921 from 9th Bengal Lancers and 10th Duke of Cambridge's Own Bengal Lancers. (The regiment was first known as 9th/10th Cavalry, changed 1922 to 4th Duke of Cambridge's Own Hodson's Horse, and 1927 to the final version.) On partition, its Punjabi Muslim squadron went to Pakistan's Guides Cavalry in exchange for its Dogra squadron. Around January 1948 the Dogra squadron went to the Scinde Horse in exchange for its Sikh squadron. Redesignated 1950 as 4th Horse, although "Hodson's Horse" continued to be used unofficially.

7th Light Cavalry is the former 28th Light Cavalry. On partition, its Punjabi Muslim squadron went to Pakistan's 6th Duke of Connaught's Own Lancers in exchange for that regiment's Jat squadron.

Regimental Badge: Crossed lances, with a crown at the intersection and a three-part scroll across the bottom of the lances, reading "LIGHT" "7" and "CAVALRY", all in silver. As with other regiments, declaration of the republic saw the crown replaced by the Ashoka Lions.

8th King George V's Own Light Cavalry was formed in 1922 from 26th King George's Own Light Cavalry and 30th Lancers (Gordon's Horse). (At first numbered as 26th/30th but soon changed to 8th; was "King George's Own" until 1937 when changed to "King George V's Own.") On partition, its Punjabi Muslim squadron when to Pakistan's 6th Duke of Connaught's Own Lancers in exchange for that regiment's Sikh squadron. Redesignated 1950 as 8th Light Cavalry.

Regimental Badge: Crossed lances, with the numeral "8" at the intersection, a crown above, and the letters "KGO" between the bottom of the lances, all in silver. After1950, the "KGO" was replaced by a scroll reading "LIGHT CAVALRY" and the crown replaced by the armoured fist of the Armoured Corps.

The Royal Deccan Horse (9th Horse) was formed from in 1921 by amalgamation of the 20th Deccan Horse and 29th Lancers (Deccan Horse). (At first designated 20th/29th Horse, changed 1922 to 9th Royal Deccan Horse and 1927 to the final form.) On partition, its Punjabi Muslim squadron went to Pakistan's Probyn's Horse in exchange for that regiment's Dogra squadron. Redesignated 1950 as 9th Horse, but sometimes also shown as The Deccan Horse (9th Horse).

Regimental Badge: Crossed lances behind the ribbon and motto (Honi Soit Qui Mal y Pense) of the Order of the Garter; above the ribbon a crown; within the ribbon the script letters "RDH"; below, a scroll reading "ROYAL DECCAN HORSE", all in silver.

The redesign replaced the crown with the Ashoka Lions and the Garter ribbon with a circle, containing laurel leaves at the bottom and non-English lettering at the top; the numberal "9" replaced the "RDH" within the circle, and the scroll was changed to read "THE DECCAN HORSE", all still in silver.

The Scinde Horse (14th Prince of Wales's Own Cavalry) was formed in 1922 from 35th Scinde Horse and 36th Jacob's Horse. (At first designated 35th/36th Cavalry but soon changed to 14th Prince of Wales's Own Scinde Horse and 1927 to final version.) On partition, sent its Ranghar squadron to Pakistan's Guides Cavalry and received a Sikh squadron from Pakistan's Probyn's Horse. Around January 1948 the new Sikh squadron went to Hodson's Horse [4th] in exchange for that regiment's Dogra squadron. Redesignated 1950 as 14th Horse.

Regimental Badge: A mounted trooper with upraised lance; below, a scroll reading "THE SCINDE HORSE" and a scroll rising up between that and the horse reading "P.W.O.", all in silver. The authors have been unable to find an illustration of the post-1950 badge.[305]

16th Light Cavalry is the former 27th Light Cavalry. In 1946 it converted to all South India classes.

Regimental Badge: Crossed lances with the numerals "16" at the intersection, a crown above, and a scroll across the bottom of the lances reading "LIGHT CAVALRY". The crown was replaced by the Ashoka Lions following 1950.

The Poona Horse (17th Queen Victoria's Own Cavalry) formed in 1921 from 33rd Queen Victoria's Own Light Cavalry and the 34th Prince Albert Victor's Own Poona Horse. (Originally designated as 33rd/34th Cavalry but soon changed to 17th Queen Victoria's Own Poona Horse and in 1927 to final version.) On partition, transferred its Kaimkhani squadron to Pakistan's Guides Cavalry in return for a Sikh squadron from that regiment. Redesignated 1950 as 17th Horse.

Regimental Badge: The ribbon and motto (Honi Soit Qui Mal y Pense) of the Order of the Garter, somewhat elongated; above the ribbon a crown; within the ribbon the royal cipher; below, a scroll reading "QUEEN VICOTRIA'S OWN POONA HORSE", all in silver.

The crown was replaced by the Ashoka Lions and the ribbon by a circle, with non-English lettering at the top; within the circle an open hand palm outwards; below, a scross reading "THE POONA HORSE", all in silver.

18th King Edward VII's Own Cavalry was formed in 1922 from 6th King Edward's Own Cavalry and the 7th Hariana Lancers. (At first designated as 6th/7th Cavalry but soon changed to 18th King Edward's Own Cavalry and 1936 to 18th King Edward VII's Own Cavalry.) On partition, transferred its Kaimkhani squadron to Pakistan's Probyn's Horse and received a Sikh squadron from Pakistan's 11th Prince Albert Victor's Own Cavalry. Around January 1948 transferred the new Sikh squadron to 3rd Cavalry and received a new Hindustani Muslim squadron from 2nd Royal Lancers. Redesignated 1950 as 18th Cavalry.

Regimental Badge: Crossed lances; just above the intersection, the Prince of Wales's plume, coronet and motto "ICH DIEN"; just below the intersection the numeral "18"; across the base of the lances a scroll reading "K.E.O.

---

[305] It is the only armoured regiment whose badge is not illustrated in Sharma, op. cit., and is one of those missing from the photographs at empiretocommonwealth.webs.com/armyreg04.htm.

CAVALRY", all in silver. After 1950, the Prince of Wales's device was replaced by the Ashoka Lions and the scroll changed to read simply "CAVALRY".

When the **20th Lancers** were formed in 1956, they were considered a re-raising of the disbanded 20th Lancers.[306] That regiment's badge was crossed lances, with a crown at the intersection, a scroll below reading "LANCERS" and the numberals "XX" in between the crown and scroll. The new regiment simply replaced the crown with the Ashoka Lancers.

The Central India Horse (21st King George V's Own Horse) was formed in 1921 by amalgamating the 38th and 39th King George's Own Central Indian Horse. (At first designated 38th/39th Cavalry, but soon changed to 38th/39th King George's Own Light Cavalry, then in 1923 to The Central India Horse (21st King George's Own Horse) and in 1937 to the final version.) On partition transferred its Punjabi Muslim squadron to Pakistan's 19th King George V's Own Lancers in exchange for the 19th's Jat squadron. Redesignated 1950 as The Central India Horse.

Regimental Badge: Crossed lances with a crown between the pennants, all in gold; at the intersection the intertwined letters "CIH" in silver. Following 1950 the Ashoka Lions replaced the crown.

The **45th Cavalry** was considered a re-raising of the Second World War regiment with that designation, making it the last regiment with a tie the pre-partition Army. However, it adopted a completely new regimental badge: the outline of a PT-76 tank with the numerals "45" centered on the hull below the turret and a scroll below with non-English lettering, all in silver.

---

306 14th Murray's Jat Lancers and 15th Lancers (Cureton's Multanis) were amalgamated in 1921 as 14th/15th Lancers and then redesignated in 1922 as 20th Lancers. They became a training regiment in 1937 and were disbanded in 1941.

Appendix E: Class Composition of Armoured Regiments

This Appendix provides the class composition of armoured regiments.

Key	Class
AIC	All India Composition [mixed]; the term All India All Classes is sometimes used
D	Dogras
J	Jats
K	Kaimkhanis
M	Marathas
OIC	Other Indian Communities
R	Rajputs
RM	Rajput Muslims
S	Sikhs
SIC	South Indian Communities

In the table below, mixed units are in equal proportions unless otherwise indicated. In all cases the pre-1947 classes had been different; see the details in the prior Appendix on the exchanges of squadrons between regiments going to India and Pakistan.

1st Horse	R, J, S
2nd Lancers	R, J
3rd Cavalry	R, J, S
4th Horse	S, D
5th Armoured	AIC
6th Armoured	AIC
7th Cavalry	J, S
8th Cavalry	SIC
9th Horse	D, J, S
10th Armoured	AIC
11th Armoured	AIC
12th Armoured	AIC
13th Armoured	AIC
14th Horse	S, D
15th Armoured	AIC
16th Cavalry	SIC
17th Horse	R, J
18th Cavalry	J, R, RM
19th Armoured	AIC

20th Lancers	J, R
21st Horse	J, D, J, All Classes
40th Armoured	AIC
41st Armoured	AIC
42nd Armoured	AIC
43rd Armoured	AIC
44th Armoured	AIC
45th Cavalry	SIC (2/3), OIC (1/3)
46th Armoured	AIC
47th Armoured	AIC
48th Armoured	AIC
49th Armoured	AIC
50th Armoured	AIC
51st Armoured	AIC
52nd Armoured	AIC
61st Cavalry	R, M, K
62nd Cavalry	D, J, S
63rd Cavalry	J, R, S
64th Cavalry	J, R, S
65th Armoured	AIC
66th Armoured	AIC
67th Armoured	AIC
68th Armoured	AIC
69th Armoured	AIC
70th Armoured	AIC
71st Armoured	J, D, SIC
72nd Armoured	AIC
73rd Armoured	S, R, K
74th Armoured	AIC
75th Armoured	AIC
76th Armoured	AIC
81st Armoured	AIC
82nd Armoured	AIC
83rd Armoured	AIC
84th Armoured	AIC
85th Armoured	AIC
86th Armoured	AIC
87th Armoured	AIC
88th Armoured	AIC
89th Armoured	AIC
90th Armoured	AIC

As can be seen, the trend has clearly been to make the new armoured regiments All India Composition, while leaving the older regiments with their traditional class composition.

[This Appendix is taken from Gautam, op.cit., Table 5.3 (p 46). However, he seems to have omitted the 40th Armoured Regiment.]

Appendix F: Identified Engineer Companies

Because these were the standard unit before the creation of regiments after 1965, those identified have been listed here. The primary source is the Corps official history, which only runs through the 1971 war. Very few group affiliations are known for the companies. Any company listed with no other information is from Sharma, op. cit., and the company would have been active during the late 1980s or later.

1st Field	Refugee escort Sep 1947. Under 629 AEG, Kashmir, Feb 1948. With 4th Mtn Div 1965 war.
3rd Field	Hyderabad Sep 1948 (detached from 623 AEG). To Kashmir Nov 1948. To Nagaland Aug 1956. HQ 632 CTE took over coy Sep 1956 and redesignated 20th Div Engrs. Left 1958. With 623 FAEG to Nepal for roadbuilding Sep 1959.
3rd Fd Survey	At Dehra Dun Aug 1947. Elements to Kashmir 1947-48. Enlarged 1963 as 501st Fd Survey Engr Gp.
4th Field	Refugee escort Sep 1947.
6th Cons	With 623 FAEG to Nepal for roadbuilding Sep 1959.
7th Field	Under 623 AEG, Hyderabad, Sep 1948.
7th Plant	Road building Ladakh 1961.
8th E&M[307]	Sent to help with Mahandi Delta floods Jul 1961. With II Corps 1971 war.
8th (I) Field	(Bengal Gp)
9th Field	Refugee escort Sep 1947. Under 624 AEG, Hyderabad Sep 1948. Served in Ladakh during 1962 war.
10th Field	Refugee escort Sep 1947. Under 623 AEG, Hyderabad, Sep 1948. With 67th Inf Bde 1965 war.
11th Fd Park	Under 623 AEG, Hyderabad, Sep 1948.
12th Field	In Kashmir May 1948. 7 Engr Regt 1971 war.
13th Field	(Madras Gp) Refugee escort Sep 1947. In Kashmir Feb 1948. Joined Sri Div Engrs May 1948. Sent to Congo with 99th (I) Inf Bde Apr 1961; left Feb 1962. Joined 1st Armd Div Sep 1965. *Honours*: Zoji La, Jammu & Kashmir 1947-48; Jammu & Kashmir 1965

[307] Electrical and Mechanical.

14th Field	(Madras Gp) Punjab Aug 1947. Refugee escort Sep 1947. With 50th Para Bde to Kashmir Oct 1947. With 625 AE to NEFA Jun 1960 for road building. Later **14th Assault Field**. 1st Armd Div Engrs 1965 war. *Honours*: Jammu & Kashmir 1947-48; Punjab 1965
15th Field	Hyderabad Sep 1948 (detached from 623 AEG). With 625 ATE to Allahabad Oct 1953 work work along the Ganges. With 625 ATE to Nepal for roadbuilding 1954-55. With 625 ATE to NEFA Jun 1960 for road building. Detached to 4th Inf Div during 1962 war. 201 Army Engr Regt 1971 war.
16th WS & Park[308]	Detachment under 624 AEG, Hyderabad Sep 1948.
18th Field	With 624 CTE to NEFA for road-building Jul 1960. Detached to 4th Inf Div during 1962 war. Kirkee under 624 CTE, to Nagaland 1963.
19th Field	(Bombay Gp) To Kashmir mid Jul 1948. With 624 CTE to NEFA for road-building Jul 1960. Detached to 4th Inf Div during 1962 war. Kirkee under 624 CTE, to Nagaland 1963. *Honours*: Jammu & Kashmir 1947-48
20th Field	At Shillong Apr 1956, sent to Nagaland. HQ 632 CTE took over coy in Nagaland Sep 1956 and redesignated 20th Div Engrs. Left 1958. Served in Ladakh during 1962 war. With 191st Inf Bde 1965 war.
21st Field	(Bombay Gp) In Kashmir by Apr 1948. 20th Div Engrs Goa Dec 1961. *Honours*: Jammu & Kashmir 1947-48
22nd Field	(Bombay Gp) Kashmir from Dec 1947. To NEFA and 640 NTE for road building by end 1952. Joined 99th (I) Inf Bde in Congo Mar 1962; left ca Mar 1963. 6th Mtn Div Engrs 1965 war. *Honours*: Jammu & Kashmir 1947-48
23rd Field	17th Div Engrs Goa Dec 1961. With 643 CTE Bhutan road building 1962. 108 Engr Regt 1971 war.
29th Field	Committed in NEFA during 1962 war.
30th Field	In Kashmir during 1965 war.
31st Field	55 Engr Regt/15th Inf Div 1965 war.
32nd Assault	(Madras Gp) 1st Armd Div Engrs 1947. To Kashmir Nov 1947. (1st Armd Div Engrs served as JA Div Engrs 1948.) *Honours*: Jammu & Kashmir 1947-48

---

308 Workshop and Park.

36th Para Fd	(Madras Gp) 2nd Abn Div Engrs 1947. Punjab Aug 1947. Refugee escort Sep 1947. Kashmir by May 1948. (2nd Abn Div Engrs served as Sri Div Engrs 1948.) Later **36th Field**. With 625 ATE to Allahabad Oct 1953 work work along the Ganges. 5 Engr Regt/26th Inf Div 1965 war. *Honours*: Jammu & Kashmir 1947-48
37th Assault	(Bombay Gp) 1st Armd Div Engrs 1947. To Kashmir Nov 1947. (1st Armd Div Engrs served as JA Div Engrs 1948.) *Honours*: Rajaori, Jammu & Kashmir 1947-48
38th Assault Sqn	Flail tanks, XI Corps, 1965 war.[309]
39th Assault Fd Park	(Bengal Gp) 1st Armd Div Engrs 1947. To Kashmir Nov 1947. (1st Armd Div Engrs served as JA Div Engrs 1948.) *Honours*¨ Jammu & Kashmir 1947-48
40th Abn Fd Park	(Bengal Gp) 2nd Abn Div Engrs 1947. Punjab Aug 1947. Refugee escort Sep 1947. (2nd Abn Div Engrs served as Sri Div Engrs 1948.) With 625 ATE to Allahabad Oct 1953 work work along the Ganges. Later **40th Fd Park**. To Nagaland Aug 1956. HQ 632 CTE took over coy Sep 1956 and redesignated 20th Div Engrs. Left 1958. 19th Div Engrs 1965 war. *Honours*: Jammu & Kashmir 1965
41st Fd Park	Refugee escort Sep 1947. Supported road building 1961. 4th Div Engrs 1962 (?) during 1962 war.
45th Fd Park	(Bombay Gp) Raised 1947. With 7th Inf Div 1965 war.
46th Fd Park	(Bombay Gp) Raised 1947. With 624 CTE to NEFA for road-building Jul 1960. Kirkee under 624 CTE, to Nagaland 1963.
49th Cons	Under 624 AEG, Hyderabad Sep 1948. With 625 ATE to Nepal for roadbuilding 1954-55.
52nd Cons	Punjab Aug 1947. Refugee escort Sep 1947. With 625 ATE to Nepal for roadbuilding 1954-55. Worked on new airfield at Leh 1963.
56th Field	In IV Corps area 1971 war.
61st Field	Kirkee under 624 CTE, to Nagaland 1963. In I Corps area 1971 war.
62nd Field	With 16th Inf Bde 1965 war.
63rd Field	With 29th Inf Bde 1965 war.
64th Field	In XI Corps area 1965 war.

309 Designated as a squadron rather than company, but an engineer squadron is essentially the same as a company.

65th Field	(Madras Gp) Under 623 AEG, Hyderabad, Sep 1948. With 625 ATE to Allahabad Oct 1953 work work along the Ganges. 23rd Div Engrs early 1958. Built quarters in J&K 1961. Served in Ladakh during 1962 war (2nd Div Engrs?). Later **65th Assault Field**. 1st Armd Div Engrs 1965 war. *Honours*: Punjab 1965
68th Field	(Bengal Gp) *Honours*: Jammu & Kashmir 1965
69th Field	Kashmir from Dec 1947. Placed under 631 AEG Jan 1948. 23rd Div Engrs early 1958.
70th Field	Sent to Rann of Kutch Mar 1965.
71st Field	55 Engr Regt/15th Inf Div 1965 war.
72nd Field	58 Corps Engr Regt 1972 war.
73rd Field	(Bengal Gp) 19th Div Engrs 1965 war (?).58 Corps Engr Regt 1972 war. *Honours*: Jammu & Kashmir 1965
74th Field	(Platoon sent to Korea 1953-54.) Road building in Ladakh 1961. With 6th BRTF Ladakh road building 1962. With 2nd Armd Bde 1965 war.[310]
75th Field	Road building Uttar Pradesh 1962.
76th Field	Road building Uttar Pradesh 1962.
77th Field	With 4th Mtn Div 1965 war.
78th Field	(Bengal Gp) With 451 CTE in Rann of Kutch 1965 and then 1965 war. *Honours*: Rajasthan 1965
79th Field	Road building Himachal Pradesh 1962-63.
82nd Field	With I Corps in 1965 war.
83rd Field	55 Engr Regt/15th Inf Div 1965 war.
84th Field	(Bengal Gp) Former Tehri Garhwal Fd Co, joined 1950.
85th Field	(Bengal Gp) "Newly raised" at time of 1965 war; with 451 CTE in support of 11th Inf Div. *Honours*: Rajasthan 1965
89th Field	(Bengal Gp) With 624 ATE, Damodar Valley, 1954. Sent to J&K Sep 1965. *Honours*: Jammu & Kashmir 1965
93rd Field	In XI Corps area 1965 war.
94th Field	With 7th Inf Div 1965 war. 59 Engr Regt 1971 war.
95th Field	(Bengal Gp) Former Mandi Field Co, joined 1952. Detachment to NEFA and 640 NTE for road building in 1954. Served in Ladakh during 1962 war. With 7th Inf Div 1965 war.
98th Field	With 7th Inf Div 1965 war.

[310] Also operated in support of 7th Infantry Division earlier. The official history refers to it as both 74th Assault Field and 74th Field Company.

99th Field	(Bombay Gp) Under 629 AEG, Kashmir, Feb 1948. To Nagaland, 20th Div Engr, Oct 1958. (20th Div Engrs became 23rd Div Engrs Sep 1959.) Left early 1962. *Honours*: Jammu & Kashmir 1947-48
100th Field	(Bengal Gp) Former Sirmoor Fd Co, joined 1950. 4th Div Engrs 1962(?), with 7th Inf Bde. With 4th Mtn Div 1965 war. *Honours*: Punjab 1965
101st Cons	101st RW Cons Aug 1947, Punjab. Kashmir 1948.
104th Cons	Raised at Allahabad. With 4th BRTF Nov 1960.
108th RW Op[311]	Punjab Aug 1947. Disbanded by 1955.
108th Cons	To Sikkim for road building 1961.
109th Cons	To Sikkim for road building 1961.
119th Cons	To Sikkim for road building 1961.
127th Cons	Bhutan road building 1961-62.
130th Cons	With 4th BRTF Nov 1960.
132nd Cons	To Sikkim for road building 1962.
136th Cons	With 643 CTE Bhutan road building 1962.
137th Cons	With 643 CTE Bhutan road building 1962.
138th Cons	With 643 CTE Bhutan road building 1962.
155th Cons	Roadbuilding in the Himalayas 1970.
160th Cons	Worked in Bangladesh following 1971 war.
165th Cons	With 29th BRTF in Bhutan during 1971 war.
183rd Cons	Bhutan road building 1962.
235th IWT Op[312]	(Bombay Gp) Raised 1947. Sent to help with Mahandi Delta floods Jul 1961.
252nd Bomb Disp	(Bengal Gp)
261st Bomb Disp	(Madras Gp)
262nd Bomb Disp	(Madras Gp)
276th Field	In XXXIII Corps area 1971 war (13, 52 or 111 Engr Regt).
282nd Field	63 Engr Regt 1971 war.
283rd Field	63 Engr Regt 1971 war.
284th Field	63 Engr Regt 1971 war.
302nd Fd Park	Worked on new airfield at Leh 1963.
303rd Fd Park	23rd Div Engrs early 1958.
305 (Fd Park?)	(Bombay Gp) *Honours*: Jammu & Kashmir 1965
310th Fd Park	55 Engr Regt/15th Inf Div 1965 war.
325th Field	

[311] Railway Operating.
[312] Inland Water Transport Operating.

344th WS & Park	In Kashmir by early 1948.
350th WS & Park	To Sikkim for road building 1961.
353rd WS & Park	With 643 CTE Bhutan road building 1962.
358th Field	113 Engr Regt 1971 war.
361st Field	15 Engr Regt 1971 war.
362nd Field	Hyderabad Sep 1948. To Kashmir Nov 1948. To NEFA and 640 NTE for road building by end 1952. 23rd Div Engrs early 1958.
368th Field	(Bengal Gp) Former Faridkot Fd Co, joined 1950.[313] Served in Ladakh during 1962 war (2nd Div Engrs?).
369th Field	(Bengal Gp) Former Malerkotla Field Co, joined 1951. To Nagaland Aug 1956. HQ 632 CTE took over coy Sep 1956 and redesignated 20th Div Engrs. Left 1958. With 623 FAEG to Nepal for roadbuilding Sep 1959. With 9th BRTF Ladakh road building 1962. Placed under 10th Inf Div Sep 1969. 58 Corps Engr Regt 1971 war. *Honours*: Jammu & Kashmir 1965
369th Plant	Road building Ladakh 1961.
370th Field	17th Div Engrs Goa Dec 1961.
371st Field	With 625 ATE to Nepal for roadbuilding 1954-55. 23rd Div Engrs early 1958. With 6th BRTF Ladakh road building 1962.
372nd Field	Served in Ladakh during 1962 war.
373rd Field	To NEFA and 640 NTE for road building by end 1952. With 31st Inf Bde Gp Rann of Kutch 1965 (probably detached from 451 CTE). 451 CTE in 1965 war.
374th Field	(Bengal Gp) Detachment to NEFA and 640 NTE for road building by late 1953. 19th Div Engrs 1965 war (?). 56 Engr Regt 1971 war. *Honours*: Jammu & Kashmir 1965
376th Field	17th Div Engrs Goa Dec 1961.
377th Field	17th Div Engrs Goa Dec 1961. Sent with 48th Inf Bde to NEFA Nov 1962.
380th Field	20th Div Engrs Goa Dec 1961.
386th (I) Field	Angola (UNAVEM III) 1995-97.
391st Field	In XXXIII Corps area during 1971 war.
401st Assault Field	To Nagaland, 20th Div Engr, Oct 1958. (20th Div Engrs became 23rd Div Engrs Sep 1959.) Later **401st Fd Coy** (ca 1959?). Left early 1962.
410th (I) Field	(Bengal Gp)

[313] As 1st Faridkot Field Company, entered J&K January 1948 with 631st AEG.

411th Para Field	(Bombay Gp) 2nd Abn Div Engrs 1947. To Kashmir early Jul 1948. With 50th (I) Para Bde from ca 1950. [With 625 ATE to Allahabad Oct 1953 work work along the Ganges.] *Honours*: Jammu & Kashmir 1947-48
412th (I) Field	(Madras Gp)
413th (I) Field	(Bengal Gp)
415th (I) Field	(Madras Gp)
417th (I) Field	(Madras Gp) Angola (UNAVEM III) 1995-97.
418th (I) Field	(Bengal Gp)
419th Assault Sqn	(Madras Gp)
421st Field	Worked on new airfield at Leh 1963. In I Corps area 1971 war.
428th Field	(Madras Gp) 6th Mtn Div Engrs 1965 war. *Honours*: Punjab 1965
430th Field	In XI Corps area 1965 war.
432nd Field	15 Engr Regt 1971 war.
433rd Field	(Madras Gp) In Kashmir late Apr 1948. With 625 ATE to Allahabad Oct 1953 work work along the Ganges. To Nagaland, 20th Div Engr, Oct 1958. (20th Div Engrs became 23rd Div Engrs Sep 1959.) [Deployed in Sikkim 1960.] Left early 1962. 201 Army Engr Regt 1971 war. *Honours*: Zoji La, Jammu & Kashmir 1947-48
434th Field	Bhutan road building 1961-62. 15 Engr Regt 1971 war.
435th Field	15 Engr Regt 1971 war.
439th Field	Uner 41st Mtn Bde Sep 1965.
482nd (I) Field	Raised Kirkee. To Sikkim for road building 1962.In Southern Cmd 1971 war.
484th Field	108 Engr Regt 1971 war.
614th E&M	Punjab Aug 1947.
620th E&M	(Bombay Gp) Raised 1947.
651st Engr Plant	With 643 CTE Bhutan road building 1962.
652nd Engr Plant	Bhutan road building 1961. With 643 CTE Bhutan road building 1962.
653rd Engr Plant	Detachment to NEFA and 640 NTE for road building by end 1952. Road building in Ladakh 1961. In J&K 1971 war.
661st Earth Moving Plant	Bhutan road building 1961-62.
664th Engr Plant	To Kashmir Dec 1947. To NEFA Jul 1960 to support road building.
667th Cons Equip	To Sikkim for road building 1961.
670th Cons	Road building Ladakh 1961.

682nd Fd Park	Punjab Aug 1947. To Kashmir late Jun 1948.
683rd Fd Park	To Nagaland, 20th Div Engr, Oct 1958. (20th Div Engrs became 23rd Div Engrs Sep 1959.) Left early 1962.
684th Fd Park	With 625 AE to NEFA Jun 1960 for road building.
701st Engr Plant	Kirkee under 624 CTE, to Nagaland 1963.
702nd Engr Plant	Worked on new airfield at Leh 1963.
755th Engr Plant	Detachment to NEFA and 640 NTE for road building by end 1952.
Army HQ Survey	Established by 1948 to handle map storage and distribution and Army HQ printing jobs. Enlarged 1963 as 502nd Photo Mapping Engr Gp.

Appendix G: Jammu and Kashmir 1947-48

This Appendix contains a list of units and formations known to have served in Jammu and Kashmir 1947-48. Brigade HQs are listed in the order of their induction into the theatre. Battalions are listed by regiment, since they were frequently shifted during the course of the fighting. Known brigade assignments are also shown, but these are partially snapshots rather than a list of all assignments and should not be considered a complete record of a battalion's assignments.

V Corps was established October 1948 at Srinagar to control operations. It was created from HQ Jammu and Kashmir Force, initially an ad hoc command element established at Srinagar ca November 1947.

Two division HQs were created in May 1948: Sri Division (later numbered as 19th) at Srinagar and JA Division (later numbered as 26th) at Jammu.

161st Infantry Brigade [Nov 1947]
50th Parachute Brigade [Nov 1947]
268th Infantry Brigade [Nov 1947]
80th Infantry Brigade [Dec 1947]
19th Infantry Brigade [Feb 1948]
163rd Infantry Brigade [by May 1948][314]
77th Parachute Brigade [May 1948]
5th Infantry Brigade [Oct 1948]
19th Infantry Brigade [Nov 1948]

7th Light Cavalry [armoured cars] [from Nov 1947]
Central India Horse ca 1948

1st (Para) Punjab (161st Inf Bde Nov 1947; 50th Para Bde Nov 1947; gone Feb 1948; 19th Inf Bde Nov 1948)
2nd Punjab (50th Para Bde by Jan 1948, gone Feb 1948; ad hoc bde Rajauri Nov 1948)
2nd (Para) Madras (77th Para Bde May 1948; gone by Sep 1948)
4th Madras (5th Inf Bde Oct 1948)
1st Grenadiers (in theatre by Sep 1948)
1st Maratha LI (in theatre 1948)
3rd (Para) Maratha LI (50th Para Bde Nov 1947 and Feb 1948)
5th Maratha LI (77th Para Bde Sep 1948; gone Oct 1948)

---

[314] Raised 1948 at Srinager as ad hoc "Z" Brigade and later numbered.

2nd Rajputana Rifles (19th Inf Bde Feb 1948 and Nov 1948)
5th Rajputana Rifles (5th Inf Bde Oct 1948)
6th Rajputana Rifles (161st Inf Bde May 1948)
1st Rajput (50th Para Bde by Jan 1948; gone Feb 1948)
3rd (Para) Rajput Nov 1947 and Feb 1948)
4th Rajput (80th Inf Bde Dec 1947; 77th Para Bde Oct 1948)
3rd Jat (77th Para Bde Sep 1948; gone Oct 1948)
6th Jat (in theatre 1948)
1st Sikh (161st Inf Bde Nov 1947; Z/163rd Inf Bde May 1948)
7th Sikh (161st Inf Bde May 1948)
2nd Dogra (161st Inf Bde May 1948)
4th Dogra (19th Inf Bde Feb 1948)
3rd Garhwal Rifles (80th Inf Bde Dec 1947; Z/163rd Inf Bde May 1948)
1st (Para) Kumaon (161st Inf Bde Nov 1947; 19th Inf Bde Nov 1948)
4th Kumaon (161st Inf Bde Nov 1947 and May 1948)
3rd Assam (ad hoc bde Rajauri Nov 1948)
2nd Bihar (in theatre by June 1948)
1st Mahar [MG] (1947-48)

2/3 GR (77th Para Bde May 1948; gone by Sep 1948)
1/4 GR (5th Inf Bde Oct 1948)
2/4 GR (to Ladakh 1948)
1/5 GR (77th Para Bde Sep 1948)
2/8 GR (to Ladakh 1948)
6/8 GR ad hoc bde Rajauri Nov 1948)
1/9 GR (80th Inf Bde Dec 1947)
3/9 GR (in theatre 1948)

Sawai Man Guards [Jaipur] (77th Para Bde May 1948; gone by Sep 1948)[315]
1st Patiala (268th Inf Bde Nov 1947; 80th Inf Bde Dec 1947; 50th Para Bde Jan 1948, Feb 1948; 77th Para Bde Sep 1948)[316]

Artillery was shifted around quite a bit during the course of the fighting.
A detachment of 13th Field Regiment, sent as infantry with 1st Sikh, was equipped with four 3.7" mountain howitzers from Patiala and reorganized as the 17th Mountain Battery.
32nd Field Battery (11th Field Regiment) arrived Jammu 3 Nov 1947
4th (Hazara) Mountain Battery flown into Punch by elements 13 Dec 1947 and Jan 1948
7th (Bengal) Mountain Battery was in theatre by Dec 1947

---

[315] From 1 April 1951 17th Rajputana Rifles (Sawai Man).
[316] From 1 April 1951 15th Punjab (Patiala).

RHQ 16th Field Regiment in theatre Dec 1947 along with 5th Mountain Battery. By early Jan 1948 it also had 7th (Bengal) Mountain Battery and 30th Field Battery (11th Field Regiment) under command.

RHQ 22nd Mountain Regiment in theatre by end Jan 1948 and given 7th (Bengal) Mountain Battery and 30th Field Battery

Artillery in the Jhangar area Mar 1948 included RHQ 16th Field Regiment, 5th and 7th Mountain Batteries, 30th Field Battery, troop of 37th AT Battery (3" mortars), and troop of 45th Field Battery. Scindia Field Battery joined May 1948.

RHQ 11th Field Regiment and its last field battery (31st) in theatre by May 1948.

36th and 47th Field Batteries were in theatre by Oct 1948.

51st Parachute Field Battery was in theatre by Nov 1948.

The Jammu and Kashmir State Forces are known to have included the 1st, 2nd, 4th, 7th, 8th and 9th Infantry, 3rd Rifles, and the J&K Mountain Battery (which was raised in 1948).

Engineer units, like infantry, could be shifted around during the course of the fighting.

1st Armoured Division Engineers (32nd and 37th Assault Field and 39th Assault Park Companies) was sent in November 1947, and served as JA Division Engineers from May 1948.

2nd Airborne Division Engineers (36th and 411th Parachute Field and 40th Parachute Field Park Companies) was sent in May 1948 to serve as Sri Division Engineers.

14th and 22nd Field Companies were both sent in 1947, in that order, followed by 69th Field Company in January 1948.

Field companies arriving during 1948 included 3rd, 21st, 362nd, 411th Parachute and 433rd.

Initial LOC work fell to 631st Army Engineer Group (69th and 1st Faridkot Field Companies) in January 1948 and 629th Army Engineer Group (1st and 99th Field Companies) the next month. 13th Field Company later joined 631st AEG. HQ 644th Plant Company served over varying numbers of plant platoons, and 344th Workshop and Park Company was also present. Later on, 620th Army Engineer Group was sent, and 101st Railway Construction Company was also on LOC duties. 571st Engineer Park was established in April 1948 to provide stores for the theatre, replacing a detachment of 344th Workshop and Park Company which had been operating as an engineer sub park. This was later supplemented by 572nd Engineer Sub Park.

[This Appendix is primarily based upon information in the text of Praval, op. cit., Ch Three; the official Regiment of Artillery history, Ch X; and the official Corps of Engineers history, Ch III]

Appendix H: Hyderabad (1948) and Goa (1961)

Between the onset of fighting in Jammu and Kashmir in 1947 and the 1962 war with China, the two major operations of the Indian Army were the accession of the last holdout princely state, Hyderabad—the so-called 100 hour war—and the last territory on the subcontinent still under European control.

Hyderabad

The Nawab of Hyderabad (second in size only to Jammu and Kashmir) hoped to remain sovereign and apart from India. Following negotiations, the government two parties executed a Standstill Agreement. By mid 1948 deteriorating conditions within Hyderabad and the unwillingness of the Nawab to budge led to a military resolution. The advance began on 13 September and resistance ended four days later. The overall operation was under Southern Command.

Because 1st Armoured Division Engineers had gone to Jammu and Kashmir, 623 Army Engineer Group was moved from Roorkee to join them at Poona. Three companies (7, 10 and 65) joined the three brigades, two (3 and 15) became Command Reserves, and the field park company (11) remained under command at Poona. 624 Army Engineer Group (9 Field Company, 49 Construction Company, and detachment 16 Workshop and Park Company) moved to Sholapur to prepare the division's concentration area.

[1] The main (western) thrust, in four groups, was a Task Force (1st Armoured Division HQ) from Sholapur:

1st Armoured Brigade [Smash Force]
- 3rd Cavalry (- two squadrons) [Shermans]
- 17th Horse (- one squadron) [Shermans]
- 14th Rajput
- 4th Gwalior Infantry
- company, 9th Dogra
- 1st Field Regiment (SP) (- one battery)
- 2nd Battery, 40th Medium Regiment
- 7 Field Company (- detachment) [from 623rArmy Engineer Group]

Strike Force
- 1st Horse (- one squadron) [Stuarts]
- 9th Dogra (- one company)
- battery, 1st Field Regiment (SP)
- detachment 7 Field Company

7th Infantry Brigade [Kill Force]
- 2nd Sikh
- 3rd Grenadiers
- 9th (Parachute) Field Regiment (- one battery)
- battery, 34th Anti-tank Regiment
- 65 Field Company [from 623 Army Engineer Group]

9th Infantry Brigade [Vir Force]
- squadron, 3rd Cavalry
- troop, 18th Cavalry
- 3rd/2nd Punjab Regiment
- 2/1 Gorkha Rifles
- 1st Mewar Infantry
- battery, 9th (Parachute) Field Regiment
- 10 Field Company [from 623 Army Engineer Group]

34th Anti-tank Regiment (- one battery)

In addition, four infantry battalions were placed to guard the flanks of the main advance: 9th/2nd Punjab, 3rd Sikh Light Infantry, 6th Jat and 6th Kumaon.

3/11 Gorkha Rifles and a squadron 8th Cavalry operated from the north and coordinated with 9th Infantry Brigade during part of the fighting.

[2] A secondary advance (Eastern Striking Force), under control of Madras Area, was from Vijawada:

2/5 Gorkha Rifles
squadron (- a troop), 17th Horse
troop, 19th Field Battery
platoon, 362 Field Company

[3] Operations on the southern border (provisional force "Mycol") were also under the control of Madras Area:[317]

5/5 Gorkha Rifles
1st Mysore Infantry
Mysore Lancers [horsed]

[317] These were assisted from 15 September by ad hoc companies formed from the Training and Depot Battalions, Madrass Engineer Group and Centre.

[4] A final advance was under the control of Bombay Area:

One column
- 3/5 Gorkha Rifles
- Two companies 17th Sikh
- composite squadrons of Stuart tanks and armoured cars from the Armoured Corps School
- 20th Field Battery
- 362 Field Company [Engineers] (- one platoon)

Another column
- 3rd Sikh
- company 2nd Jodhpur Infantry

[5] 3/11 Gurkha Rifles and elements 8th Cavalry

Goa

This operation was also under the control of Southern Command. The main thrust, from the east, would be by 17th Infantry Division and its two brigades,[318] with another thrust from the north by 50th (Independent) Parachute Brigade. The advance began the night of 17/18 December 1961 and the last Portuguese surrendered on the 20th. The main thrusts were by the 50th and 63rd Brigades.

There was extensive Engineer support, with 20th Division Engineers moving with 50th (Independent) Parachute Brigade, and 640 and 643 Corps Troops Engineers sent as well. The Madras Engineer Group and Centre was ordered to raise a brigade HQ for overall command, and HQ 417 Engineer Brigade was ready to function three days after raising, on 14 December. The 17th Infantry Division's actual advance would be supported by its engineers and 643 Corps Troops Engineers.

17th Infantry Division
48th Infantry Brigade
63rd Infantry Brigade
- 2nd Bihar
- 3rd Sikh
- 4th Sikh

50th (Independent) Parachute Brigade
- 1st Parachute
- 2nd Parachute

[318] Its third brigade (99th) had been relieved for service in the Congo.

[50th (Independent) Parachute Brigade]
 2nd Sikh Light Infantry
 411th Parachute Field Company

1st Maratha Light Infantry
4th Madras
20th Rajput

[This Appendix is primarily based upon information in the text of Praval, op. cit., Ch Three; the official Corps of Engineers history, Ch III; L N Subramanian, “100 Hour War – Hyderabad Police Action,” www.bharat-rakshak.com/LAND-FORCES/History/1948-62/260-100-Hour-War.html; and Dr. B.C. Chakravort, “Operation Vijay,” www.bharat-rakshak.com/LAND-FORCES/History/1961Goa/262-Operation-Vijay.html.]

Appendix I: Indian Army October 1962

Army HQ Reserve

1st Armoured Division (Jullunder)
1st Armoured Brigade
43rd Lorried Infantry Brigade

2nd Independent Armoured Brigade (Babina)
50th Independent Parachute Brigade (Agra)
65th Independent Infantry Brigade (Secundrabad)

Western Command
(HQ Simla)

27th Infantry Division (Jullunder) [Army HQ reserve formation]
64th Infantry Brigade
123rd Infantry Brigade
U/I Infantry Brigade

XV Corps (HQ Srinager)

19th Infantry Division (Baramula)
104th Infantry Brigade (Tithwal)
161st Infantry Brigade (Uri)
268th Infantry Brigade (Baramula)

25th Infantry Division (Poonch)
80th Infantry Brigade
93rd Infantry Brigade
120th Infantry Brigade

26th Infantry Division (Jammu)
19th Infantry Brigade
36th Infantry Brigade
168th Infantry Brigade

114th (I) Infantry Brigade (Leh)
163rd Infantry Brigade (Srinager) (newly raised)

XI Corps (HQ Jullunder)

5th Infantry Division (Ferozepur)
Brigades unknown

17th Infantry Division (Ambala)[319]
48th Infantry Brigade
63rd Infantry Brigade
164th Infantry Brigade

82nd (Independent) Infantry Brigade (Jodhpur. AOR: Rajasthan)
U/I Independent Brigade (Jamnager. AOR: Rann of Kutch)

Sugar Sector (Pooh, Himachal Pradesh)
five companies Punjab and Himachal Pradesh Armed Police forces
one infantry battalion earmarked from 4th Division

The Command had other infantry brigades, mainly in Uttar Pradesh, which went under Central Command when it was created during the war, but their designations are known.

Eastern Command
(HQ Lucknow, later Calcutta)

202nd (I) Infantry Brigade (Calcutta: command reserve)

Central Sector (UP – Nepal – Tibet border)
9th Infantry Brigade (ex 20th Infantry Division)
4th Special Task Force (armed police) sectors (HQ Moradabad, UP)

IV Corps (HQ Tezpur; raised 4 Oct 1962)

4th Infantry Division (Tezpur) (AOR: NEFA)
5th Infantry Brigade (Along. AOR: Subansiri, Siang, Lohit FDs)
7th Infantry Brigade (Tawang, AOR Kameng Frontier Division)
11th Infantry Brigade (Darjeeling. AOR Sikkim; but was in Nagaland)

---

[319] Newly raised, replacing 4th Division after its shift to Eastern Command 1959-60.

XXXIII Corps (HQ Shillong; AOR Nagaland [CI] and East Pakistan)

20th Infantry Division (Ranchi; to Gangtok 16 Nov 1962)
66th Infantry Brigade (raised Dinapur, Bohar Aug 1962)
165th Infantry Brigade (possibly at Ramgarh)

23rd Infantry Division (Nagaland) (also Command Reserve)
73rd Infantry Brigade
192nd (?) Infantry Brigade
301st Infantry Brigade

Southern Command
(HQ Poona)

6th (I) Brigade (Secundrabad: an Army HQ Reserve)
U/I Infantry Brigade (Madras/Trivandrum)

[This is an edited and somewhat revised version of Mandeep Singh Bajwa & Ravi Rikhye, The Indian Army on the Eve of the 1962 War: A Note. (2008).]

Appendix J: 1962 War Orders of Battle

The forces facing the Chinese in the 1962 war were part of Eastern Command (Lt Gen L.P. Sen), which was then at Lucknow and about to shift to Calcutta. Next came IV Corps (Lt Gen B.M. Kaul), which was newly raised for NEFA/Eastern Bhutan at Tezpur, taking over part of the area under XXXIII Corps.[320] Thus, this new headquarters had no operational or administrative experience. In addition, General Kaul was replaced on account of illness at the very beginning of the Chinese offensive by Lt Gen. Harbaksh Singh from Western Command, returning four days later to resume command.[321]

114th Infantry Brigade at Chushul

Raised in 1959 at Leh as 114th (Independent) Infantry Brigade, the brigade began with only two battalions; when the Ladakh border was handed over to the Army in April 1960, 14th Jammu and Kashmir Militia screened the northern half of the 480-kilometer long sector Demchok to Daulet Beg Oldi, and 7th Jammu and Kashmir Militia screened the southern half.[322] They were joined April 1961 by 1/8 Gorkha Rifles, which took over part of the front. 5th Jat arrived in April 1962 and also took over part of the front. With all four battalions at the (480 km) front, there was no reserve until 13th Kumaon arrived at Leh in September 1962.

At that point the new 3rd Infantry Division, raised 26 October 1962 at Leh, took assignment of the brigade, which was no longer independent. The two J&K Militia battalions left, replaced by 1st Jat. In addition, the brigade's front was shortened, with 70th Infantry Brigade (9th Dogra and 3/4 GR; arrived 1 November) taking over part and 163rd Infantry Brigade forming the division reserve at Leh. 114th Infantry Brigade had one battalion at the front, with brigade HQ and the remainder at Chushul.

---

[320] Because GOC XXXIII Corps repeatedly protested the unprofessional arrangements underway to evict the Chinese from their positions, the corps area of responsibility was divided.

[321] Lt Gen Kaul was finally replaced 30 November 1962 by Lt Gen SHFJ Manekshaw (later COAS and first field marshal in the Indian Army).

[322] While not truly militia, the regiment had not yet been regularized as the Jammu and Kashmir Light Infantry.

The 114th Infantry Brigade order of battle for Chushul[323] was:

1/8 Gorkha Rifles
1st Jat Regiment
5th Jat Regiment
13th Kumaon Regiment
38th Battery, 13th Field Regiment [eight 25-pounder guns][324]
32nd Heavy Mortar Battery [4.2"]
company, Mahar Machine Gun Regiment
HQ B Squadron and two troops, 20th Lancers [AMX-13]
one field engineer company

The Chinese attack on 20 October 1962 destroyed the 114th Infantry Brigade despite its fierce resistance. India's highest decoration for bravery is the Param Vir Chakra (PVC), and this fighting was the first time a single formation won two of these, with majors from two of its battalions posthumously honored for action within a span of three weeks.[325]

11th Infantry Brigade at Walong

Walong was originally the responsibility of a single battalion, 6th Kumaon, and an Assam Rifles company. HQ 11th Infantry Brigade arrived 31 October 1962. After the initial clashes, 2nd Infantry Division (Maj Gen M.S. Pathania) was raised at Teju to take over the eastern sector of NEFA while 4th Infantry Division was responsible for the west. The new division planned to replace the 11th at Walong with the 181st Infantry Brigade, but this was cancelled after protests by the local commanders. Neither it not the other brigade in the division (5th Infantry) figured in the battle.

11th Infantry Brigade (Brig N.C. Rawlley)[326]

3/3 Gorkha Rifles
4th Dogra
4th Sikhs
6th Kumaon
71st Heavy Mortar Battery
troop, 17th Parachute Field Regiment

---

[323] The Battle of Chushul is more commonly refered to as the Battles of Gurung Hill and Rezang La within the Indian Army.

[324] Only F Troop was present at the beginning; the remainder of the battery was flown in 27 October 1962. The balance of the regiment was sent to Leh, with the other two batteries deployed with the other two brigades of 3rd Infantry Division.

[325] Not until the 1999 Kargil War would there again be two PVCs awarded to a single unit.

[326] Who would serve as GOC XI Corps in the 1971 war.

platoon, 6th Mahar Machinegun Regiment, one platoon
engineer platoon
company, Assam Rifles

A counterattack 13 November 1962 captured a hill northwest of the town of Walong after a hard fight. However, concerted Chinese attacks dislodged them, and the forces in the area retreated down the Lohit Valley.

7th Infantry Brigade at Namkachu

This brigade came under 4th Infantry Division (Maj Gen Nirinjan Prasad) at Bombdila. The battle extended in phases during October and resulted in the sacrifice of the brigade for no purpose. It ceased to exist and played no role in the subsequent battle of Bomdila.

7th Infantry Brigade (Brig John Dalvi) [became a POW]
1/9 Gorkha Rifles
2nd Rajputs[327]
4th Grenadiers
9th Punjab
company, 6th Mahar Machine Gun Regiment
E Troop, 17th Parachute Field Regiment[328]
34th (Maratha)Heavy Mortar Battery (minus a platoon; no ammunition)
100th Field Company
platoon Assam Rifles

There were also 450 civilian road construction crew from the Border Roads Organization, used as porters.

4th Infantry Division at the Battle of Bomdila

What is here called the Battle of Bomdila was actually a series of three battles, fought at Se La, Dirang Dzong, and Bomdila. The battle is also sometimes referred to as the Battle of Se La.

4th Infantry Division had gone to the NEFA in 1959 with three infantry brigades. 7th Infantry Brigade went to the northwest corner of NEFA and 5th Infantry Brigade went to the northeast corner. 11th Infantry Brigade was

---

[327] Lost 282 KIA, 81 WIA, and 90 POW in a single day; only 60 personnel escaped. The battalion began with only 513 other ranks, less than 2/3 of authorized strength.
[328] Which had four guns (two operational), 260 rounds, and no sights or forward observers.

detached for CI Operations in Nagaland; it arrived only on 31 October 1962 and went to the new 2nd Infantry Division.

The 4th Infantry Division (HQ at Dirang Dzong) was strung out along 100 km of mountain terrain, with its logistics base at Misamari, 200 km away—a journey so arduous it took three days each way by truck. From north to south, came Se La, then Dirang Dzong, and then Bomdila. The division was reinforced during the course of the fighting. However, because battalions were simply being picked up from all over India and rushed into battle, they arrived without their vehicles and heavy equipment, and were also lacking some of their administrative and support elements. xxxx understrength

4th Infantry Division (Maj Gen Nirinjan Prasad, replaced by Maj Gen. A.S. Pathania)

Division Troops
- B Squaron, 7th Light Cavalry [Stuarts]
- 4th Artillery Brigade
  - 5th Field Regiment
  - 6th Field Regiment
  - 22nd Mountain Regiment
  - 34th Heavy Mortar Battery (-)
  - 116th Mortar Battery
  - 7th (Bengal) Mountain Battery

7th Infantry Brigade was destroyed during October and played no further role in the fighting. This left the division with only one of its three original brigades.

HQ 4th Artillery Brigade was placed in charge of a scratch force at Tawang: 1st Sikh and 4th Garwhal Rifles, plus 13th Dogra from 62nd Infantry Brigade. It also had the 2nd (Derajat) and 7th (Bengal) Mountain Batteries from 22nd Mountain Regiment and 97th Field and 114th Heavy Mortar Batteries. This force was dissolved when Tawang fell and the artillery brigade HQ joined the division HQ.

<u>5th Infantry Brigade</u> (Brig G.S. Gill) was the only remaining original brigade from the division, and was understrength.

- 1/4 Gorkha Rifles
- 2nd J&K Rifles
- section, 6th Mahar Machine Gun

48th Infantry Brigade (Brig Gurbax Singh) was part of 17th Infantry Division at Ambala. (The 17th had been raised to replace the 4th when the latter went to the NEFA.) It left Ambala on October 23rd, a day after the PLA opened its offensive, and by October 28th had concentrated at Misamari, the railhead for Bombdila. On November 6th, it reached Bomdila. At Bomdila, 4th Sikh LI was detached to Se La as part of 62nd Infantry Brigade. 1st Madras replaced it coming from Nagaland.

5th Guards
1st Sikh LI
1st Madras

Artillery support for the brigade at Bomdila was provided by RHQ 22nd Mountain Regiment, in command of its own 2nd (Derajat) and 7th (Bengal) Mountain Batteries, 88th Field Battery (6th Field Regiment), and a troop of 135th Heavy Mortar Battery.

62nd Infantry Brigade (Brig Hoishiar Singh, killed in action during the retreat) was stationed at Ramgarh as part of 20th Infantry Division. It left for Tezpur (HQ IV Corps) on 15-16 September with 4th Sikh, 4th Garhwal Rifles, and 2/8 Gorkha Rifles. At Jorhat, 2/8th GR was taken away for 5th Infantry Brigade and 4th Sikhs was taken away for 11th Infantry Brigade. On 25 October, HQ 62nd Infantry Brigade moved to Se La, and 1st Sikh was placed under its command. This battalion had left the ill-fated 7th Infantry Brigade on normal rotation. 4th Sikh LI from 48th Infantry Brigade and 2nd Sikh LI joined the brigade at Se La.

4th Garhwal Rifles
1st Sikh LI
2nd Sikh LI
4th Sikh LI
13th Dogra

65th Infantry Brigade (Brig G.M. Saeed, replaced by Brig A.S. Cheema) was at Hyderabad in southern India and left for Siliguri (XXXIII Corps) on 14-15 October. The destination was changed to Misamari. It arrived there 23 October with only two battalions. It then moved to Dirang Dzong along with division HQ.

4th Rajput[329]
19th Maratha LI

---

[329] Arrived with just 8 officers, 15 JCOs, and 575 ORs, roughly 2/3 of their authorized strength.

<u>67th Infantry Brigade</u> (Brig M. Chatterjee) started arriving at Bomdila just hours before a badly depleted 48th Infantry Brigade was overrun. A reinforcement from another division.

3rd J&K Rifles
5/5 Gorkha Rifles
6/8 Gorkha Rifles

[This appendix is an edited version of four documents: Indian 114 Infantry Brigade at the Battle of Chushul, 1962; India 1962: 11th Infantry Brigade at the Battle of Walong; India 7th Infantry Brigade at the Battle of the Namkachu 1962; Ravi Rikhye & Dave Sandhu, India 1962: 4th Infantry Division at the Battle of Bomdila; and Maj Gen (Retd) SV Thapliyal {former GOC 3rd Infantry Division}, "Battle of Eastern Ladakh: 1962 Sino-Indian Conflict." The Regiment of Artillery official history was used to improve the information on that arm.]

Appendix K: Orders of Battle 1965.

Rann of Kutch April 1965

The Rann of Kutch initially came under HQ Gujarat and Maharashtra Area. In April, a separate Kilo Force was created, and on April 17, 1965, it was renamed as Kilo Sector.

HQ Gujarat and Maharashtra Area
- 2nd Grenadiers
- 11th Field Regiment
- 1673rd Field Battery

112th Infantry Brigade
- 7th Grenadiers
- 5th Rajputana Rifles

HQ Kilo Sector
31st Infantry Brigade
- 1st Mahar
- 2nd Sikh Light Infantry
- 17th Rajputana Rifles
- two companies State Reserve Police (lightly armed)

50th (Independent) Parachute Brigade
- 2nd Parachute
- 3rd Parachute
- 4th Parachute
- 17th Parachute Field Regiment

Western Command May 1965

I Corps
- 14th Infantry Division

XI Corps
- 15th Infantry Division (HQ Amritsar)
- 4th Mountain Division (HQ Fazilka)
- 7th Infantry Division (HQ Bhikiwind)
- 2nd (I) Armoured Brigade

XV Corps

3rd Infantry Division

70th Infantry Brigade
- 2nd Assam
- 5th Garhwal Rifles
- 14th Rajputana Rifles
- 17th Punjab
- A/Ladakh Scouts

114th Infantry Brigade
- 1st Assam
- 2nd Jat
- 3rd Kumoan
- 2/3 GR
- 6th Bihar
- 7th J&K Rifles
- C and H/ Ladakh Scouts

163rd Infantry Brigade

Division Artillery Brigade
- 32nd Light Regiment [to 121st (I) Infantry Brigade]
- 43rd Field Regiment
- 62nd Field Regiment
- 63rd Field Regiment

19th Infantry Division

68th Infantry Brigade <initially in corps reserve; independent brigade>
- 1st Parachute
- 19th Punjab
- 4th Rajput
- 6th J&K Militia

104th Infantry Brigade
- 1st Sikh
- 2nd Rajput
- 4th Kumaon
- 8th Kumaon
- 3/8 GR

161st Infantry Brigade
- 7th Maratha LI
- 20th Maratha LI
- 6th Dogra
- 4th Sikh LI
- 6th Bihar
- 7th Bihar

[19th Infantry Division]
268th Infantry Brigade
- 6th Guards
- 3rd Sikh
- 3rd J&K Rifles
- 2nd J&K Militia
- 13th J&K Militia

7th Field Regiment
164th Field Regiment
37th Light Regiment
Two composite mountain batteries
One medium battery

25th Infantry Division
2nd Sikh
62nd Mountain Brigade [reinforcement, not part of the division]
- 2nd Dogra
- 14th Kumaon
- 4/5 GR
- 3/11 GR
- 11th J&K Militia

80th Infantry Brigade
- 1st Madras
- 5th Sikh LI
- 2nd Bihar
- 4/3 GR
- 4/8 GR
- 9th J&K Militia (- one coy)

93rd Infantry Brigade
- 7th Madras
- 8th Grenadiers
- 3rd Rajputana Rifles
- 3rd Rajput
- 7th Sikh
- 3rd Dogra

120th Infantry Brigade
- 22nd Maratha LI
- 14th Jat
- 2nd Garhwal Rifles
- 10th Mahar

[25th Infantry Division]
25th Division Artillery Brigade
- 23rd Composite Mountain Regiment <from XV Corps Artillery Brigade>
- 52nd Composite Mountain Regiment (-two batteries)
- 42nd Field Regiment
- 169th Field Regiment
- 31st Light Regiment
- one section 39th Medium Regiment
- 163rd Field Regiment [attached from 26th Infantry Division, on call]

26th Infantry Division
19th Infantry Brigade
- 14th Dogra
- 8th J&K Rifles
- 2/1 GR

162nd Infantry Brigade
- 6th Jat
- 7th Jat
- 1st Sikh LI

168th Infantry Brigade
- 9th Mahar
- 5/4 GR

Armour
- 18th Cavalry
- 62nd Cavalry

13th Field Regiment
168th Field Regiment
38th Medium Regiment <from XV Corps Artillery Brigade>
126th Divisional Locating Battery

SRI Force[330]
163rd Infantry Brigade (ex 3rd Infantry Division)[331]
- 1st Maratha LI
- 2/9 GR

HQ 31 ComZ Sub Area
- 8th J&K Militia (- one coy)

---

[330] Established to protect Srinagar area from infiltrators while the corps' infantry divisions were busy on the border.
[331] Composition per the official history. Rikhye and Sandhu show 1st and 6th Guards and 6th Rajput, although 6th Guards is shown in 268th Infantry Brigade by both sources used.

[SRI Force]
HQ J&K Militia
12th J&K Militia (- two coys)

121st Infantry Brigade Group
1st Guards
17th Punjab
1st J&K Militia
Two coys 12th J&K Militia
85th Light Regiment (- one battery)
32nd Light Regiment (ex 3rd Infantry Division)

191st Infantry Brigade Group
9th Punjab
6th Rajput
6th Sikh LI
3rd Mahar
3rd J&K Militia
15th Kumaon [available for 26th Inf Div on 6 hours notice]
B Sqn 20th Lancers
14th Field Regiment
39th Medium Regiment (- one battery and one section)
85th Light Battery

squadron 21st CIH (less one troop)

25th LAA Regiment (- one bty)

HQ XV Corps Artillery Brigade
23rd Composite Mountain Regiment (Pack)—with 25th Infantry Division
52nd Composite Mountain Regiment (Pack)
38th Medium Regiment (- one battery)—with 26th Infantry Division
39th Medium Regiment (- one troop)
27th LAA Regiment
No 2 AOP Flight

41st Mountain Brigade [Corps Reserve]
3rd Kumaon
6/5 GR
1/8 GR

Command Reserve

1st Armoured Division
- 1st Armoured Brigade
- 43rd Lorried Infantry Brigade

28th Infantry Brigade <later moved Pathankot to Damana, under XV Corps>
- 2nd Grenadiers
- 5/8 GR
- 1/1 GR
- 161st Field Regiment

67th Infantry Brigade

XI Corps August 1965

XI Corps

4th Mountain Division
9th Horse
7th Mountain Brigade
- 4th Grenadiers
- 7th Grenadiers

33rd Mountain Brigade
62nd Mountain Brigade
- 1/9 GR
- 18th Rajputana Rifles
- 9th J&K Rifles
- 13th Dogra

7th Infantry Division
48th Infantry Brigade
65th Infantry Brigade
- 17th Rajput
- 4th Sikh
- 9th Madras
- 16th Punjab

67th Infantry Brigade

15th Infantry Division <newly raised>
38th Infantry Brigade
    1st Jat
    1/3 GR
    3rd Garhwal Rifles
54th Infantry Brigade
    13th Punjab
    3rd Jat
    15th Dogra

29th Infantry Brigade
    2nd Madras
    2nd Raj Rifles
    1/5 GR

57th Infantry Brigade
    included 61st Cavalry [horsed]

Corps Reserve
2nd (I) Armoured Brigade
    3rd Cavalry
    7th Cavalry
    8th Cavalry
    9th Horse ?? detached
96th Infantry Brigade <detached from 15th Inf Div; returned Sep>
    6th Kumaon
    16th Dogra
    7th Punjab
50th (I) Parachute Brigade arrived 10 Sep 1965
    2nd Para
    3rd Para
    6th Para

23rd Mountain Division (less one brigade), in Assam, was ordered to move west but arrived too late to play any role in the September fighting.

Sialkot Sector September 1965

I Corps

I Corps HQ was raised in mid May 1965 and arrived at Kaluchack by 4 September 1965. None of the assigned formations had previously served under it.

1st Armoured Division

1st Armoured Brigade
- 4th Horse [Centurions]
- 16th Cavalry [Centurions]
- 17th Horse [Centurions]
- 9th Dogra

43rd Lorried Infantry Brigade
- 5th Jat
- 5/9 GR
- 8th Garhwal Rifles

2nd Lancers [Shermans] and 62nd Cavalry u/c for operations

1st Artillery Brigade[332]

35th Infantry Brigade later u/c of division, then to 6th Mountain Division

6th Mountain Division[333]

69th Mountain Brigade
- 3rd Madras
- 4th Madras
- 9th Kumaon

99th Mountain Brigade
- 6th Garhwal Rifles
- 2/5 GR
- 4th Rajputana Rifles

35th Infantry Brigade later u/c after leaving 1st Armd Div

14th Infantry Division <in process of raising>

35th Infantry Brigade <detached to 1st Armoured, then 6th Mountain Divisions>

58th Infantry Brigade
- 14th Rajput
- 4th J&K Rifles
- 3/1 GR

116th Infantry Brigade <joined Aug 1965>
- 5th Rajputana Rifles, later detached
- 5/5 GR
- 18th Madras

---

[332] Two SP field regiments, one medium regiment, one light AA regiments.

[333] This division, with two brigades, was raised in March 1963 and had been serving on the Himalayan border before transfer to the plains around Sialkot.

26th Infantry Division
162nd Infantry Brigade
- 6th Jat
- 1st Sikh LI

168th Infantry Brigade
- 2/1 GR
- 4/4 GR
- 8th J&K Rifles

52nd Mountain Brigade added after ops started
- 5/11 GR
- 10th Mahar
- 1st Madras

XI Corps September 1965

XI Corps (Lt Gen J.S. Dhillion)

2nd (Independent) Armored Brigade (Brig T.K. Theograj)[334]
- 3rd Cavalry [Centurions]
- 7th Cavalry [PT-76]
- 8th Cavalry [AMX-13]
- 1st (SP) Field Arillery [Sextons[335]]

Corps Artillery
- 60th Heavy Regiment [7.2 inch]
- 20th Locating Regiment

Patti, corps reserve
- Three unidentified infantry battalions

Dera Baba Nanak sector

29th Infantry Brigade (Brig. Pritam Singh)
- 2nd Rajputana Rifles
- 1/5 Gorkha Rifles
- B Squadron, 14th Horse
- 5th Field Regiment
- 16th Bn, Punjab Armed Police (PAP)

---

[334] While brigade was a corps reserve, its motor battalion (1st Dogra) and all or part of its armour were scattered to other formations. Note that every regiment had a different type of tank, with two (7th and 8th) equipped with light tanks.
[335] World War II vehicle: 25-pounder gun on a Canadian Ram tank chassis (similar to Sherman).

In mid-September 2nd Rajputana Rifles and 16th PAP were put in charge of this sector and the rest of the brigade was pulled out to become a corps reserve at Bhikkiwind.

Atari-Dograi axis

15th Infantry Division (Maj Gen. Niranjan Prasad; Maj Gen. Mohinder Singh from 9 September]
1st Horse
14th Horse [Sherman V]
54th Infantry Brigade (Brig M.S. Rikh, wounded; Brig. Niranjan Singh wef 12 September)
- 3rd Jat
- 13th Punjab
- 15th Dogra

38th Infantry Brigade (Brig Pathak, Brig. U.K. Gupta wef 13 September)
- 1st Jat
- 3rd Garhwal Rifles
- 1/3 Gorkha Rifles

96th Infantry Brigade (Brig Malhotra)
- 6th Kumaon
- 7th Punjab
- 16th Dogra

50th (Independent) Parachute Brigade (Brig Nambiar) – arrived 10 September
- 2nd Parachute
- 3rd Parachute
- 6th Parachute
- 17th Parachute Field Regiment
- 411th Parachute Field Company

41st Mountain Brigade (Brig M.R. Rajwade) – arrived 12 September; left 19 September for 4th Mountain Division[336]
- 1/8 Gorkha Rifles
- 6th Rajput
- 9th Mahar

7th Mountain Brigade – arrived 19 September from 4th Mountain Division

---

[336] The brigade, when the reserve for XV Corps, originally had 1/8 Gorkha Rifles, 3rd Kumaon, and 6/5 Gorkha Rifles. When it shifted to Akhnur, it took only the first of the three battalions with it. It was given 6th Rajput from 163rd Infantry Brigade (Sri Force, ex- 3rd Infantry Division, and 9th Mahar from 26th Infantry Division. We believe that it kept these battalions when it went to XI Corps.

Rajatal Force – to cover gap between 15th and 7th Infantry Divisions
1st Dogra (less two companies) [2nd Armoured Brigade's motor battalion]
Fighting Troop 2nd Armoured Brigade [two Shermans]
C Squadron, 3rd Cavalry (less HQ and two troops) [six Centurions]
14 September replaced by Bharat Force
1st Dogra (less two companies)
1st Horse
14th Horse
B Squadron, 7th Cavalry
A Squadron, 8th Cavalry
troop, 3rd Cavalry

Khalra-Barki axis

7th Infantry Division (Maj Gen. S.K. Sibbal)
Central India Horse
19th Rajput
29th Infantry Brigade: detached to Dera Baba Nanak sector, north of 15th Infantry Division
48th Infantry Brigade (Brig Shahane, replaced by Brig Piara Singh)
3rd Guards
6/8 Gorkha Rifles
65th Infantry Brigade (Brig L. Farras)
4th Sikh: detached to 4th Mountain Division September 11
9th Madras
16th Punjab[337]

Khem Karan sector

4th Mountain Division (Maj.-Gen. Gurbakhsh Singh)
9th (Deccan) Horse[338] [Sherman IV/V]
7th Mountain Brigade (Brig Sidhu)
4th Grenadiers
7th Grenadiers
9th Jammu and Kashmir Rifles

---

[337] Arrived from Northeast without vehicles, RCL, or radio sets; vehicles arrived at war's end. The battalion had one map of the area.
[338] The CO, Lt Col A.S. Vaidya, was later Chief of the Army Staff.

[4th Mountain Division]
62nd Mountain Brigade
1/9 Gorkha Rifles
13th Dogra
18th Rajputana Rifles
33rd Mountain Brigade was away in another sector
40th Medium Regiment operated in support of the division

Fazilka sector

67th (Independent) Infantry Brigade Group (Brig Bant Singh)
2nd Maratha Light Infantry
3/9 Gorkha Rifles
14th Punjab
61st Cavalry [horsed]
Independent Squadron, 14th Horse
144th Field Artillery Regiment (Territorial Army)
Armed Police[339]
Punjab Armed Police Battalion, Firozpur
Punjab Armed Police Battalion, Madot
Punjab Armed Police Battalion, Jalalabad
Punjab Armed Police Battalion, Fazilka
Rajasthan Armed Police Battalion, Ganganager
Rajasthan Armed Police Battalion, Raisingh Nager

The brigade arrived in its operational area with only one of its own battalions, other units having been shifted out. Of the units, only one infantry battalion had recent familiarity with the area. Units were under strength as personnel were on leave. Concentrated by 5 September, a day before XI Corps launched its offensive, the artillery regiment did not get its first line ammunition until 7 September. The Brigade had no lines of small arms ammunition till that day, and was still awaiting arrival of essential stores. One battalion was deployed at Ferozepur, to the north of the brigade.

I Corps, Operation Neptune, September 1965

HQ I Corps (Lt General P.O. Dunn)

Raised recently at Jhansi as a spare HQ, without assigned troops, to be sent where needed. Arrived 4 September 1965, two days ahead of the offensive it

---

[339] The state armed police were equipped with bolt-action rifles.

was to command. General Dunn met his subordinate commanders for the first time that day.

I Corps Artillery Brigade
- 24th Medium Regiment (ex XXXIII Corps)
- 38th Medium Regiment
- 71st Medium Regiment
- 73rd Composite Bty from 20th Locating Regiment

26th Infantry Division (Maj Gen M.L. Thapan) (formerly under XV Corps, given to I Corps 4 September 1965 for Operational Nepal)
18th Cavalry [Shermans] replacing 2nd Lancers on rotation, division tank regiment
62nd Cavalry, also a division tank regiment, sent to 1st Armored Division
19th Infantry Brigade (Brig Aban Naidu) (all battalions detached for Ablaze)
162nd Infantry Brigade (Brig R.S. Sheoran) (one battalion detached for Ablaze)
- 1st Sikh Light Infantry
- 6th Jats
- 7th Jats
- C Squadron, 18th Cavalry

168th Infantry Brigade (Brig A.K. Luthera)
- 2/1 Gorkha Rifles
- 2/4 Gorkha Rifles
- 8th Jammu and Kashmir Rifles
- A Squadron,18th Cavalry
- 168th Field Regiment

1st Armoured Division (Maj Gen R.S. Sparrow)
4th Horse (Hodson's) [Centurions] division reserve, with one motor company
62nd Cavalry [Shermans} (3rd Cavalry detached to XI Corps)
1st Armoured Brigade (Brig K.K. Singh)[340]
- 16th Cavalry [Centurions]
- 17th Horse (Poona) [Centurions]
- 9th Dogra (motor battalion)

43rd Lorried Infantry Brigade (Brig H.S. Dhillon)
- 2nd Lancers [Shermans]
- 5th Jats
- 8th Garwahl Rifles
- 5/9 Gorkha Rifles

---

[340] Would command I Corps in 1971.

[1st Armoured Division]
1st Division Artillery Brigade (Brig O.P. Malhotra)
- 2nd Field (SP) Regiment
- 101st Field (SP) Regiment
- 29th Air Defence Regiment [joined after operation started]

6th Mountain Division (Maj.-General S.K. Korla)[341]
69th Mountain Brigade (Brigadier Eric Vas)
- 3rd Madras
- 4th Madras
- 9th Kumaon

99th Mountain Brigade
- 4th Rajputana Rifles
- 6th Garhwal
- 2/5 Gorkha Rifles (Frontier Force)

6th Mountain Artillery Brigade
- Included 93rd Mountain Composite Regiment and 86th Light Regiment

14th Infantry Division[342] (Maj Gen R.K. Ranjit Singh)
58th Infantry Brigade (detached to Pathankot in lieu of 28th Infantry Brigade which reinforced Chaamb)
35th Infantry Brigade (sent to 6th Mountain Division as reserve)[343]
116th Infantry Brigade
- 5th Rajputana Rifles
- 5/5 Gorkha Rifles-
- 18th Madras

10th Infantry Division, Battle for Chaamb, September 1965

HQ XV Corps (Lt Gen K.S. Katoch) at Srinager was in overall command. It was responsible for 950 km of border, of which 750 km was with Pakistan.

HQ 10th Infantry Division (Maj Gen D.B. Chopra) was a new forming HQ with 30% of its establishment, transferred from Hyderabad/Secunderabad as war with Pakistan became imminent. The division was initially given 191st Infantry Brigade Group and 80th Infantry Brigade from 25th Infantry Division, thus shortening that division's line.

---

[341] Raised 26 March 1963, this was the division's first time in operational area, and it had only two brigades.
[342] Still forming and was not functional as a division. This was its first time in the area. 35th and 58th Infantry Brigades were deployed on the UP-Tibet border.
[343] 166th Field Regiment detached to support 35th Infantry Brigade.

191st Infantry Brigade Group was on counterinsurgency duty in the Chaamb-Jaurian area against Pakistani infiltrators. Its commander, Brig Masters, had been killed on 15 August and Brig M.M. Singh was arriving to take over. On 16 August it was directly under HQ XV Corps and it sector ran to 115 kilometers screened by 66 border posts, manned by armed police and regular troops. The brigade had two infantry battalions (3rd J&K Militia and 3rd Mahar) along with 3rd Punjab Armed Police (entirely at border posts). When the Pakistani 12th Infantry Division launched an offensive against Chaamb on 1 September, XV Corps sent reinforcements.

191st Infantry Brigade Group 31 August-1 September 1965
- 3rd J&K Militia
- 3rd Mahar
- 9th Punjab
- 6th Rajput (arriving from 163rd Infantry Brigade, 3rd Infantry Division, Leh)
- 6th Sikh Light Infantry (from 1 September)
- 15th Kumaon (from 1 September)
- B Squadron, 20th Lancers [AMX-13 light tanks]
- 14th Field Regiment
- 85th Light Battery
- 39th Medium Regiment (- one battery and one section)
- 3rd Punjab Armed Police

HQ 10th Infantry Division arrived at Akhnur 2-5 September 1965 and assumed control.

191st Infantry Brigade Group (Brig M.M. Singh)

Akhnur
- 15th Kumaon
- 6th Sikh Light Infantry
- 6th Rajput
- 6/5th Gorkha Rifles
- remnants 3rd Punjab Armed Police
- elements 14th Field Regiment

Kalidhar/Sundarbani [Hill subsector to the NWW of Chaamb]
- 3rd Mahar
- 3rd Jammu & Kashmir Militia
- 9th Punjab
- one troop 123rd Medium Regiment

41st Mountain Brigade (Brig Rajwade) arrived 2 September from corps reserve, where it has been inducted from outside the theatre during the anti-infiltrator operations. It was deployed at Jaurian-Troti (behind – to the NNE – of Chaamb, protecting the route to Akhnur).

- 9th Mahar
- 1/8 Gorkha Rifles
- 161st Field Regiment
- 123rd Medium Regiment (minus one battery and the troop at Sundarbani)

28th Infantry Brigade (Brig Pritpal Singh) from Pathankot, went into corps reserve to replace 41st Mountain Brigade, but was also immediately deployed to 10th Infantry Division and located at Damana/Fatwal Ridge.

- 1/1 Gorkha Rifles
- 2nd Grenadiers
- 5/8 Gorkha Rifles

52nd Mountain Brigade arrived 11September XI Corps, to which it had been sent earlier as a reinforcement from outside the theatre.

- 1st Madras
- 10th Madras
- 5/11 Gorkha Rifles

11th Infantry Division in Operation Barrel

Before 1965, leave alone the deep desert, anything south of Ganganager was regarded as too remote for military action. However, the post-1962 War buildup included two divisions (11th and 12th) for Southern Command. By the 1965 war with Pakistan, only the 11th had been raised and it was incomplete. The division's 30th Infantry Brigade fought most of the war in the desert; with no other action to divert the division commander (Maj Gen N.C. Rawlley)or GOC Southern Command (Lt Gen Moti Sagar), both focused on this one brigadier and his brigade.

30th Infantry Brigade (Brig J.C. Guha)

- 1st Garhwal
- 3rd Guards
- 5th Maratha Light Infantry
- 17th Madras arrived 15 September
- D Squadron, 13th Grenadiers [mounted on camels]
- 3rd (I) Armoured Squadron (-one troop) [Shermans] arrived 7 September
- 95th Mountain Composite Regiment left 13 September
- 1673rd Field Battery, 167th Field Regiment
- 85th Field Company

[30th Infantry Brigade]

6th Bn, Rajasthan Armed Constabulary (put under command 11 September)

7th Bn, Rajasthan Armed Constabulary (put under command 11 September)

On 21 September, the newly raised HQ 85th Infantry Brigade arrived from Ahmedabad. Forces were split between the two brigades:

85th Infantry Brigade (Brig H.N. Summanwar)

5th Maratha LI (left the brigade shortly thereafter)
17th Madras
1673rd Field Battery [no prime movers]
3rd (I) Armoured Squadron (- two troops)

30th Infantry Brigade

1st Garhwal
3rd Guards
two troops 3rd (I) Armoured Squadron
an artillery battery (?)

[This appendix has been compiled initially from information in various chapters of the official history—B. C. Chakravorty, *History of the Indo-Pak War, 1965*—which varies in the level of detail provided. Much additional information came from the following documents: Ravi Rikhye & Dave Sandhu, Indian XI Corps: Orbat September 1965 (2002); Ravi Rikhye, Indian 67th Brigade at the Battle of Fazilka 1965 (2002); Agha Humanyun Amin et al, The Battle of Assal Uttar: Pakistan and India 1965 (2002); Ravi Rikhye, Indian Army I Corps, September 1965, Operation Nepal (2002); Ravi Rikhye & Dave Sandhu, Indian 10th Division at the Battle for Chaamb, 1965 (2002); Ravi Rikhye, Indian 11th Infantry Division in Operation Barrel, 1965 (2002); Ravi Rikhye and David Sandhu, Indian XV Corps, Kashmir 1965 (2002). The history of the Regiment of Artillery provided some additional information.]

Appendix L: Indian Army December 1971

Information is as of 3 December 1971 unless otherwise noted.

Chief of the Army Staff: General S. H. F. J. "Sam" Manekshaw

Troops Committed Against East Pakistan.

EASTERN COMMAND
(Lt Gen Jagjit Singh Aurora)

312th Independent Air Defence Brigade
342nd Air Defence Brigade

II Corps (Lt Gen T. N. "Tappy" Raina)[344]

58 Corps Engineer Regiment
203 Army Engineer Regiment
268 Army Engineer Regiment

4th Mountain Division (Maj Gen Mohinder Singh Barar)
A squadron, 45th Cavalry [PT-76]
7th Mountain Brigade (Brig Zail Singh)
- 22nd Rajput
- 5th Jat
- Naga Regiment

41st Mountain Brigade (Brig A. E. "Tony" Michigan)
- 5th Guards
- 9th Dogra
- 5/1 Gorkha Rifles

62nd Mountain Brigade (Brig Rajendra Nath)
- 5th Maratha Light Infantry
- 4th Sikh Light Infantry
- 2/9 Gorkha Rifles

4th Mountain Artillery Brigade
- 22nd Mountain Regiment [76mm]
- 194th Mountain Regiment [76mm]
- 7th Field Regiment [25 pounder]

---

[344] General Raina had been OC 114th Infantry Brigade in 1962, and was later Chief of the Army Staff.

[4th Mountain Division
[4th Mountain Artillery Brigade]
    181st Light Regiment [120mm mortar]
    battery, 78th Medium Regiment [130mm]
63 Engineer Regiment

9th Infantry Division (Maj Gen Dalbir Singh)
45th Cavalry [PT-76] (A Squadron detached to 4th Mountain Division)
B Squadron, 63rd Cavalry [T-55]
32nd Infantry Brigade (Brig M. Tewari)
    7th Punjab [mechanised: SKOTs]
    8th Madras
    13th Dogra
42nd Infantry Brigade (Brig J. S. Gharaya > Brig K. L. Kochar)
    14th Punjab
    19th Maratha Light Infantry
    2nd Sikh Light Infantry
350th Infantry Brigade (Brig H. S. Sandhu)
    26th Madras
    4th Sikh
    1st J&K Rifles
9th Artillery Brigade
    6th Field Regiment [25 pounder]
    14th Field Regiment [25 pounder]
    67th Light Regiment [120mm mortar]
    78th Medium Regiment (less one battery) [130mm]
    264th SBRL Increment (Grad P rocket launcher)
    201st Division Locating Battery
102 Engineer Regiment

IV Corps (Lt Gen Sagat Singh)

4 Engineer Regiment
62 Engineer Regiment

8th Mountain Division (Maj Gen K. V. Krishna Rao)
5th ad hoc Ind Armoured Squadron [Ferret scout cars]
84 BSF
85 BSF
93 BSF
104 BSF

[8th Mountain Division]
59th Mountain Brigade (Brig C. A. "Bunty" Quinn)
9th Guards
6th Rajput
4/5 Gorkha Rifles
1st East Bengal Regiment[345]
81st Mountain Brigade (Brig Raja C. V. Apte)
3rd Punjab
4th Kumaon
10th Mahar
8th East Bengal Regiment
108 Engineer Regiment
Echo Sector (Brig M. B. Wadke)
5/5 Gorkha Rifles
86 BSF
3rd East Bengal Regiment
BSF Sector (Brig Kulwant Singh)
87 BSF

23rd Mountain Division (Maj Gen R. D. "Rocky" Hira)
1st Ind Armoured. Squadron [PT-76]
61st Mountain Brigade/57th Mountain Division (Brig K. P. "Tom" Pande)
7th Rajputana Rifles
2nd Jat
12th Kumaon
83rd Mountain Brigade (Brig Bhupinder S. Sandhu)
2nd Rajput
3rd Dogra
8th Bihar
9th East Bengal Regiment
181st Mountain Brigade (Brig Y. P. "Yash" Bakshi)
6th Jat
9th Kumaon
14th Kumaon
301st Mountain Brigade (Brig Harinder Singh Sohdi)
14th Jat
3rd Kumaon
1/11 Gorkha Rifles

---

[345] The East Bengal Regiment was part of the Pakistan Army, and its battalions either revolted or were interned. The 1st and 8th East Bengal were also nominally grouped as the 1st East Bengal Brigade under control of the division.

[23rd Mountain Division]
Kilo Force (Brig Anand Saroop)
31st Jat
32nd Mahar
4th East Bengal Regiment
10th East Bengal Regiment
3 Engineer Regiment

57th Mountain Division (Maj Gen Ben F. Gonsalves)
5th Ind Armoured Squadon [PT-76]
91 BSF
61st Mountain Brigade (Brig K. P. "Tom" Pande) (detached to 23rd Division)
7th Rajputana Rifles
2nd Jat
12th Kumaon
73rd Mountain Brigade (Brig Tuli)
14th Guards
19th Punjab
19th Rajputana Rifles
311th Mountain Brigade (Brig R. N. Mishra)
4th Guards
18th Rajput
10th Bihar (detached to Sierra Force)
57th Mountain Artillery Brigade
59th Mountain Regiment
65th Mountain Regiment
197th Mountain Regiment
82nd Light Regiment
Sierra Force
10th Bihar
2nd East Bengal Regiment
11th East Bengal Regiment
15 Engineer Regiment

Special Frontier Force (Maj Gen Sujan Singh Uban)

XXXIII Corps (Lt Gen Mohan L. Thapan)

HQ Brigadier Armour XXXIII Corps (Brig Gurcharn Singh Sandhu)
63rd Cavalry [T-55] (B Squadron detached to 9th Division)
69th Armoured [PT-76]

471 Engineer Brigade
- 13 Engineer Regiment
- 52 Engineer Regiment
- 111 Engineer Regiment
- 235 Army Engineer Regiment

6th Mountain Division (Maj Gen. P. C. Reddy) (initially Army HQ reserve for Bhutan)

9th Mountain Brigade (Brig Tirath Verma)
- 5th Grenadiers (detached to 71st Infantry Brigade on 14 December)
- 4th Rajput
- 12th Garhwal Rifles

99th Mountain Brigade
- 18th Sikh
- 11th Garhwal Rifles
- 16th Kumaon

20th Mountain Division (Maj Gen Lachman Singh Lehl)

66th Mountain Brigade (Brig G. S. Sharma)
- 1st Guards
- 6th Guards
- 17th Kumaon

165th Mountain Brigade (Brig Raghuvir S. Pannu)
- 20th Maratha Light Infantry [mechanized: SKOTs]
- 16th Rajput
- 6th Assam

202nd Mountain Brigade (Brig Farhat P. Bhatty)
- 8th Guards
- 22nd Maratha Light Infantry
- 5th Garhwal Rifles

340th Mountain Brigade Group (Brig Joginder Singh Bakshi)
- 4th Madras
- 2/5 Gorkha Rifles
- 5/11 Gorkha Rifles

52 Engineer Regiment (?)[346]

71st Mountain Brigade/8th Mountain Division (Brig Pran Nath Kathpalia) (under XXXIII Corps initially, under 6th Mountain Division as of 5 December)
- D Squadron (ad hoc), 69 Cavalry [PT-76]
- 7th Maratha Light Infantry
- 12th Rajputana Rifles

---

[346] The 13th Engineer Regiment also operated in the area of this division.

[71st Mountain Brigade]

21st Rajput
12th Garhwal Rifles
107th Infantry Battalion (TA)
73 BSF
75 BSF
78 BSF
82 BSF
103 BSF
5th Grenadiers/9th Mountain Brigade (from 14 December)

50th (I) Parachute Brigade (Brig Mathew Thomas)[347]

2nd Para
7th Para
8th Para

Bengal Area (Maj Gen P. Chowdry)

1/3 Gorkha Rifles (later to Romeo Force)
two companies 11th Bihar (later to Romeo Force)

Romeo Force (Brig S. S. Rai)

1/3 Gorkha Rifles
two companies 11th Bihar

101 Communications Zone (Maj Gen Gurbax Singh Gill > Maj Gen Gandharva C. Nagra)

95th Mountain Brigade/8th Mountain Division (Brig Hardev Singh Kler)

13th Guards
1st Maratha Light Infantry
13th Rajputana Rifles
5/5 Gorkha Rifles (detached to Echo Force)
56th Mountain Regiment [76mm]

5th Mountain Brigade/2nd Mountain Division (released for employment on 8 December)

2nd Rajput
2nd Dogra
2nd Garhwal Rifles

---

[347] Elements came under command II Corps 6-10 December 1971 and then the brigade shifted to Western Command.

[101 Communications Zone
167th Mountain Brigade/8th Mountain Division (Brig Adi A. Irani) (released for employment on 8 December)
6th Sikh Light Infantry
7th Bihar
10th Jammu and Kashmir Rifles
FJ Sector (Brig Sant "Baba" Singh)
6th Bihar/167th Mountain Brigade
83 BSF

Troops on the China Border.

XXXIII Corps (Rear HQ under Corps Chief of Staff Maj Gen J. S. Nakai)

17th Mountain Division

27th Mountain Division

303rd Mountain Brigade/8th Mountain Division

164th Mountain Brigade
9th Grenadiers
1st Assam
2/1 Gorkha Rifles

IV Corps (Rear HQ under Corps Chief of Staff Maj Gen O. P. Malhotra)

2nd Mountain Division (Maj Gen Gandharva C. Nagra)
5th Mountain Brigade detached on 8 December

5th Mountain Division
167th Mountain Brigade detached on 8 December

Uttar Pradesh/Tibet Border
one brigade of 6th Mountain Division

Troops on Counterinsurgency Duty.

Nagaland and Manipur (Maj Gen Jagjit Singh)
56th Mountain Brigade/8th Mountain Division
Assam Rifles

Mizo Hills Range (regular battalions later assigned to Kilo Force)
- 31st Jat
- 14th Mahar (formerly 31st Mahar)
- Assam Rifles
- BSF

BSF Troops on the East Pakistan Border

in Hilli (301 Brigade) Sector
- 70 BSF
- 74 BSF
- 77 BSF

in 71st Brigade Sector
- 70 BSF
- 74 BSF
- 77 BSF

Forces in the West

WESTERN COMMAND
(Lt Gen K. P. Candeth)

12th Guards [SS-11 ATGM]
11th Sikh Light Infantry on airfield defense
103rd Infantry Battalion (TA) on airfield defense
118th Infantry Battalion (TA) various duties in the Delhi area
124th Infantry Battalion (TA) on airfield defense
126th Infantry Battalion (TA) at Pathankot
123rd Mountain Brigade (sent west from Eastern Command on 6 December)

XV Corps (Lt Gen Sartaj Singh)
9th Paracommando

3rd Infantry Division (Maj Gen S. P. Malhotra)
20th Punjab
14th Dogra
4/4 Gorkha Rifles (C Company detached to Partapur Sector)
70th Infantry Brigade
114th Infantry Brigade

Partappur Sector (Brig Udai Singh)
D, G and K Companies, Ladakh Scouts[348]
Nubra Guards [local levy]
C Company, 4/4 Gorkha Rifles

121st Independent Infantry Brigade[349] (Brig M. L. Whig)
7th Guards
18th Punjab
5/3 Gorkha Rifles
2/11 Gorkha Rifles
9th Jammu & Kashmir Militia
13th Jammu & Kashmir Militia
87th Light Regiment
101st Field Battery, 15th Field Regiment

19th Infantry Division (Maj Gen Eustace D. D'Souza)
Gallies (or BSF) Sector (Brig Randhawa)
1st Jammu & Kashmir Militia
three BSF battalions
104th Infantry Brigade
6th Rajputana Rifles
8th Rajputana Rifles
9th Sikh
3rd Bihar
BSF battalion
161st Infantry Brigade (Brig K. K. Nanda)
8th Sikh
7th Sikh Light Infantry
4th Rajputana Rifles
5th Mahar
2nd Assam
3rd Maratha Light Infantry
two BSF battalions
268th Infantry Brigade (initially in reserve, later HQ Gulf Sector at Gulmarg)
2nd Guards
12th Grenadiers
4th Mahar

---

[348] G and K Companies were both minus a platoon. During the subsequent fighting, they were formed into a four-platoon composite company; D Company joined after the war began.
[349] 7th Guards, 18th Punjab and 2/11 GR were assigned to the brigade, while the other three battalions (per the 1971 official history) "were available in the area to support any actions." (p 305)

V Sector (Maj Gen Patankar)
- battalion from 268th Infantry Brigade?
- four or five BSF battalions
- Kilo-Gulf Sector (Brig A. J. Texeira) (Kaunrauli-Gulmarg)

25th Infantry Division (Maj Gen Kundan Singh)
3rd Jammu & Kashmir Militia
7th Mahar
93rd Infantry Brigade (Brig A. V. Natu)
- 6th Sikh
- 8th Jat
- 13th Mahar (from 33rd Infantry Brigade)
- 1/4 Gorkha Rifles
- 11th Jammu & Kashmir Militia
- 9 BSF
- 50 BSF

33rd Infantry Brigade/39th Infantry Division
- 13th Mahar

120th Infantry Brigade (Brig Hari Singh)
- 21st Punjab
- 9th Rajputana Rifles
- 14th Grenadiers
- 6/11 Gorkha Rifles

80th Infantry Brigade
- 4/9 Gorkha Rifles
- 4th Garhwal Rifles
- 11th Rajputana Rifles
- 5th Sikh Light Infantry

10th Infantry Division (Maj Gen Jaswant Singh)
9th Horse [T-54]
51 BSF
57 BSF
3rd Medium Regiment
216th Medium Regiment
28th Infantry Brigade (Brig M. V. Natu)
- 5th Rajput
- 2nd Jammu & Kashmir Rifles
- 7th Jammu & Kashmir Militia
- 8th Jammu & Kashmir Militia

191st Infantry Brigade (Brig R. K. Jasbir Singh)
- 5th Sikh
- 5th Assam

[10th Infantry Division]
[191st Infantry Brigade]
- 10th Garhwal Rifles
- 4/1 Gorkha Rifles

68th Infantry Brigade (Brig R. T. Morlin)
- 7th Kumaon
- 9th Jat
- 5/8 Gorkha Rifles
- 3/4 Gorkha Rifles (from 52nd Infantry Brigade)

52nd Infantry Brigade
- 16th Punjab
- 7th Garhwal Rifles
- 3/4 Gorkha Rifles (detached to 68th Infantry Brigade)

3rd (Independent) Armoured Brigade (Brig B. S. Irani)
- 72nd Armoured Regiment [T-55]
- 2nd Ind Armoured Squadron [AMX13]
- 8th Light Cavalry (detached)
- Central Indian Horse (detached)
- 7th Grenadiers [BTR60] (detached)

61 Engineer Regiment

26th Infantry Division (Maj Gen Z. C. "Zoru" Bakshi)
8th Light Cavalry [Vijayanta] (from 3rd Independent Armoured Brigade)
Central Indian Horse [T-55] (from 3rd Independent Armoured Brigade)
7th Grenadiers [BTR60] (from 3rd Independent Armoured Brigade)
10th Garhwal Rifles
5th Kumaon
4th Dogra
9th Rajput
19th Infantry Brigade (Brig Mohinder Singh)
- 3/5 Gorkha Rifles
- 7/11 Gorkha Rifles
- 11th Guards
- A/9th Paracommando
- squadon, 8th Light Cavalry

36th Infantry Brigade
162nd Infantry Brigade
- 3/3 Gorkha Rifles
- 6th Garhwal Rifles

107 Engineer Regiment

I Corps (Lt Gen K. K. Singh)[350]

41st Independent Artillery Brigade

416 Engineer Brigade
- 5 Engineer Regiment
- 7 Engineer Regiment
- 201 Army Engineer Regiment
- 237 Army Engineer Regiment
- 267 Army Engineer Regiment
- 31 Maintenance Task Force (from BRO)

X Sector (later assumed by HQ/39th Infantry Division)
31st Independent Artillery Brigade
323rd Infantry Brigade/39th Infantry Division
- 6/8 Gorkha Rifles
- 19th Madras

168th Infantry Brigade/26th Infantry Division
- 2/4 Gorkha Rifles
- 5th Jammu and Kashmir Rifles
- 19th Madras (detached to 323rd Infantry Brigade)

54th Infantry Division (Maj Gen W. A. G. Pinto)
6th Madras
47th Infantry Brigade (Brig A. P. Bharadwaj)
- 3rd Grenadiers
- 16th Madras
- 16th Dogra

74th Infantry Brigade (Brig Ujaggar Singh)
- 8th Grenadiers
- 6th Kumaon
- 9th Maratha Light Infantry

91st Infantry Brigade (Brig A. Handoo)
- 3rd Garhwal Rifles
- 16th Dogra
- 3/1 Gorkha Rifles

9 Engineer Regiment

---

[350] General Singh had been OC 1st Armoured Brigade in the same sector in 1965.

16th Independent Armoured Brigade (Brig Arun S. Vaidya)
    4th Horse [Centurion]
    16th Light Cavalry [Centurion]
    17th Cavalry [Centurion]
    18th Rajputana Rifles [Topas]
    90th Ind Recce Squadron [AMX-13]

39th Infantry Division (Maj Gen B. R. Prabhu)
87th Infantry Brigade (to 36th Infantry Division after 12 December)
    3/9 Gorkha Rifles
72nd Infantry Brigade/36th Infantry Division (Brig J. M. Vohra)
    1st Mahar from 115th Infantry Brigade/36th Infantry Division
    15th Grenadiers
    22nd Punjab
    3rd Sikh Light Infantry
323rd Infantry Brigade (detached to X Sector)
113 Engineer Regiment

2nd Independent Armoured Brigade (Brig R. N. Thumby)
    1st Cavalry [T-55]
    7th Light Cavalry [T-55]
    14th Cavalry [T-55]
    1st Dogra [mechanized: Topas]
    91st Ind Recce Squadron [AMX-13]

36th Infantry Division (Maj Gen Balwant Singh Ahluwalia)
6th Madras
18th Infantry Brigade (Brig Prithvi Raj)
72nd Infantry Brigade (detached to 39th Infantry Division)
115th Infantry Brigade (Brig Hriday Kaul)
    4th Grenadiers
    10th Guards
    1st Mahar (detached to 72nd Infantry Brigade with 39th Infantry Division)
104 Engineer Regiment

XI Corps (Lt Gen N. C. Rawlley)

21st Independent Artillery Brigade

474 Engineer Brigade

- 15th Infantry Division (Maj Gen B. M. Bhattacharjee)
- 66th Armoured Regiment [Vijayanta]
- 86th Infantry Brigade (Brig Gauri Shankar)
    - 71st Armoured Regiment/14th Ind Armoured Brigade [T-55]
    - 10th Dogra
    - 1/9 Gorkha Rifles
    - 4/8 Gorkha Rifles
    - 17th Rajput
    - 21 BSF
- 58th Infantry Brigade/14th Infantry Division (Brig Narinder Singh)
    - 24th Punjab
- 96th Infantry Brigade (Brig A. E. Joseph)
    - 15th Maratha Light Infantry
    - 8th Sikh Light Infantry
- 54th Infantry Brigade (Brig G. N. Sinha)
    - 2nd Sikh
    - 9th Punjab
    - 11th Grenadiers
    - 23 BSF
    - 27 BSF
- 38th Infantry Brigade
    - 16th Grenadiers
    - 4th Assam
    - 8th Garhwal Rifles

- 7th Infantry Division (Maj Gen Freemantle)
- 3rd Cavalry [Centurions]
- 5th Dogra
- 65th Infantry Brigade
    - 14th Rajput
    - 14th Jammu & Kashmir Rifles
    - 3rd Madras
- 48th Infantry Brigade (Brig Menon)
    - 6th Mahar
    - 1/5 Gorkha Rifles
    - 9th Sikh Light Infantry
- 29th Infantry Brigade
    - 9th Bihar
    - 15th Punjab (detached to 35th Infantry Brigade)
- 35th Infantry Brigade/14th Infantry Division (Brig Pran Anand)
    - 15th Punjab/29th Infantry Brigade
    - 13th Punjab
    - 15th Dogra

[7th Infantry Division]
[35th Infantry Brigade]
3rd Guards
25 BSF
31 BSF
109 Engineer Regiment

14th Infantry Division (Maj Gen Harish K. Bakshi > Maj Gen Onkar Singh Kalkat)
35th Infantry Brigade (detached to 7th Infantry Division initially)
58th Infantry Brigade (detached to 15th Infantry Division)
116th Infantry Brigade
1st Parachute
17th Madras
3/11 Gorkha Rifles (later detached to 67th Infantry Brigade)
8 Engineer Regiment

Foxtrot (F) Sector (Maj Gen Ram Singh)
70 Armoured Regt [SS-11 ATGM] (A Squadron detached to Southern Command)
67th Infantry Brigade (Brig Surjit Singh Chaudhry > Brig G. S. Reen > Brig Piara Singh)
4th Ind Armoured Squadron [Shermans]
B Squadron, 18th Cavalry, 14th Armoured Brigade [T-54]
4th Jat
3rd Assam
15th Rajput
22nd BSF
28th BSF
115th Infantry Battalion (TA) (added on 7 December)
51st Independent Parachute Brigade (Brig E. A. Thyagaraj)
squadron, 18th Cavalry,14th Armoured Brigade (T-54)
3rd Parachute
4th Parachute
11th Dogra
Juliet Sub Sector (defending Abohar along Gang Canal)
C Squadron, 18th Cavalry/14th Armoured Brigade [T-54]
19th Rajput
163rd Infantry Brigade
92nd Ind Recce Squadron [PT-76]
5th Bihar
2/8 Gorkha Rifles

[Foxtrot (F) Sector]
Abohar Fortress
112th Infantry Battalion (TA)
10 Engineer Regiment
60 Engineer Regiment
109 Engineer Regiment

Mike Force (Col P. C. Mehta > Brig Gurcharn Singh Sandhu)
18th Cavalry (- 2 sqdns) [T-54]
62nd Cavalry [T-55]
Company, 1/8 Gorkha Rifles [mechanized: Topas]

1st Armoured Division (Maj Gen Gurbachan Singh)
93 Ind Recce Squadron [AMX-13]
1st Armoured Brigade (Brig. N. S. Cheema)
2nd Lancers [Vijayanta]
65th Armd Regt [Vijayanta]
67th Armd Regt [Vijayanta]
68th Armd Regt [Vijayanta]
43rd Lorried Infantry Brigade (Brig. Ramesh Chandra)
1st Madras [Topas]
1st Jat [Topas]
1st Garhwal Rifles[Topas]
Division Artillery Brigade
two field regiments [Abbott SP 105mm]
one medium regiment [130mm]
one light AA regiment [40mm] (attached during the war)

14th Independent Armoured Brigade (Brig R. Christian)
18th Cavalry (T-54) (detached to F Sector)
62nd Cavalry (T-55) (detached to F Sector)
64th Cavalry (T-54)
70th Armoured Regiment [SS-11] (detached to F Sector)
71st Armoured Regiment [T-55] (detached to 15 Division)
1/8 Gorkha Rifles [Topas] (one company detached to M Force)
92 Ind Armoured Squadron [PT-76] (detached to F Sector)

SOUTHERN COMMAND
(Lt Gen G. G. Bewoor)

10th Para-Commando
27th Madras (later detached to Kutch Sector)
101st Infantry Battalion (TA) at Jodhpur

117th Infantry Battalion (TA) at Barmer
123rd Infantry Battalion (TA) in Rajasthan on airfield defense

270 Army Engineer Regiment

Kilo (Bikaner) Sector
- 13th Grenadiers (camels)
- 11 BSF
- 12 BSF

Jaiselmer Sector

12th Infantry Division (Maj Gen R. K. Khambatta)
20th Lancers [AMX-13]
6th Ind Armoured Squadon [T-55]
30th Infantry Brigade
- 6/5 Gorkha Rifles
- 17th Rajputana Rifles
- 9th Jammu & Kashmir Rifles

45th Infantry Brigade (Brig R. O. Kharbanda)
- 23rd Punjab
- 3rd Rajputana Rifles
- 8th Dogra
- 14 BSF
- 18 BSF (from 5/6 December)

322nd Infantry Brigade [detached 12 December]
- 4th Maratha Light Infantry
- 3rd Jat
- 13th Kumaon

56 Engineer Regiment

Barmer Sector

11th Infantry Division (Maj Gen R. D. R. Anand)
3rd Ind Armoured Squadron [T-55]
17th Grenadiers (camels)
2nd Grenadiers
17 BSF
85th Infantry Brigade (Brig Gurjeet Singh Randhawa)
- 2nd Rajputana Rifles
- 2nd Mahar
- 10th Sikh
- 10th Sikh Light Infantry

[11th Infantry Division]
31st Infantry Brigade
    15th Kumaon
    9th Madras
    18th Madras
    20th Rajput
330th Infantry Brigade
57 Engineer Regiment

Kutch Sector
    A Squadron, 70th Armoured Regt [SS-11]
    Two or three BSF battalions
    116th Infantry Battalion (TA)
    27th Madras (arrived approximately 17 December)

Bhuj
    109th Infantry Battalion (TA)

Note: Mukti Bahini. The Mukti Bahini were the liberation or freedom forces raised by the Bengalis in opposition to the Pakistan military in East Bengal, the future Bangladesh. While not part of the Indian Army, they were supported by them and helped fight the Pakistanis. The battalions of Pakistan's East Bengal Regiment in East Bengal mutinied at various dates in 1971: June (1st, 3rd and 8th, at Tura, Meghalaya, and 2nd and 4th in Tripura) and September (9th, 10th and 11th). The officers and men who managed to escape to India became the nucleus of the Mukti Bahani's regular forces, and units were re-raised in India. Some of these battalions are included in the order of battle above, where they were with Indian formations 3 December. A field battery was raised in August 1971 with four 3.7" mountain howitzers, and two more in October and November 1971 with six Italian 105mm mountain howitzers each. At the end of November 1971 these forces were organized as follows:

    K Force (or K Brigade): 10th and 11th East Bengal; No 3 Field Battery
    S Force (or S Brigade): 2nd, 4th and 9th East Bengal; No 1 Field Battery
    Z Force (or Z Brigade): 1st, 3rd and 8th East Bengal; No 2 Field Battery

In addition, there were two units of the Niyomito Bahini (the regular Bangladesh Army): Swadhin Bangla Regiment and Mukti Fauj (Fauj is a word common through North India and means army). These were supplemented by various irregular units.

Note on Kashmir. During the 1971 war the 121st (Independent) Infantry Brigade, 19th Infantry Division and 25th Infantry Division were all well above the normal strength for a brigade (three battalions) or division (nine battalions).

The 121st had six battalions, the 19th some 18, and the 25th 15-16. This was in part a result of the 1 January 1949 cease-fire, which limited troops and Jammu and Kashmir and Ladakh. Instead of moving in more division and brigade HQs as the forces increased, the Army simply kept adding battalions. In a sense this did not matter because India's posture in Kashmir was static and defensive, but it made the launching of any real offensive difficult as the formations were so unwieldy for effective control.

Note on APCs. The Topas is the OT-62, developed by Poland and Czechoslovakia. It is a tracked amphibious vehicle, developed from the Soviet BTR-50 (a variant of the PT-76 amphibious tank chassis). The SKOT is an 8x8 amphibious APC developed by Czechoslovakia and Poland. It is essentially an improved version of the Soviet BTR-60. Thus, as with tanks, the Indian Army had a variety of APCs, some wheeled and some tracked.

[This Appendix began with the information in the Appendix in John H. Gill,. *An Atlas of the 1971 India-Pakistan War*, supplemented by S. N. Prasad (ed.), *History of Indo-Pak War, 1971*, Ravi Rikhye, Indian I Corps in the 1971 War (2002); Ravi Rikhye, Indian II Corps in the East Bengal Campaign, 1971 (2002); Ravi Rikhye, Indian XXXIII Corps in the East Bengal Campaign, 1971 (2002); Ravi Rikhye, Indian Southern Command in the 1971 War (2002); Ravi Rikhye, Indian 10th Division in the Battle for Chaamb, 1971 (2002); Ravi Rikhye, Indian 19th Division in the 1971 War (2002); and Ravi Rikhye, India: The Partapur and 121st Brigade Sectors in the 1971 War (2002). Some additional material on the Partappur Sector and 121st (I) Infantry Brigade, drawn from *Trishul: Ladakh and Kargil 1947-93*, (written by an assistant commander of 3rd Infantry Division), was provided to the authors by Mr Rohit Vats. In the case of discrepancies, I have normally followe Gill. The note on the Mukti Bahini is based on Ravi Rikhye, Mukti Bahini: Bangladesh Forces in the Liberation War 1971 (2002). Information on the Engineers is from their official history.]

Appendix M: Foxtrot Sector 1971

The area covered by Foxtrot Sector, XI Corps, during the 1971 war was originally held by 67th (Independent) Infantry Brigade, facing a Pakistani brigade. In 1970, however, Pakistan raised HQ II Corps at Multan as a strike corps. As India built up to the 1971 War, the lack of troops in this sector became a matter of concern, particularly when it became evident that Pakistan's II Corps would strike between Jalalabad (Punjab) and Anupgarh (Rajasthan).

Foxtrot sector was formally raised in July 1971, commanded by a major general headquartered at Abohar, Punjab. 67th (Independent) Infantry Brigade was at Fazilka. 51st (Independent) Parachute Brigade was brought down from Sugar Sector (Himachal Pradesh) facing Tibet as India assessed the probability of the Chinese opening a second front to aid Pakistan during the planned Indian winter campaign in the East was low. It was at Ganganagar. Finally, 163rd Infantry Brigade from 3rd Infantry Division was shifted from Ladakh and placed at Suratgarh. (Foxtrot Sector's front is roughly the same area now covered by X Corps, with three divisions.) They were supported by three engineer regiments acting as infantry and, on mobilization, a TA infantry battalion. In addition, a provisional armoured unit known as Mike Force—drawn from 14th (Independent) Armoured Brigade—was assembled east of Ganganager, with part of a regiment of T-54 tanks, a regiment with T-55 tanks, and a mechanized infantry company. (This would later become the 6th (Independent) Armoured Brigade.)

During the war, 116th Infantry Brigade from 14th Infantry Division was sent as a reinforcement, going to Jalalabad-Muktsar.

The intent of forming Foxtrot Sector, effectively an ad hoc division, was to absorb Pakistan II Corps' attack without calling on the Indian Army HQ strike reserve, the 1st Armoured and 14th Infantry Divisions. (Although the 14th was split up during the fighting, with one brigade—as noted—going to Foxtrot Sector and another sent elsewhere in XI Corps.) In the event the ceasefire was called and Pakistan cancelled its II Corps offensive.

[This Appendix is based on information provided by Ravi Rikhye as well as details from the prior Appendix.]

Appendix N: Kargil Order of Battle 1999

Overall command was provided by XV Corps of Northern Command. Artillery support included units of the XV Corps Artillery Brigade.

8th Mountain Division (HQ ex Sharifabad, Valley)
8th Mountain Artillery Brigade [division artillery]
121st (Independent) Infantry Brigade Group (Kargil)[351]
- 16th Grenadiers
- 4th Jat
- 3rd Punjab
- 10th Garhwal Rifles
- BSF Bn
- detachment 17th Guards [ATGM]

56th Mountain Brigade (Matayan)
- 16th Grenadiers[352]
- 18th Grenadiers
- 8th Sikh
- 1st Naga
- 2nd Rajputana Rifles
- 18th Garhwal Rifles
- 13th J&K Rifles
- 1/3 GR
- 9th Parachute Commandos
- detachment 17th Guards [ATGM]

50th (Independent) Parachute Brigade[353] [ex Army HQ Reserves]
- 6th Parachute
- 7th Parachute
- 1st Parachute Commandos
- detachment 19th Guards [ATGM]

192nd Mountain Brigade
- 18th Grenadiers
- 8th Sikh
- 9th Parachute Commandos
- detachment 17th Guards [ATGM]

---

[351] Normally assigned to Kargil sector.
[352] The reason many infantry battalions are mentioned under different formations is that they fought the war at different times under different brigades.
[353] 50th (I) Parachute Brigade were successively Army HQ reserve, Northern Command reserve and XV Corps reserve ultimately fighting the war under 8th Mountain Division. They were kept close by for purposes of acclimatization the contingency plan calling for them to be dropped north of the Line of Control.

79th Mountain Brigade (Dras)
- 17th Jat
- 28th Rashtriya Rifles
- 12th Mahar
- 13th J&K Rifles
- 2nd Naga
- 9th Parachute Commandos
- detachment 17th Guards [ATGM]

3rd Infantry Division (HQ Leh)
3rd Artillery Brigade [division artillery]
70th Infantry Brigade Group (ex Demchok, China border)
- 1/11 GR
- 12 J&K Light Infantry
- 10th Parachute Commandos
- 1st Bihar
- Ladakh Scouts
- 17th Garhwal Rifles
- 5th Parachute
- 14th Sikh
- detachment 19th Guards [ATGM]

102nd (Independent) Infantry Brigade Group[354] (Shyok River Valley)
- 11th Rajputana Rifles
- 9th Mahar
- 13th Kumaon
- 27th Rajput
- Detachment High Altitude Warfare School Permanent Cadre
- detachment 19th Guards [ATGM]

Kargil Theatre Artillery: these artillery units took part in the War serving under various formations:[355]
- 4th Field Regiment
- 15th Field Regiment
- 41st Field Regiment
- 108 Medium Regiment
- 139th Medium Regiment
- 141st Field Regiment
- 153rd Medium Regiment

---

[354] Normally under command 3rd Infantry Division despite the independent designation.
[355] The authors of the original document were not able to find out which artillery regiment served with which artillery brigade; therefore they've all been grouped together.

158th Medium Regiment
197th Field Regiment
212th Rocket Regiment
244th Heavy Mortar Regiment
253rd Medium Regiment
255th Field Regiment
286th Medium Regiment
305th Medium Regiment
307th Medium Regiment
315th Field Regiment
1861st Light Regiment
1889th Light Regiment

Other battalions (higher HQ unclear)[356]
5th Special Frontier Force (Vikas Force)[357]
663 Reconnaissance & Observation Squadron [Army Aviation Corps]
668 Reconnaissance & Observation Squadron [Army Aviation Corps]
Ladakh Scouts: Karakoram & India Wings
13th Punjab
12th Grenadiers
22nd Grenadiers
9th Rashtriya Rifles
14th Rashtriya Rifles
17th Rashtriya Rifles
11th Sikh
3rd J&K Rifles
16th Dogras
Dogra Scouts
5th Rajput

The following two battalions might have served, or might be errors:
7th Jat
14th Sikh Light Infantry

[This Appendix is an edited version of Mandeep S. Bajwa and Ravi Rikhye, Indian Army – Kargil War 1999 (2006).]

[356] This list is compiled from newspaper and casualty reports.
[357] Normally operates in companies; not clear if the whole battalion was present.

Appendix O: Peacekeeping Operations.

With a large, well-trained and disciplined Army, India has been an active participant in UN and other peacekeeping operations. According to the Army's web site, they are ranked as the third largest troop contributor to the UN.

Korea [1953-54]

India contributed a medical unit (60th Parachute Field Ambulance) to the 1st Commonwealth Division during the fighting. Following the Armistice, a major problem was the refusal of many North Korean and Chinese POWs to be repatriated. India was chosen to take over security for those POW camps during the process of Chinese and North Korean personnel attempting to persuade their compatriots to return. This was known as Indian Custodian Force in Korea. The first battalion, 3rd Dogra sailed 19 August 1953. They were joined by 2nd Parachute, 5th Rajputana Rifles, 6th Jat, and 3rd Garhwal Rifles. The Indian troops completed custody of the non-repatriates 24 September 1953. The mission ended in January 1954.

Sinai [1956-1967]

UN Emergency Force I (UNEF I) was deployed November 1956-June 1967. It began on the armistice demarcation line and later n the Egyptian side of the international frontier in the Sinai. Two Indian officers served tours as the Force commander: Lt Gen P. S. Gyani (December 1959-January 1964) and Maj Gen Indar J. Rikhye (January 1966-June 1967).

3rd Parachute sent out Nov 1956, replaced a year later by 1st Parachute. Battalions were replaced each year until May 1967 when the force was withdrawn at the request of Egypt, but the identities of those after 1957 are not known.

Lebanon [1958]

The UN Observation Group in Lebanon (UNOGIL) was in existence June-December 1958, along the Lebanese-Syrian border. India contributed, but the UNOGIL total was only 591 military personnel at its peak.

Congo [1960-1964]

The UN Operation in the Congo (ONUC) was in existence from July 1960 to June 1964.

India contributed the 99th (Independent) Infantry Brigade Group, which had been formed November 1960 as part of the 17th Infantry Division. There were basically two rotations of troops under the brigade, one 1961-62 and the next 1962-63. The brigade withdrew in March 1963.

1961-62 rotation:
- 5th Independent Armoured Car Squadron [drawn from 63rd Cavalry]
- 2nd Jats
- 1st Dogras
- 3/1 GR
- A Company, 4th Mahar [MG]
- 120th Heavy Mortar Battery
- 13th Field Company Engineers

1962-63 rotation:
- 4th Madras
- 2/5 GR
- 4th Rajputana Rifles
- D Company, 4th Mahar [MG]
- 121st Heavy Mortar Battery
- 22nd Field Company Engineers

In addition, there were a number of service and support units during each rotation.

Sri Lanka [1987-1990]

This operation was outside the auspices of the UN, intended to oversee the disarming of various groups in that country following a negotiated agreement. Apparently the government did not think that the force, designated Indian Peace Keeping Force (IPKF) would have to fight. HQ for the IPKF was established at Madras, under the control of Southern Command.

The first troops landed in August 1987: the 54th Air Assault Division and 340th (Independent) Infantry Brigade, which was trained for amphibious operations. These were followed, probably in 1988, by the 4th Infantry Division (two brigades only) and the 57th Mountain Division, the only formation that had actually trained for jungle warfare. The 18th Infantry Brigade was also sent out. The IPKF was around 80,000 personnel at its peak ans suffered some 1,500 troops killed in action.[358]

---

[358] For an evaluation of the IPKF's performance, see the article at www.bharat-rakshak.com/LAND-FORCES/History/1987-90/300-Appendix-A.html.

Following election of new governments in India and Sri Lanka in 1989, the IPKF began to withdraw. The last contingents left Sri Lanka in March 1990. HQ IPKF remained active, and was soon redesignated as HQ XXI Corps.

The following units served with the IPKF (artillery units have not been identified):

65th Armoured Regiment
13th, 16th Guards
3rd, 6th, 13th, 15th, 16th, 19th Mechanised Infantry[359]
3rd, 19th, 21st, 26th Punjab
2nd, 5th, 7th, 11th, 12th, 19th, 25th Madras
12th, 18th, 19th Grenadiers
1st, 5th, 8th, 17th Maratha LI
5th, 7th, 11th, 16th, 19th Rajputana Rifles
4th, 5th, 6th, 17th, 25th Rajput
4th, 12th, 14th, 15th Jat
7th, 16th, 17th, 22nd Sikh
1st, 4th, 7th, 13th, 14th Sikh LI
9th, 10th, 13th, 15th Dogra
4th, 5th, 11th, 12th, 13th, 16th, 18th Garhwal Rifles
7th, 9th, 11th, 16th, 18th Kumaon
4th, 5th, 7th Assam
4th, 7th, 9th, 15th Bihar
4th, 8th, 19th Mahar
2nd J&K Rifles
1st, 11th J&K LI
1, 4, 5/1 GR
1, 3, 4/5 GR
6, 7/8 GR
1, 3/11 GR
3rd, 4th, 5th, 7th Parachute
1st, 9th, 10th Para-Commando
3rd, 4th, 8th, 16th, 51st, 53rd, 110th, 115th, 270th Engineer Regiments

Maldives [1988]

Another non-UN operation. The government of the Maldives requested assistance in helping to counter an attempted coup. India airlifted parts of 50th (Independent) Parachute Brigade: 6th Parachute Battalion, 10th Para-Commando Battalion, and elements of 17th Parachute Field Regiment. The operation was completed in three days (3-6 November 1988).

[359] Usually used in a dismounted role.

Cambodia [1992-1993]

The UN Transitional Authority in Cambodia (UNTAC) served from February 1992 to September 1993. India sent the 1st Assam, later joined by 4th J&K Rifles. There was an earlier United Nations Advance Mission in Cambodia (UNAMIC), November 1991-March 1992.

Angola [1995-1997]

The Indian Army participated in UN Angola Verification Mission – III (UNAVEM – III), which lasted from February 1995 to June 1997. The following units served with UNAVEM – III:

16th Guards
14th Punjab
company from 21st Mechanised Infantry
386th (I) Field Company [engineers]
417th (I) Field Company [engineers]

Somalia [1993-1994]

India contributed a large contingent for UN Operations in Somalia II (UNOSOM – II), which lasted from March 1993 to December 1994. The force itself was established in May 1993. India contributed the following units:

HQ 66th (I) Infantry Brigade Group
3rd Mechanised Infantry
1st Bihar
5th Mahar
3rd J&K Light Infantry
squadron 7th Cavalry
8722nd Light Battery
6th Reconnaissance and Observation Flight [Army Aviation Corps]

Sierra Leone [1999-2001]

The UN Observer Mission in Sierra Leone (UNOMSIL), July 1998 to October 1999, was succeeded by the UN Assistance Mission in Sierra Leone (UNAMSIL), which ran November 1999 to February 2001.

India sent a battalion group in December 1999, 18th Grenadiers. Companies from 14th, 23rd and 11th Mechanised Infantry served at various times. The force also included an artillery battery, two engineer companies, and a medical unit. The Indian units withdrew September 2000-February 2001.

Congo [1999 to date]

The UN Mission in Congo (MONUC) began in November 1999 and is continuing.

Indian troops assigned to this mission have been under the control of 301st Infantry Brigade. The following battalions have served: 10th Bihar, 3rd Mahar, 22nd Grenadiers, 5th Parachute, 2/11 GR, 15th Kumaon, 26th Madras, 1st J&K Rifles, 15th Maratha Light Infantry, 2nd Rajputana Rifles, 6th Sikh Light Infantry, and a company of 9th Parachute (SF). In addition, the Army Aviation Corps' 5th and 8th and 9th (I) Recce and Observation Flights have participated.

Other UN Operations

The following are known UN operations for which Indian Army personnel qualified for a clasp to the Videsh Seva Medal. It is probable that small numbers of personnel were involved.[360]

UNYOM: Yeman 4 September 1963-4 September 1964
UNTAG: United Nations Transitional Assistance Group in Namibia, April 1989-March 1990
ONUSAL: United Nations Observer Mission in El Salvador, July 1991-April 1995
ONUMOZ: United Nations Operation in Mozambique, December 1992-December 1994
UNOMIL: United Nations Observer Mission in Liberia, September 1993--?
UNMIH: United Nations Mission in Haiti, September 1993-June 1996
UNAMIR: United Nations Assistance Mission in Rwanda, October 1993-March 1996
UNMIBH: United Nations Mission in Bosnia and Herzegovina, December 1995--?

[360] Taken from a cached web site on Indian Army medals and decorations last updated in 1999 (see Ed Haynes in Sources), so this is unlikely to be complete.

Appendix P: Ranks and Awards

Ranks

The basic rank structure is that of the pre-independence Army, and the rank insignia is copied as well, with the elimination of crowns and their replacement by the national emblem.

Officers

Field Marshal[361] [gold national emblem (Ashoka Lions) over gold crossed batons surrounded by a gold lotus wreath][362]
General[363] [gold national emblem over gold sun over gold crossed baton and scimitar, all outlined in red]
Lieutenant General [gold national emblem over gold crossed baton and scimitar, both outlined in red]
Major General [gold star over gold crossed baton and scimitar, both outlined in red]
Brigadier [gold national emblem over three gold stars in a triangular formation]
Colonel [gold national emblem over two gold stars]
Lieutenant Colonel [gold national emblem over gold star]
Major [gold national emblem]
Captain [three gold stars]
Lieutenant[364] [two gold stars]

---

361 Field marshal is more an honorary rather than a normal active rank. The Army Chief during the 1971 war, S.H.F.J. Manekshaw, was elevated to field marshal two weeks before completing his term of office. The rank was also awarded retroactively to K.M. Cariappa, the first Indian Commander-in-Chief, in 1986, many years after his 1953 retirement.

362 The illustration in the Wikipedia article shows a crossed baton and scimitar. However, the flag of a field marshal shows crossed batons rather than a crossed baton and scimitar. See www.crwflags.com/fotw/flags/in^rank.html#fm, and this is consistent with the British rank insignia, which also has crossed batons.

363 This rank appears to be restricted to the Chief of the Army Staff. Otherwise, lieutenant general is the highest rank.

364 All officers are now commissioned as lieutenants and the former rank of Second Lieutenant is no longer used. The insignia of that rank was one gold star.

Junior Commissioned Officers[365]

Subedar Major [gold national emblem with red/gold/red stripe below]
Subedar/Risaldar [two gold stars with red/gold/red stripe below]
Naib Subedar/Naib Risaldar <also known as Jemadar until 1965> [one gold star with red/gold/red stripe below]

Non Commissioned Officers and Enlisted[366]

Company Havildar Major/Squadron Daffadar Major [national emblem]
Company Quarter Master Havildar/Squadron Quarter Master Daffadar [three rank chevrons with national emblem above]
Havildar/Daffadar [Sergeant; three rank chevrons]
Naik/Lance Daffadar [Corporal; two rank chevrons]
Lance Naik/Acting Lance Daffadar [Private First Class; single rank chevron]
Sepoy/Sowar [Private; no insignia]

Two appointments, Regimental Havildar and Regimental Quartermaster Havildar, are obsolete and disappearing. While having distinctive rank insignia, they were not technically higher ranks than Company Havildar Major or Squadron Daffadar Major.

Sepoy is the generic name for the lowest rank, or private; in the Armoured Corps, the equivalent is Sowar. However, there are numerous alternatives depending on the regiment: e.g., Grenadier, Rifleman, Paratrooper, Gunner, Signalman, Commando, Sapper, Craftsman, Guardsman, etc. Soldiers below officer rank are often referred to collectively as Jawans.[367]

Officers and Junior Commissioned Officers wear their rank on each shoulder. Rank badges for NCOs are worn only on the right sleeve. Company Havildar Major or Squadron Daffadar Major are appointments rather than true ranks; their insignia are worn on leather straps on the wrist of the right hand.

---

[365] These are a carryover from the Viceroy Commissioned Officer ranks of the old Indian Army. They are awarded to long-serving NCOs, and serve as a bridge between officers and other ranks. (When created, of course, they were a bridge between British officers and Indian other ranks.) Unlike other armies, officers do not command platoons: the Naib Subedar or Naib Risaldar do.

[366] Where two alternatives are given (e.g., Havildar/Daffadar) the first is for the Army generally and the second is for units of the Armoured Corps.

[367] The term has also been used to refer to personnel of various paramilitary organizations. It can be used in the singular, Jawan, in lieu of soldier.

Awards

Until 14 August 1947, personnel of the Indian Army were eligible for British gallantry awards, including the Victoria Cross. The Republic of India created a distinctive set of national awards effective 26 January 1950. Those for gallantry (Param Vir Chakra, Maha Vir Chakra and Vir Chakra) had been settled in 1948 and were awarded retroactively to 15 August 1947. "A perusal of the British and Indian awards will show that the Param Vir Chakra to the Victoria Cross, the Maha Vir Chakra to the Indian Order of Merit and the Vir Chakra is equivalent to the Military Cross. The other group of awards i.e. the Ashoka Chakra series, [created later] meant for gallantry other than in the face of the enemy, was probably meant to replace the George Cross, Albert Medal and George Medal."[368] Various types of medals (gallantry and non gallantry) were instituted beginning 1952 and in subsequent years.

Except for the campaign stars, Indian medals are circles, generally of one metal with a design, hanging from a plain horizontal bar. Campaign stars are normally five-pointed, with a central circular design, although the Op Vijay star has five points plus a top attachment to the ribbon, giving it the appearance of a six-pointed star.[369]

Gallantry Awards

Param Vir Chakra ("Bravest of the Brave Medal") is the highest decoration that may be awarded. It is awarded "for most conspicuous bravery or some daring or pre-eminent act of valour or self sacrifice, in the presence of the enemy, whether on land, at sea, or in the air." It is open to all members of the Armed Forces and may be awarded posthumously.[370] Subsequent awards are indicated by a Bar attached to the riband.

The medal is a circular bronze disc, with the Sate Emblem (Ashoka Lions) in the center on a raised circle. Around this are four replicas of Indra's Vajra (mythical weapon of the ancient Vedic King of Gods). (The rear contains the words Param Vir Chakra in Hindi and English, separated by lotus flowers.) The

---

[368] Unless otherwise indicated, quotations are from the official Indian Army web site. This was done to ensure accuracy in the descriptions for entitlement.

[369] Color illustrations of the medals and ribbons can be found at Global Security, www.globalsecurity.org/military/world/india/awards-gallantry.htm for gallantry awards and www.globalsecurity.org/military/world/india/awards-non-gallantry.htm for non-gallantry.

[370] Unless otherwise indicated, lesser gallantry awards are also open to all members of the Armed Forces, may be awarded posthumously, and subsequent awards are indicated by a Bar.

medal is worn from a suspension bar and a purple ribbon. Twenty members of the Army have received the PVC, thirteen of them posthumous.[371] To date, no Bars have been awarded.

Ashok Chakra is awarded "for most conspicuous bravery, or some act of daring or pre-eminent act of valour or self-sacrifice otherwise than in the face of the enemy."[372] This award could be made to civilians as well. Until a 1999 modification, members of Police Forces were explicitly excluded from eligibility. The ribbon is dark green with a very narrow (2mm) central saffron stripe.

Maha Vir Chakra ("Extraordinary Bravery Medal") awarded for "acts of gallantry in the presence of the enemy on land, at sea or in the air." The ribbon is divided vertically white and orange, with the orange on the wearer's left.

Kirti Chakra awarded "for conspicuous gallantry otherwise than in the face of the enemy." As with the Ashok Chakra, the award can also be to civilians and (from 1999) to members of Police Forces. The ribbon is dark green with two narrow (2mm) saffron stripes effectively dividing it in thirds.

Vir Chakra awarded for "acts of gallantry in the presence of the enemy, whether of land or at sea or in the air."[373] The ribbon is divided vertically dark blue and organge-saffron.

Shaurya Chakra is awarded "for gallantry otherwise than in the face of the enemy." As with the Ashok Chakra, the award can also be to civilians and (from 1999) to members of Police Forces. The ribbon is dark green with three evently spaced narrow (2mm) saffron stripes.

Sena Medal is awarded "for such individual acts of exceptional devotion to duty or courage as have special significance for the Army." There are similar medals for the Air Force and Navy.

---

[371] Their pictures and information on the awards can be found on the Indian Army website at indianarmy.nic.in/Site/FormTemplete/frmPhotoGallery.aspx?MnId=ChynJzU8M60%3d&ParentID=+XtwXAaidZ0%3d. These individuals are shown earlier under their regiment. Two were earned by the Armoured Corps (both members of the same regiment), 17 in the Infantry, and one by the Corps of Engineers.

[372] Until 1967 the Ashok Chakra was known as the Ashoka Chakra, Class I; with the Kirti Chakra and Shaurya Chakra as Classes II and III of the Ashoka Chakra.

[373] This is abbreviated VrC when following a name, to distinguish it from the Victoria Cross, abbreviated VC.

Mention in Dispatches entitles the named individual to wear a lotus leaf on the ribbon of the campaign medal relating to the campaign for which mention was made. Mention in Dispatches was established "to recognize distinguished and meritorious service in operational areas and acts of gallantry which are not of a sufficiently high order to warrant the grant of gallantry awards...." Names may be included posthumously and an individual can be mentioned in more than one dispatch.

At the lowest level are Chief of the Army Staff and Vice Chief of the Army Staff Commendation Cards, awarded "for a specific act of bravery or distinguished service or special service" which does not qualify for any higher award. It cannot be made posthumously. This entitles the awardee to a COAS Commendation Badge for wear on the uniform, or (for VCOAS and other commendations) to the Army Commendation Badge.

Non Gallantry Awards

Sarvottam Yudh Seva Medal is awarded "for distinguished service of the most exceptional order during war/conflict/hostilities."

Param Vishisht Seva Medal is awarded "for distinguished service of the most exceptional order."

Uttam Yudh Seva Medal is awarded "for distinguished service of an exceptional order during war/conflict/hostilities."

Ati Vishisht Seva Medal is awarded "for distinguished service of an exceptional order."

Vishisht Seva Medal is awarded "for distinguished Service of a high order."

Parakram Padak was formerly known as the **Wound Medal**. It is awarded to "personnel who sustained/sustain wounds as a result of direct enemy action in any type of operations or counterinsurgency operations." Police Forces and various other types of paramilitaries are also eligible for this award. The medal is not awarded posthumously.

As with other armies, there are also a number of *campaign medals*; following British practice, they are known as stars or star medals:

- The **Samar Seva Star** is for service in the 1965 war with Pakistan, requiring at least ten days' active service with "a unit/formation operating or located in the qualifying areas" during the period 5 August 1965-25 January 1966.[374]

- The **Poorvi Star** is for service "in operations in and around Bangladesh" in 1971. Those who served in the West during the 1971 war are entitled to the **Paschimi Star**.
- The **Op Vijay Star** was instituted for service in the 1999 Kargil War.[375]

There is a **Siachen Glacier Medal** for service during the 1984 operations there.

The **Samanya Seva Medal** was created in 1965 for services rendered for particular operations, indicated by a clasp:

KUTCH KARGIL 1965 [Rann of Kutch operations]
NAGALAND [1975 on; for earlier service see GS Medal 1947]
NATHULA CHOLA
MIZORAM [1975 on; for earlier service see GS Medal 1947]
TIRAP
MANIPUR

There is also **General Service Medal 1947**, awarded for service in particular operations, indicated by a clasp:

JAMMU AND KASHMIR [1947-1949]
OVERSEAS KOREA 1950-53
GOA 1961
LADAKH 1962
NEFA 1962
NAGA HILLS [1955-56]
MIZO HILLS [1966-75]

There is a **Special Service Medal**, which has two clasps:

SRI LANKA [for Operation Pawan, the IPKF, 1987-90]
SURAKSHA

The **Sainya Seva Medal** is given in recognition of non-operational service under conditions of hardship and severe climate in specified areas recognized by clasps:

JAMMU AND KASHMIR [service qualifying for GS Medal excluded]

---

[374] As with all types of campaign medals in various countries, there are detailed qualifications spelled out for service in a battle zone, operational sorties, naval personnel, etc.

[375] In addition, there is an Op Vijay Medal for those outside of the battle zone who were mobilized in support of operations or at headquarters involved in planning mobilization or operations.

NEFA [later renamed as ARUNACHAL][376]
ANDAMAN AND NICOBAR [one year's service after 20 May 1966]
BENGAL-ASSAM [one year's service after 26 October 1962]
MARUSTHAL

There is the **Videsh Seva Medal**, for services rendered outside India, which has 32 clasps providing a look at how extensive India's contributions to peacekeeping and humanitarian operations has been:

KOREA[377]
NEPAL[378]
INDO-CHINA[379]
UAR [service with UNEF]
ETHIOPIA [two periods of service, 1957 and 1961 to unknown dates]
LEBANON [service with UNIFIL]
IRAQ [service on loan to Iraqi government November 1959 to ?]
GHANA [service on loan to Ghanaian government March 1959 to ?]
CONGO [service with ONUC]
BHUTAN[380]
NIGERIA
YEMEN [service with UNYOM]
BANGLADESH
MAURITIUS
AFGHANISTAN
ZAMBIA
SRI LANKA[381]
ANGOLA[382]

---

[376] Given for one year's roadbuilding service 7 October 1952-15 November 1958, or for personnel seconded to the Assam Rifles for service there for one year after 15 August 1947.

[377] For service with the Neutral Nations Repatriation Commission (NNRC) or the Indian Custodial Force in Korea, 22 November 1950-17 March 1954. Service during the Korean War was recognized by a clasp to the Indian General Service Medal 1947. All clasps have minimum qualifying periods which are not given here.

[378] Awarded for roadbuilding service 15 April 1952-15 April 1958; signal communications during the Nepali election 26 November 1958-3 May 1959; or for service with the Indian Military Training Mission or the Military Advisory Training Group 1 August 1952 and later.

[379] Service on the staff of the International Commission for Supervision and Control in Viet-Nam, Laos, and Cambodia (ICSC), 7 August 1954 to some unknown date.

[380] For service with the Indian army team in Bhutan, 27 May 1961-22 September 1962; or for service with the Indian Military Training Team, 27 August 1962-?; or for service with a unit employed on road construction in Bhutan, 3 April 1961-?

[381] For service with the IPKF 1987-90; personnel awarded this also received the the Special Service medal with a bar for Sri Lanka.

NAMIBIA [service with UNTAG]
EL-SALVADOR [service with ONUSAL]
CAMBODIA [service with UNAMIC]
SOMALIA [service with UNOSOM I and UNOSOM II]
MOZAMBIQUE [service with ONUMOZ]
LIBERIA [service with UNOMIL]
RWANDA UNAMIR]
BOSNIA-HERZEGOVINA [service with UNMIBH]
IRAN/IRAQ
NICARAGUA
GUATEMALA
LEBANON
NORTHERN IRAQ
LESOTHO
ZAMBIA
SUDAN
BOTSWANA
TANZANIA
SEYCHELLES
HONDURAS
COSTA RICA
IRAQ-KUWAIT
NEW YORK
QATAR
SIERRA LEONE
YUGOSLAVIA
LAOS
TAJIKISTAN

There are still more medals of various types, such as those for various periods of long service and good conduct and for personnel on the strength of units at various dates, such as 15 August 1947 (the **Independence Medal**), 5 August 1965 (the **Raksha Medal**), and 3 December 1971-20 December 1972 (the **Sangram Medal**).

---

[382] Service with UNAVEM I, UNAVEM II, and UNAVEM III, January 1989-June 1997 or with with the United Nations Observer Mission in Angola (MONUA), July 1997--?.

Appendix Q: Equipment

Main Battle Tanks

	2002	2005	2008	2010
Arjun	14	14	15	124
T-90S	10	124	330	620
T-72/T-72M1	1,500	1,900	1,925	1,950
Vijayanta	1,200	1,200	1,008	700
T-55/T-55 Mod	450	450	450	450
PT-76	90	90	100	90
Total	5,266	5,783	5,836	5,944

The Indian Armoured Corps has always had a variety of MBTs, generally with different main armament and different characteristics. This creates obvious problems in terms of ammunition, supplies, repair and doctrine. In addition, the Army has often found itself with a number of older or obsolescent tanks. The PT-76 tanks will be phased out sometime after 2010 and the T-55s will be gone after 2015.

Development of the **Arjun** (named for one of the main characters in the Mahabharata) dates back to 1972 but mass production was not ordered until 1996 and trials (which uncovered a number of problems) did not really begin until 2008. Initial orders were for 124 tanks, enough for two regiments (45 each, plus spares and training vehicles). Following the 2010 tests, an order for additional 124 tanks (two more regiments) were placed.[383] There do not appear to be any current plans to go beyond the 248 ordered. The tank mounts a 120mm rifled gun as its main armament. The first regiment received the new tank in May 2009, but these were used to continue trials and testing.[384] It is not clear how the four regiments, when finally equipped, will be assigned: e.g., one full brigade and an extra regiment, or divided one or two regiments each to two or more brigades.

---

[383] See Government of India, Press Information Bureau, 17 May 2010 Press Release on the decision as well as praise about the performance of the tank, www.pib.nic.in/release/release.asp?relid=61870.

[384] *Hinudstan Times*, 26 May 2009, www.hindustantimes.com/News-Feed/newdelhi/Arjun-rumbles-to-life-Army-raises-maiden-regiment/Article1-414590.aspx.

The T-90 is the most modern of Soviet tanks, with initial production in 1993; the **T-90S** export version was offered beginning in 1997. The T-90S Bhisma (named after a warrior in the Mahabharata) is an improved version. In 2001, India bought 310 T-90S tanks, some complete and some in kits. In 2006 India bought another 300 and signed a contract to produce up to 1,000 additional tanks with local materials. The first of the locally produced T-90S Bhisma tanks were delivered in August 2009. The goal is to have 310 T-90S and 1,330 T-90M by 2020. The main weapon is a 125mm smoothbore gun.

The **T-72** (which entered Soviet service in 1973) was introduced in 1979, intended as an interim MBT while the Arjun was under development. All were imported into India, the bulk in 1982-86. Efforts to overhaul and modernize them began in the 1990s, and 968 have been upgraded within India. The T-72M1 Ajeya is the modernized version. The main weapon, as with the T-90, is a 125mm smoothbore gun.

The **Vijayanta** (Victorious) was an Indian-built licensed variant of the Vickers MBT Mk 1 developed in the United Kingdom. The prototype was completed in 1963 and the first tanks entered service in 1965. 90 tanks were built by Vickers in the United Kingdom; production in India continued through 1983 with about 2,200 built. The main weapon is a 105mm gun.

The **T-55** tank was originally introduced in 1958 and production continued through 1981 although it was probably obsolescent by then and replaced in first-line Soviet units by newer tanks. The main weapon is a 100mm rifled gun. The numbers in the table reflect the number still operational; there were around 700 on strength as late as 2000 and some 200 of those are in storage.

The **PT-76** is a light amphibious tank which entered service in 1954 and is little more than an obsolete recce vehicle, under-gunned (76mm rifled gun) and under-armoured. However, it does have excellent amphibious abilities.

Recce Vehicles

The Indian Army has little in the way of recce vehicles (or units) with 255 of the BRDM-2 (BTR-40-P2). This vehicle dates back to 1959, and is a four-wheel drive amphibious vehicle with a small turret containing a 14.5mm machine gun. These are found in the recce and support battalions with armoured and RAPID divisions.

AIFVs/APCs

The Indian Army did not acquire any APCs until 1971; until then the motor battalions in armoured formations were carried in lorries and other wheeled vehicles.[385]

The **BMP-1** dates to the 1960s. It is amphibious and has a low velocity 73mm gun in a turret. It can carry eight infantry in addition to the crew of three. There were in excess of 350 from 2000, 600 in 2005 and 700 from 2008. These are being phased out in favor of the newer BMP-2.

The **BMP-2 Sarath** (Chariot of Victory) is a locally produced licensed version of the Soviet vehicle. This is essentially an updated BMP-1 with a 30mm gun. The initial order was in 1986, and was later amended to provided for 750 vehicles 1991-92. They were overhauled beginning in mid 2000 (completion date of 2006), at the rate of 100 a year; the upgraded vehicle is designated BMP-2M. The overhaul included improved ATGM armament. Strength since 2000 is in excess of 1,000 vehicles. Production is around 100 vehicles a year, to be increased to 125.

The **OT-62** and **OT-64** (SKOT) APC are still in use in limited numbers. The former is a tracked amphibious vehicle (a member of the PT-76 family) and the latter is an eight-wheeled vehicle with a 14.5mm machine gun. The OT-62 can carry 18-20 passengers plus a crew of two; the OT-64 can carry 15 personnel in addition to the crew of two. Since 1995 the Indian Army has had 157 of both types combined.

Around 160 Casspirs are in inventory. These were originally developed by South Africa to aid their police in CI operations. It is designed to be mine-resistant. A four-wheel drive vehicle, it can carry 12 in addition to the crew of two.

Artillery

SP Artillery

The Indian Army currently has very little SP artillery. There are about 80 of the old 105mm SP Abbot in storage and 20 130mm M-46 Catapults. The latter involves a towed 130mm M-46 weapon mounted on the chassis of the Vijayanta tank. Some 100 conversions were made, with 80 of them now in storage. There are plans to have a new 155 SP weapon (185 units) by 2015,

---

[385] Praval, op. cit., p 550.

with a competition underway between two different vehicles. However, all artillery procurements have been mired in corruption allegations and other problems (see the discussion in the next section).

Towed Artillery

There are a variety of calibers and weapons in the towed artillery. There are in excess of 1,300 105mm weapons, 700 light field guns and 600 plus Indian field guns. The light field gun can be heli-lifted in mountainous areas.

The next step up are 450 122mm D-30[386] and 1,200 130mm M-46 guns. Both are standard Soviet weapons. There are two different towed 155mm weapons, the Soviet M-46 (200)[387] and the Swedish FH-77B (400). The FH-77B, newest of the towed artillery, were acquired in the mid 1980s, and about 100 of them are not in service due to their age and poor repair.

The Army is looking for a new towed 155mm gun and a light weight version 155mm gun. However, this process has gone slowly due to allegations of corruption and kickbacks in procurement and the blacklisting of several foreign companies offering the weapon. In mid 2009, the announced goal was to acquire by purchase (200) and then manufacture (614) enough towed weapons for 40 field regiments and enough SP howitzers for five regiments (100).[388] Trials for the SP weapons were to be held in mid 2010, but it is unclear when the actual procurements will be made.

In early 2010 there was a decision to acquire 145 British-designed ultra-light M777 155mm howitzers from the US. These are intended for the two newly-authorized mountain divisions.[389] However, the main contract for a towed 155mm howitzer had to be re-bid in mid 2010, extending a process already eight years long, and it appears that the M777 and SP contracts are also

[386] One hundred of the 550 purchased were used for the Catapult SP vehicle.
[387] This involves upgraded the M-46 carriage to take a 155mm howitzer barrel. An additional 220 upgrade kits will be ordered.
[388] *The Times of India*, 24 August 2009, timesofindia.indiatimes.com/news/india/Rs-20k-cr-deals-may-end-Armys-artillery-drought/articleshow/4926262.cms. See also their article from 10 June 2009, timesofindia.indiatimes.com/India/Scandals-haunt-Armys-artillery-plans/articleshow/4637127.cms.
[389] *The Telegraph* (Calcutta), 1 January 2010, www.telegraphindia.com/1100102/jsp/nation/story_11934631.jsp.

affected.[390] The plan (or hope) is to have all artillery converted to modern 155mm weapons by 2020.

Mobile Rocket Launchers

There arc very small numbers of these weapons: 80 214mm Pinaka and 38 300mm 9K58 Smerch; a further order of 24 is to be completed in 2010. The Pinaka is a locally developed multibarrel rocket launcher, with 12 barrels on a launch vehicle. The Smerch is a Soviet weapon, with 12 barrels on an 8x8 truck. The Pinaka is to replace the 122mm multi-barrelled BM-21, of which there are 150 of the modernized version.

Anti Tank Guided Missiles

There are a wide variety of these in service. Production of the locally-developed Nag (Cobra) was approved in July 2009, with an order for 443 to be produced in three years. The Nag is being produced both for land mounts and for use on the new light combat helicopter. It is a third generation "fire and forget" ATGM with imaging infra-red guidance. It has a range up to 4km (land) or 7km (air).

India produced the Milan 1 under license, and bought the Milan 2T from France. Milan was developed in France and the first version entered service in 1972. It is wire-guided, which requires the sight to be kept on the target. Its range is up to 2km.

The Israeli Lahat is used with the Arjun tank. It has a semi-active laser guidance system and a range of 6-8km.

There are a few different Soviet ATGMs: the 9M119 Svir used with the T-90S, the 9M113 Konkurs, and the newer 9M133 Kornet. The old 9M111 Fagot is being phased out. The Svir is laser-guided and designed to be fired from smooth bore 125mm guns. It dates to the 1980s and has 4-6km range. The Konkurs is wire-guided missile, dating to the 1970s with a range to 4km. It is designed to be fired from vehicles and is integral to the BMP and BRDM. The Kornet (entering service around 1994 in Russia) is a heavy laser-guided missile with a range to 5.5km. It is normally fired from a tripod launcher.

---

[390] 24 July 2010 flash news item at www.indian-military.org/news-archives/indian-army-news/839-flash-indian-155mm-52cal-towed-gun-competition-scrapped-a-record-third-time-re-tender-signalled.html.

Missiles

The Brahmos missile (named after two rivers, the Brahmaputra and the Moskva) was a joint development between India and Russia. The **Brahmos Block-I** was taken into service by the Army in June 2007. (There are versions developed for land-based firing, sea-based firing, and launching from aircraft.) The Army formed one regiment (861st) with the Brahmos Block-I, with five launchers. The missile has a range of 300 km, flies at a high rate of speed, and can carry a 660 pound warhead. It can also carry a nuclear warhead of 200kg.

Testing began in 2009 on the **Brahmos Block-II**, with new software and improved accuracy. The Army wants to raise two new regiments equipped with the Brahmos Block-II, with an ultimate order of some 80 launchers over ten years. It is thought that the new regiments would have between four and six batteries of three to four launchers each.[391]

The **Prithvi** (Earth) is a short range missile developed in India. The Army version is designated Prithvi I. The maximum warhead is 1,000 kg and the range is 150 km. It entered service in 1994. It can carry a nuclear warhead. The production order is believed to be for 100 missiles, which will went to the Army's 333rd Missile Group.

The **Agni** (Fire) series of missiles began testing in 1989. Agni I is another relatively short range missile, (800-900 km) with a 1,000 kg warhead. It is a single-stage missile, can carry a nuclear warhead, and has a road mobile launcher. Agni II (two stages) is an intermediate range missile (2,000-3,000 km). It has a launcher that can be moved by road or rail. It went into service in 2002, and production may have been as low as 25. The Agni III (also(two stages) is an intermediate range missile (3,000-5,500 km) that can carry warheads up to 1.5 tons. These all can carry nuclear warheads (15 to 250 kilotons). It is rail mobile. Operational deployment is said to be 2010-2011. An intercontinental ballistic missile, the Agni V, is under development; it would have a range of 5,000-6,000 km.

---

[391] The information in this paragraph is taken from a January 2010 Strategy Page article, "Indian Army Demands More Missile Regiments", www.strategypage.com/htmw/htart/20100126.aspx, and the Wikipedia entry on the Brahmos missile, en.wikipedia.org/wiki/BrahMos.

Air Defence Artillery

Anti Aircraft Guns

India has 1,920 of the towed 40mm L/70 Bofors AA gun (with the older L/60 version phased out of service) as well as 800 of the towed twin-barrel 23mm Soviet AA gun (ZU-23-2).

There are small numbers (75) of the ZSU-23-4 quad 23mm SP AA gun, mounted on a modified PT-76 tank chassis, and 24 of the 2S6M (Tunguska-M1) tracked vehicle, which has two pairs of 30mm AA guns and eight SA-19 SAMs. This is the follow-on to the ZSU-23-4.

Surface to Air Missiles

There are 180 of the medium range **SA-6** SAMs, mounted on a tracked armored vehicle (three missiles) and with a maximum effective range of 24,000 meters. These systems (and the SA-8 below) were upgraded and improved ca. 2002. India has been working on an indigenous replacement, the **Akash** (Sky) SAM since the 1980s; they went into service with the Indian Air Force in 2009. An order for the Army was only placed in June 2010.

Shorter range SAMs include 250 of the **SA-13**, mounted on a light tracked armoured vehicle with four ready to fire missiles and eight reloads. The effective range is up to 5,000 meters. There are also 400 **SA-9**, which are carried in a quadruple mount on a BRDM-2 chassis. Maximum range is 5,200 to 6,500 meters depending on the model. In addition, there are something over 50 of the **SA-8**, which has six missiles mounted on a 6x6 amphibious vehicle. (It was the first system to incorporate the engagement radars on the same vehicle as the missiles.) Maximum range is 15,000 meters.

In addition, the Army has large numbers of the man-portable SA-16 and earlier SA-7 SAMs.

Army Aviation

The Army Aviation Corps has a strength of around 200 helicopters. Fifty are the **SA-315B Alouette II Cheetah**, a French design manufactured under license beginning in 1976-77. They are a light helicopter (two seater, no passenber compartment) and can be used in a variety of roles, and can be fitted with armaments. A variant with the engine of the ALH, termed **Cheetal**, came into service in 2008; 20 were ordered. However, the plan is to retrofit the existing fleet with the new engine and so replace all of the Cheetahs with Chcctals.

There are 100 of the **SA 316 Alouette III Chetak**, which is considered a multipurpose helicopter. These actually date back to the early 1960s; supplied by France, they are overhauled in India. The helicopter has a compartment for four passengers in addition to two crew in front, and can be armed.

The Cheetah, Chetal, and Cheetak are all to be replaced in the recce and observation role by 197 light utility helicopters.[392] However, as with the artillery, there are problems in the acquisition process. The original tender was cancelled in December 2007, reissued in July 2008, and reports in 2010 suggested that it might again be cancelled and reissued. There are also plans for an Indian Multi Role Helicopter that could carry 10-12 troops.

The CI or light attack version of the Cheetah is the **Lancer**, and 12 were built or converted. It has two gun/rocket pods, one on each side; each carries one 12.7mm MG and three 70mm rockets.

The newest helicopter is the **Dhruv** (Polaris), a multi-role light helicopter. The first official flight was in 1992, and the Army tested the Dhruv in the 1999 Kargil War. It can carry 12 passengers or four stretchers. A production order for 20 was approved in 2006, around 44 are now on strength, and the ultimate goal is 125-150 by 2015. Of these, half will be for the utility and transport role and half will be the weapons systems integrated version. The weapons systems integrated Dhruvs have a chin-mounted 20mm gun and eight hard points on four pylons. They can carry eight ATGMs, four 68mm or 70mm rocket pods, or four tube-launched air-to-air missiles. The normal Dhruv is from the Advanced Light Helicopter (ALH) program while the armed version is termed the Light Combat Helicopter (LCH).

In addition to the aircraft, there are three Unmanned Aerial Vehicles (UAVs) in use. The Nishant (12 ordered) was developed in India and completed user trials in 2008. Its range is 160 km. It is primarily intended for intelligence gathering but can also be used for reconnaissance, artillery fire correction, and surveillance. There are 21 Searcher UAVs and 31 Heron UAVs purchased from Israel. The Heron can operate for up to 52 hours and the Searcher for 18.

---

[392] The intent is to acquire 60 already built and build the remaining 137 in India under license.

Appendix R: Battle Honours

According to the Indian Army's official web site, "Battle Honours are official commemoration of battles, actions or engagements and are awarded to Regiments whose units or sub-units have taken active and creditable part in these operations. Battle Honours may be awarded in the form of 'Battle Honour, Theatre Honour or Honour Title'." This largely tracks the British practice, and thus that of the pre-Independence Indian Army.

Units qualifying for a battle honour in a theatre automatically qualify for the appropriate theatre honour. Theatre honours are not emblazoned on colours.[393] A battle honour is earned if, in general, at least half of the unit was actively engaged "and fought creditably with distinction in the operation." For the most part, this system applies to armoured regiments, infantry battalions, artillery and air defence artillery regiments, engineer regiments, Army Aviation Corps squadrons, and signals regiments.

Honour titles may be awarded to artillery, air defence artillery, and Army Aviation Corps units "which have distinguished themselves in a battle by rendering creditable service...." However, it appears that an infantry battalion has sometimes been awarded an honour title as well.

Despite discussing battle honours in general, the Army's web site does not actually list them, regimental entries (on both the official Army and Bharat Rakshak web sites) appear to be inconsistent or incomplete in their display, and the Armoured Corps is omitted entirely. Therefore this Appendix is based entirely on unofficial sources; see the discussion at the end.

Theatre Honours

These are listed sequentially because of the relatively limited number.

Theater Honour	**Dates**
Jammu & Kashmir 1947-48	22 Oct 1947 – 31 Dec 1948
Ladakh 1962[394]	20 Oct 1962 – 24 Nov 1962
Rajasthan 1965	6 Sep 1965 – 2 Dec 1965

[393] This is one difference from the prior British practice, in which a regiment could select a theatre honour (e.g., Burma 1944-45). Also unlike the British practice, mere presence in the theatre is not enough to qualify for a theatre honour.

[394] Only four infantry battalions were awarded this theatre honour and three of them also were given a battle honour. These were not awarded until 1975.

Jammu & Kashmir 1965	5 Aug 1965 – 3 Nov 1965
Punjab 1965	6 Sep 1965 – 23 Sep 1965
East Pakistan 1971	3 Dec 1971 – 20 Dec 1971
Punjab 1971	3 Dec 1971 – 17 Dec 1971 ?
Sindh 1971	4 Dec 1971 – 13 Dec 1971 ?
Jammu & Kashmir 1971	3 Dec 1971 – 20 Dec 1971
Kargil 1999[395]	

Battle Honours

Because of the great number, these are listed alphabetically. The associated theatre honour is given after the dates.

Battle Honour	**Dates**
Akhaura	4-14 Dec 1971; East Pakistan 1971
Amritsar (Airfield)[396]	Dec 1971; Punjab 1971
Assal Uttar	9-11 Sep 1965; Punjab 1965
Banwat[397]	3-4 Dec 1971; Jammu and Kashmir 1971
Basantar River	5-17 Dec 1971; Punjab 1971
Bhaduria	10-11 Dec 1971; East Pakistan 1971
Bogra	14-16 Dec 1971; East Pakistan 1971
Brachil Pass and Wali Malik	7-12 Dec 1971; Jammu and Kashmir 1971
Burj	3-9 Dec 1971; Punjab 1971
Burki	9-10 Sep 1965; Punjab 1965
Buttar Dograndi	17 Sep 1965; Punjab 1965
Chachro	7 Dec 1971; Sindh 1971
Chakri	8-10 Dec 1971; Punjab 1971
Chamb	6-10 Dec 1971; Jammu and Kashmir 1971
Charwa	7-8 Sep 1965; Punjab 1965
Chauddagram (Laksham)	4-5 Dec 1971; East Pakistan 1971
Chushul	21 Oct-20 Nov 1962; Ladakh 1962
Darsana	3-4 Dec 1971; East Pakistan 1971
Defence of Punch	3-7 Dec 1971; Jammu and Kashmir 1971
Dera Baba Nanak	3-6 Dec 1971; Punjab 1971
Dograi	21-22 Sep 1965; Punjab 1965
Fatehpur	11-12 Dec 1971; Punjab 1971

[395] No details of the theatre honour or of any specific battle honours have been located. See the discussion at the end of the list of battle honours.
[396] The unit(s) earning this battle honour are not known.
[397] The unit(s) earning this battle honour are not known.

Gadra City	4-5 Dec 1971; Sindh 1971
Gadra Road	8 Sep 1965; Rajasthan 1965
Ganga Sagar	1-3 Dec 1971; East Pakistan 1971
Gurais s	24-29 Jun 1948; Jammu & Kashmir 1947-48
Gutrian	3-7 Dec 1971; Jammu and Kashmir 1971
Hajipir	26-31 Aug 1965; Jammu & Kashmir 1965
Harar Kalan	7-10 Dec 1971; Punjab 1971
Hilli	4-11 Dec 1971; East Pakistan 1971
Hussainiwala Bridge	19-20 Sep 1965; Punjab 1965
Jamalpur	9-11 Dec 1971; East Pakistan 1971
Jarpal	15-16 Dec 1971; Punjab 1971
Jaurain-Kalit	2-5 Sep 1965; Jammu & Kashmir 1965
Jhanger	15-18 Mar 1948; Jammu & Kashmir 1947-48
Kalidhar	1 Sep-5 Oct 1965; Jammu & Kashmir 1965
Kargil	23 Nov 1948; Jammu & Kashmir 1947-48
Khansama	13-14 Dec 1971; East Pakistan 1971
Khinsar	5 Dec 1971; Sindh 1971
Kumarkhali	16 Dec 1971; East Pakistan 1971
Lagyala Gompa	23 Oct-18 Nov 1962
Laleali-Picquet 707	3-8 Dec 1971; Jammu and Kashmir 1971
Longanewala	4-5 Dec 1971; Sindh 1971
Madhumati River	14-15 Dec 1971; East Pakistan 1971
Maharajke	7 Sep 1965; Punjab 1965
Malakpur	12-14 Dec 1971; Punjab 1971
Mian Bazar (Laksham)	3-4 Dec 1971; East Pakistan 1971
Mynamati	10-16 Dec 1971; East Pakistan 1971
Nangi Tekri	10-11 Dec 1971; Jammu and Kashmir 1971
Naushera	24 Jan-7 Feb 1948; Jammu & Kashmir 1947-48
Namka Chu	10 Oct-16 Nov 1971
Nuranang	16-18 Nov 1962; Ladakh 1962
Op Hill (NL 1053)	2-3 Nov 1965; Jammu & Kashmir 1965
Parbat Ali	8-13 Dec 1971; Sindh 1971
Phillora	11 Sep 1965; Punjab 1965
Piequet 707	*See* Laleali-Picquet 707
Point 9013	20-21 Sep 1965
Poongli Bridge	11-12 Dec 1971; East Pakistan 1971
Punch	20 Nov 1947-23 Nov 1948; Jammu & Kashmir 1947-48
Raja Picquet-Chand Tekri	5-6 Sep 1965; Jammu & Kashmir 1965
Rajaori	8-12 Apr 1948; Jammu & Kashmir 1947-48
Rezang La	18 Nov 1962; Ladakh 1962

Samba (VA/VP)[398]	Dec 1971; Punjab 1971
Sanjoi-Mirpur	3-12 Sep 1965; Jammu & Kashmir 1965
Shamsher Nagar	1-2 Dec 1971; East Pakistan 1971
Shehjra	5-6 Dec 1971; Punjab 1971
Shingo River Valley	7-17 Dec 1971; Jammu and Kashmir 1971
Siramani	16-17 Dec 1971; East Pakistan 1971
Skardu	10 Feb-14 Aug 1948; Jammu & Kashmir 1947-48
Slyhet	8-16 Dec 1971; East Pakistan 1971
Srinagar	27 Oct-13 Nov 1947; Jammu & Kashmir 1947-48
Suadih	4-5 Dec 1971; East Pakistan 1971
Syamganj	14-15 Dec 1971; East Pakistan 1971
Sylhet	8-16 Dec 1971
Thanpir	4-5 Dec 1971; Jammu and Kashmir 1971
Tilakpur-Muhadipur	19-23 Sep 1965; Punjab 1965
Tithwal	17-23 May 1948; Jammu & Kashmir 1947-48
Turtok	6-14 Dec 1971; Jammu and Kashmir 1971
Uri	19 May-19 Jun 1948; Jammu & Kashmir 1947-48
Zoji La [sometimes shown as Zojila]	3 Sep-4 Nov 1948; Jammu & Kashmir 1947-48

Kargil 1999

No details of the theatre honour and few details of any specific battle honours have been located. Initially, the only reference to it the authors found was with the Parachute Regiment's web site and (on the Bharat Rakshak site) 11 Gorkha Rifles. 11 GR are also credited with Batalik, which was a battle during that war and 1/11 GR was involved, one of their officers receiving a posthumous PVC. Apparently there has been recent controversy about the battle of Batalik, concerning the corps commander and who deserved credit for the action.[399]

Research and personal communications from T. F. Mills found some additional information on battle honours associated with this theatre honour:

Tiger Hill: Grenadiers, 18th Garhwal?
Drass: Naga, 2nd Rajputan Rifles, Bombay Sappers
Muskoh: 2nd Naga
Tololing: 2nd Rajputan Rifles

---

398 The unit(s) earning this battle honour are not known.

399 See a 28 May 2010 story at www.indianexpress.com/news/the-batalik-battle/624617/0. The article indicates that there is an official history of the war, but it seems not yet leaked.

However, he could not find any authority for them or any site that mentioned all of them.

Pre-independence battle honours: For the most part, units of the Indian Army were allowed to retain honours earned prior to August 1947. However, those determined to be "repugnant" to the new state (primarily for operations within the current boundaries of India) were to be removed.

[The lists of theatre and battle honours are from notes made some time ago from information on T. F. (Todd) Mills' Regiments.Org web site, which has disappeared except in some cached locations, one of which was consulted to doublecheck (see Sources). Mr. Mills also responded to questions concerning Kargil 1999.]

Sources

Ahmed, Col (Retd) Ali. "India's Strategic and Military Doctrines: A Post 1971 Snapshot." *USI Journal*, Oct - Dec 2009,Vol CXXXIX, No.578.[400]

Athawale, Lt Cmdr Yogesh B. "Image of the Armed Forces – Arresting Negative Trends." *USI Journa*l, April-June 2006, Vol CXXXVI, No 564.

Bajwa, Mandeep Singh. Indian Contingent UNOSOM II 1992-1994. (2006) Online [2010] at www.orbat.com/site/cimh/index.html

__________. 2nd (Independent) Armored Brigade. (2005) Online [2010] at www.orbat.com/site/cimh/index.html

__________. The Jat Regiment. (2004) Online [2010] at www.orbat.com/site/cimh/index.html

__________. Armored Regiments. (2001)[401]

__________. Class Composition of Indian Armored Regiments.

Bajwa, Mandeep Singh & Ravi Rikhye. A Note on Indian Army Tank Regiments 1947-86. (2008) Online [2010] at www.orbat.com/site/cimh/index.html

__________. 4th Infantry Division: An Outline History. (2008) Online [2010] at www.orbat.com/site/cimh/index.html

__________. The Indian Army on the Eve of the 1962 War: A Note. (2008) Online [2010] at www.orbat.com/site/cimh/index.html

__________. Indian Army—Kargil War 1999. (2006) Online [2010] at www.ordersofbattle.darkscape.net/site/history/index.html

__________. Indian Armored and Mechanized Brigades. (2004) Online [2010] at www.orbat.com/site/cimh/index.html

---

[400] The *Journal* of the United Service Institution of India has issues going back to 2006 online at www.usiofindia.org/.

[401] Documents like this one were prepared for posting at Orbat.com but a current URL cannot be located.

__________. 1st Armoured Brigade. (2005) Online [2010] at www.orbat.com/site/cimh/index.html

__________. Indian Army Formation Lineages: 3rd Independent Armored Brigade, A Case Study of the Opportunities & Difficulties. (2005) Online [2010] at www.orbat.com/site/cimh/index.html

__________. India Army: Scouts Units. (2004)

__________. Indian Army Corps 2003. (2003)

__________. Indian Army: Cavalry Regiments. (2001) Online [2010] at www.orbat.com/site/cimh/index.html

__________. Indian Army RAPID Divisions. (2001)

__________. The Jat Regiment. *Bharat Raksak Monitor*, Vol 3(4) Jan-Feb 2001, online [2010] at www.bharat-rakshak.com/MONITOR/ISSUE3-4/bajwa.html. This can also be found at www.orbat.com/site/cimh/index.html

Bharat Rakshak, Indian Army web site, at [2010] www.bharat-rakshak.com/LAND-FORCES/

Border Roads Organisation web site, [2010] www.bro.gov.in/indexab.asp

Bragg. R. J. & Roy Turner, *Parachute Badges and Insignia of the World* [Blandford Colour Series] (Poole, Dorset: Blandford Press, 1979)

Chakravorty, B. C. *History of the Indo-Pak War, 1965* (New Delhi: History Division, Ministry of Defence, Government of India, 1992)

Chappell, Mike. *The Gurkhas* [Osprey Elite Series, 49] (London: Osprey Publishing Ltd, 1993)

Cole, Howard. *Formation Badges of World War 2: Britain, Commonwealth and Empire*. (London: Arms and Armour Press, 1973.)

Conboy, Ken. *Elite Forces of India and Pakistan*. (Elite Series 41) (Oxford: Osprey Publishing Ltd, 1992)

Farwell, Byron. *Armies of the Raj From the Mutiny to Independence, 1858-1947*. (New York, W. W. Norton and Company, Inc., 1991)

Gautam, [Col (Retd)] P. K. *Composition and Regimental System of the Indian Army: Continuity and Change*. (New Delhi: Institute for Defence Studies and Analyses, 2008)

Gera, Maj Gen (Retd) Y K. "Naxalism: A Threat to India's Security." *USI Journal*, Jul - Sep 2009,Vol CXXXIX, No.577.

Gill, John H. *An Atlas of the 1971 India-Pakistan War: The Creation of Bangladesh*. (published by the Near East South Asia Center for Strategic Studies, co-located with National Defense University)

Haynes, Ed. Decorations and Medals of the Republic of India. This web site now exists only in a cached form, last updated in 1999. web.archive.org/web/20050908140108/faculty.winthrop.edu/haynese/india/medals/IndMed.html

History of the Corps of Engineers Indian Army, 1947-1972. [Compiled under the direction and authority of the Engineer-in-Chief, Army Headquarters] (New Delhi: Palit & Palit, 1980)

History of the Regiment of Artillery, Indian Army. [Published under the authority of the Director of Artillery, Army Headquarters.] (London: Leo Cooper Ltd, 1972)

Independent Armored and Mechanized Brigades. (2001)

India, Global Security website, at [2010] www.globalsecurity.org/military/world/india/army.htm

India 7th Infantry Brigade at the Battle of the Namkachu 1962. (2002) Online [2010] at www.orbat.com/site/history/historical/india/namkachu1962.html

India 1962: 11th Infantry Brigade at the Battle of Walong. (2002) Online [2010] at www.orbat.com/site/history/historical/india/walong1962.html

Indian Armored Division. (2001) Online [2010] at www.orbat.com/site/toe/index.htm

Indian Army, at Indian Military website [2020] www.indian-military.org/army.html

Indian Army Signals Units. (2001)

Indian Army website, at [2010] indianarmy.nic.in/Index.aspx?flag=LfcULYFlbeQ=

Indian Army, Wikipedia, at [2010] en.wikipedia.org/wiki/Indian_Army. In addition, there are a number of related articles which link from that page.

Indian 114 Infantry Brigade at the Battle of Chushul, 1962. Online [2010] at www.orbat.com/site/history/historical/india/114chushul.html

Jaipur, H.H. The Maharaja of, *The Indian State Forces: Their Lineage and Insignia* (London: Leo Cooper, Ltd., 1967)

Jeffrey, Robin. "The Punjab Boundary Force and the Problem of Order, August 1947." *Modern Asian Studies*, 8, 4 (1974), 491-520.

Kanwal, Brig Gunmeet. "Equipment Acquisition Imperatives of the Indian Army." *Indian Defence Review*, Vol 25.2 (June 2010), but a reprint originally published in Vol 18(4) (October-December 2003). Online [2010] at www.indiandefencereview.com/2010/06/equipment-acquisition-imperatives-of-the-indian-army.html

Kempton, Chris. *'Loyalty & Honour': The Indian Army September 1939-August 1947*. 3 vols. (Milton Keynes: The Military Press, 2003)

Library of Congress, Federal Research Division. A Country Study: India. Online [2010] at lcweb2.loc.gov/frd/cs/intoc.html

Mills, T. F. His Land Forces of Britain, the Empire and Commonwealth web site was the starting place for information on those armies. Sadly, the site lapsed. A cached version, updated through mid 2004, is at web.archive.org/web/20060110124913/www.regiments.org/regiments/index.htm

Mohan, PVS Jagan. The Brigade of The Guards. *Bharat Raksak Monitor*, Vol 3(1) Jul-Aug 2000, online [2010] at www.bharat-rakshak.com/MONITOR/ISSUE3-1/jagan.html

Parachute Regiment website, [2010] www.indianparachuteregiment.kar.nic.in/home.html

Patel, Y. I. "Dig Vijay to Divya Astra: a Paradigm Shift in the Indian Army's Doctrine," www.bharat-rakshak.com/LAND-FORCES/History/Millenium/324-A-Paradigm-Shift.html.

Prasad, S. N. (ed.). *History of Indo-Pak War, 1971*. (New Delhi: History Division, Ministry of Defence, Government of India, 1992)

Praval, Maj (Retd) K. C. *Indian Army After Independence*. (Frankfurt, IL: The Lancer International Inc., n.d.; first published New Delhi: Lancer Publishers & Distributors, n.d.)

Puri, Lt Gen Mohinder. "Kargill: A Ringside View." *Indian Defence Review*, Vol 21.4 (December 2007), online [2010] at www.indiandefencereview.com/2007/12/kargil-a-ringside-view.html

Rikhye, Maj Gen (Ret) Indar Jit. Guarding Ladakh: Raising 114 Infantry Brigade. (2004) Online [2010] at www.orbat.com/site/cimh/index.html

Rikhye, Ravi. Thumbnail Sketches of Other Jat Battalions. (2010) Online [2010] at www.orbat.com/site/cimh/index.html

_________. The Kumaon Regiment's Battalions. (2008). Online [2010] at www.orbat.com/site/cimh/index.html

_________. Indian Armor TOES. (2008)

_________. Indian 8th Division: An Outline History. (2006)

_________. Indian Cavalry Regiments to 1994. (2003) Online [2010] at www.orbat.com/site/cimh/index.html

_________. Indian Armored Divisions – An Analysis. (2003)

_________. The Rashttriya Rifles. (2003). Online [2010] at www.orbat.com/site/cimh/index.html

_________. Indian Southern Command in the 1971 War. (2002) Online [2010] at www.orbat.com/site/history/historical/india/desert71.html

_________. Indian I Corps in the 1971 War. (2002). Online [2010] at www.orbat.com/site/history/historical/india/Icorps71.html

_________. Indian II Corps in the East Bengal Campaign, 1971. (2002) Online [2010] at www.orbat.com/site/history/historical/india/IIcorps71.html

__________. Indian XXXIII Corps in the East Bengal Campaign, 1971. (2002). Online [2010] at www.orbat.com/site/history/historical/india/XXXIIIcorps71.html

__________. Indian 10th Division in the Battle for Chaamb, 1971. (2002) Online [2010] at www.orbat.com/site/history/historical/india/chaamb71.html

__________. Indian 19th Division in the 1971 War. (2002) Online [2010] at www.orbat.com/site/history/historical/india/19div71.html

__________. India: The Partapur and 121st Brigade Sectors in the 1971 War. (2002) Online [2010] at www.orbat.com/site/history/historical/india/121bde1971.html

__________. Indian 99th Independent Brigade Group in the Congo, 1961-63. (2002). Online [2010] at www.orbat.com/site/history/historical/india/99bdecongo.htm

__________. Mukti Bahini: Bangladesh Forces in the Liberation War 1971. (2002)

__________. Indian Kilo Sector, Rann of Kutch April 1965. (2002)

__________. Indian Army: Armored Corps Center and School. (2001)

__________. A Short History of Indian Division Deployments Against China. (2001)

Rikhye, Ravi and David Sandhu. Indian XV Corps, Kashmir 1965. (2002) Online [2010] at www.orbat.com/site/history/historical/india/XVCorps65.html

__________. India 1962: 4th Infantry Division at the Battle of Bomdila. (2002) Online [2010] at www.orbat.com/site/history/historical/india/bomdila1962.html

Rinaldi, Richard A. Indian Army Airborne/Special Forces Units. (2008) Online [2010] at www.orbat.com/site/cimh/index.html

Rosignoli, Guido. *Army Badges and Insignia of World War 2, Book Two.* (Macmillan Color Series) (New York: Macmillan Publishing Co, Inc, 1975)

Sandhu, Dave. Indian Peace Keeping Force (IPKF) in Sri Lanka. (2002). Online [2010] at www.orbat.com/site/cimh/india/ipkf.html

Sandhu, Dave and Ravi Rikhye. Indian Army Strike Force in the 1971 War. (2002)

Sandhu, D. S. The Rajput Regiment. *Bharat Raksak Monitor*, Vol 3(3) Nov-Dec 2000, online [2010] at www.bharat-rakshak.com/MONITOR/ISSUE3-3/sandhu.html

_________. The Sikh Regiment: Indian Army's Most Decorated Regiment. *Bharat Raksak Monitor*, Vol 3(6) May-Jun 2001, online [2010] at www.bharat-rakshak.com/MONITOR/ISSUE3-6/sandhu.html

Sainis, Sunil. "Thoughts on Operation Parakrama," www.bharat-rakshak.com/LAND-FORCES/History/Millenium/321-Op-Parakram.htm

Shankar, Lt Gen Vinay. "Army's Capability Accretion." *Indian Defence Review*, Vol 25.1 (March 2010), online [2010] at www.indiandefencereview.com/2010/03/armys-capability-accretion.html

Sharma, Lt Col (Retd) Gautam. *Indian Army (A Reference Manual)*. (New Delhi: Reliance Publishing House, 2000)

Sinha, Brig SP. "CI Operations in the Northeast." *Indian Defence Review*, Vol 21.2 (January 2007), online [2010] at www.indiandefencereview.com/2007/01/c-i-operations-in-the-northeast.html

Sinha, Dr. P. B. and Col A. A. Athale. *History of the Conflict with China, 1962*. New Delhi: Ministry of Defence, History Division, 1992. This can be found online [2010] at http://www.bharat-rakshak.com/LAND-FORCES/Army/History/1962War/PDF/

Subramanian, L. N. The Rajputana Rifles. *Bharat Raksak Monitor*, Vol 5(1) Jul-Aug 2002, online [2010] at www.bharat-rakshak.com/MONITOR/ISSUE5-1/subra.html

_________. "100 Hour War – Hyderabad Police Action," online [2010] at www.bharat-rakshak.com/LAND-FORCES/History/1948-62/260-100-Hour-War.html

Thapliyal, Maj Gen (Retd) SM. "Battle of Eastern Ladakh : 1962 Sino-Indian Conflict." *United Service Institution of India Journal*, Apr-Jun 2005, online [2010] at www.usiofindia.org/article_apr_jun05_10.htm.

Tripathi, Lt Gen (Retd) S P M. "The Truth about Military Hardware in our Armed Forces." *USI Journal*, October-December 2007,Vol CXXXVII, No.570.

Verma, Bharat. "Declining Military Prowess." *Indian Defence Review*, Vol 24.1 (January 2009), online [2010] at www.indiandefencereview.com/2009/01/declining-military-prowess.html

www.ingramcontent.com/pod-product-compliance
Ingram Content Group UK Ltd.
Pitfield, Milton Keynes, MK11 3LW, UK
UKHW051127260726
13967UKWH00010B/2914